FOREWORD [...]ATING

PETER
TRABEN HAAS

CONTEMPLATIVE CHURCH

AFTERWORDS
BY
CYPRIAN CONSIGLIO & ILIA DELIO

Published by ContemplativeChristians.com
Second Printing: October 2018
P.O. Box 164202
Austin, TX 78716

Contemplative Church: How Meditative Prayer and Monastic Practices Help Congregations Flourish

Library of Congress Cataloging-in-Publication Data

Haas, Peter Traben (1972 –   )
Contemplative Church: How Meditative Prayer and Monastic Practices Help Congregations Flourish

ISBN: 978-0-692-16666-6

1. *Spirituality – Christianity. 2. Contemplative. 3. Church Leadership. I. Title.*

Cover graphic design and artwork by Sarah Presson and *EyeLikeDesign*
Austin, TX. www.eyelikedesign.com/

"Dear brothers and sisters, we can't help but thank God for you, because your faith is flourishing and your love for one another is growing."

– 2 Thessalonians 1.3

"To lose oneself in the Unfathomable, to plunge into the Inexhaustible, to find peace in the Incorruptible...to give one's deepest to the One whose depth has no end."[1]

– Pierre Teilhard de Chardin

Dedicated to Flourishers & Evolvers –

Cynthia Bourgeault
Tim Cook
Barbara Cook
Ilia Delio
Bede Griffiths
Thomas Keating
Martin Laird
John Main
Carl McColman
William Meninger
Raimon Panikkar
Basil Pennington
Bernadette Roberts
Richard Rohr
Wayne Teasdale
...

Whose wisdom and love continue to help humankind
remember and return
to the treasures and depths of the contemplative way.

Contents

Foreword **Thomas Keating** *12*

Preface **Fellow Stewards of the Treasure** *14*

Introduction ***Remembering and Returning to the Contemplative Path*** *18*

Part One:
Realizing the Problems

Chapter One ***Realizing*** *26*
1 · The Storm of Silence
2 · Axial Moment for a New Monasticism
3 · Convergence 4 · How 5 · Become

Chapter Two ***Needing*** *44*
1 · A Collective Dark Night 2 · System Stressors
3 · Explore 4 · Reconnect with Depth

Part Two:
Rediscovering the Pathway

Chapter Three ***Defining*** *66*
1 · Inwardness 2 · Outwardness 3 · Centeredness

Chapter Four ***Deepening*** *80*
1 · A Brief Tour of Foundational Contemplatives
2 · A Brief Word on Mysticism

Chapter Five ***Centering*** *102*
1 · The Center Is Everywhere
2 · Where Did Centering Prayer Come From?

Chapter Six **Practicing** **113**
1 · A Brief Overview of Key Monastic Practices
2 · Why Monastic Practices?

Part Three:
Recovering the Possibilities

Chapter Seven ***Becoming*** ***142***

1 · Becoming a Contemplative
2 · Spiritual Reading
3 · Replenishing the Center
4 · Becoming a Contemplative Church
5· Getting Practical

Chapter Eight ***Evolving*** ***162***

1 · The Evolution of Consciousness
2 · Serve from a Deeper Place

Chapter Nine ***Flourishing*** ***171***

1 · Re-Fill in the Nook of Heaven's Stillness
2 · Nourish, Flourish and Become Love

Conclusion ***The Song of Silence*** ***177***

Afterword **From the Monastery** **Cyprian Consiglio** ***182***

Afterword **From the Academy** **Ilia Delio** ***188***

Appendices ***192***

· Selected Contemplative Scripture Passages
· Sample Contemplative Prayers and Liturgy
· Sample Contemplative Retreat Formats and Forms
· The Evolution of Meditation in the Christian Tradition

Acknowledgements ***218***

Bibliography ***220***

Endnotes ***248***

"So that we may present everyone mature in Christ..."

– Colossians 1.28-29

"The Christian of the future will be a mystic or he or she will not exist at all." [2]

– Karl Rahner

Foreword /

Thomas Keating

In this impressive and well researched presentation of the contemplative dimension of the Gospel, Peter Traben Haas respectfully and lovingly reaches out to those in the Protestant tradition, pleading with them to restore and renew the tradition of contemplative prayer and practice in their communities. That tradition was scarcely recognizable at the time of the Reformation, when Martin Luther, five-hundred years ago nailed his Ninety-Five Theses to the door of a church.

This book provides a comprehensive survey of the history of contemplative prayer and its place as an essential aspect of the Christian community. It also serves as a solid conceptual background for the teaching of contemplative prayer to churches and seminaries where leaders of Christian denominations are formed. Without leaders who practice contemplative prayer, the faithful are not likely to embrace the practice, or if they do, they may *not* feel welcome in many church communities.

Besides discussing the roots of the contemplative tradition found throughout the scriptures, Peter introduces the reader to the early sources of the contemplative tradition up through the flowering of contemplative prayer in the Middle Ages, as well as calling attention to contemporary efforts to renew this tradition and practice in our time.

Contemplative prayer practiced regularly, tends to reveal the emotional wounds of infancy and early childhood arising from a child's total emotional vulnerability and unfulfilled instinctual needs for survival and security, affection and esteem, and power and control. The practice of contemplative prayer gradually heals the emotional wounds of a lifetime while at the same time awakening an unshakeable trust in God's infinite mercy and love. To his list of contributions to the contemplative renewal Peter adds recent discoveries of contemporary science unavailable until about a hundred years ago and which reinforce the wisdom literature of earlier times. One of these is the discovery of the psychological unconscious along with its secret but profound influence on human behavior

This is a monumental presentation with an appeal to Protestant churches and denominations to become aware of the treasure Haas warns is missing in their communities: *the contemplative dimension of the Gospel.* A continued ignoring or loss of this singular positive, contemplative Christian influence on society would be a disaster for the church and for humanity.

Thomas Keating
St. Benedict's Monastery, CO

Preface /

Fellow Stewards of the Treasure

I wish for flourishing.

The flourishing I wish for may be different from the flourishing many have previously aimed toward. This flourishing is inward, silent and enduring; deeply connected to our ongoing awakening and evolution in Christ. What follows in this book is a humble treasure-map of a frequently neglected path toward flourishing – the *contemplative* path.

Today, it seems church leaders and faith communities are saddled with impossible expectations: the goal of ever-expanding membership, attendance, budgets, influence and renown. But these markers are largely external numerical indicators of *quantity*, with little to do with *quality*. What are we chasing after? Meanwhile others are just trying to keep their church afloat. Wondering who will be there to shut the doors and turn the lights out. Bearing all that in mind, it is appropriate to ask a few important questions: What makes a church *flourish,* not just grow? What can deepen us in the love of God so that we can experience the *formation of Christ within* (i.e., Galatians 4.19)?

One way of answering these questions is to acknowledge that two dynamics linger with us from the past, like a shadow, limiting our possibilities for flourishing. The first, a persistent avoidance of *meditative prayer.* The second, the initial and ongoing Protestant untethering from classic *monastic practices*.

Combined, meditative prayer and monastic practices are two foundational elements of the contemplative dimension and expression of Christianity. Ignored, they are the diminishment of the Church, her people, and even the earth we all inhabit.

Observing our times, it is easy to spot our unworkable human patterns of communication, our addiction to insatiable financial accumulation, and our depletion of vast natural resources – just to name a few indicators of the need for a wiser way of being together on this extraordinary planet we all get to call home. Given our current ecclesiastical, environmental and cultural stressors, now is an apt time for a re-discovery of the contemplative treasures and tools left behind with the Reformers in the long-casting shadow of the Reformation.

For me, such a wiser way is possible with a return to a contemplative future. Such a return is *not* regressive, or counter to the spiritual roots of the Reformation. It is a renewal of the Reformer's foundational impulse: the experiential encounter of the Word of God with our deepest human center.

I am seeking to live this renewal out in both my life and ministry as a pastor. I know others are too. I have met many fellow contemplatives on retreats around the country.[1] Even online communities flourish, with contemplatives seeking community and connection.[2]

Paradoxically, it seems our ongoing Protestant fragmentation might lead us back to the ground of humility. A ground where all things die so to become possible, and where everything can begin again – breathed to life by the creator Spirit who still fiercely furrows our soul with the living waters of silence and stillness. Perhaps this book will be a small contribution to the unfolding of a deepened contemplative renewal.

My wish for the contemplative evolution of Christianity arises from a love for the Church and a hope for her continued flourishing. These are not just words of an idealistic pastor. These words are also an expression of my hope, for I believe a season of deep spiritual crisis *and* evolution is upon us. Through the renewal of meditative prayer and contemplative, monastic practices, perhaps we can be moved beyond the splintering shadow of the Reformation into a new axial age; the age of Presence.

If not now, then certainly later in the ever-unfolding sphere of time; for the glory of God, for the flourishing of the entire human community, and for the complete joy of the global, Christian church.

Fellow wanderers in the night that is light, unite:

Sola Silence. *Sola* Stillness. *Sola* Solitude.

Peter Traben Haas
Austin, Texas

"Our times are driven by the inestimable energies of the mechanical mind; its achievements derive from its singular focus, linear direction and force. When it dominates, the habit of gentleness dies out. We become blind: nature is rifled, politics eschews vision and becomes the obsessive servant of economics, and religion opts for the mathematics of system and forgets its mystical flame."[1]

– John O'Donohue

"*But because I ask for silence,*
don't think I'm going to die.
The opposite is true;
it happens I'm going to live."[2]

– Pablo Naruda

Introduction /

Remembering and Returning to the Contemplative Path

I remember it was a blue-sky day in the Adirondack Mountains. The morning light was streaming through the tall front windows of Tibbits' Auditorium. It was Sunday morning, August 27th and I was at Camp-of-The-Woods' weekly worship service, carefully listening to the compelling New Jersey drawl of a middle-aged, rotund preacher. His down-home wisdom compelled me intellectually, but I also felt, in my solar plexus area, a peaceful, emotional draw to what he was saying.[1]

I remember that he paused his preaching. A silence rose up from the congregation, like a mist on nearby Lake Pleasant. Then, quietly, as if to each of us, the preacher, with a flick of his wrist, dispensed an invitation: "*Come down and receive Christ*," he said, "*You will never regret it*."

I came forward. It was 1989. I was seventeen years old. I walked down the century-old wooden stairs in Tibbits' Auditorium and fell to the ground on my knees near the pulpit. Unexpected emotions of a shadowed sadness rose up, perhaps unloading the hurts of a young lifetime. The wound of being human, now just a bit more healed in the light of Christ's love.

It is customary to attach religious words to describe these kinds of experiences. Words such as: Conversion. Born-again. Accepting Jesus. Getting saved. But, for me, in that still, sunlit moment, it felt as easy as breathing; as simple as being, the instinctive spiritual surrender to the Unknown God.

I could not have known then how different my life would be when I rose from the dusty floor of that Evangelical sanctuary of summertime worship, in the ancient rounds of those Adirondack Mountains. Rising tear stained, I sensed I was a very different person. I walked down a young man who rarely read a book; I rose a new man with an insatiable hunger for reading. I began the day as a teenager interested in girls and dreaming about becoming a lead singer like Bono. I ended the day studying and seeking wisdom.

Taking that first Sunday step of faith; boots knocking all the way down the wooden stairway to what certainly became a doorway to a deeper, more real way of life. Whatever happened to me that summer morning, next to my birth, I mark August 27th, 1989 as the second most important day of my life.

Life *was* never the same for me. But, the preacher was also incomplete in his presentation of the spiritual journey. As my life unfolded, it turned out that "accepting Jesus" was *not* enough for me. I know this now, having taken the journey toward a different, mostly un-tried way of being and becoming a Christian, called *contemplative.*

Two decades passed. I left a forestry program at Northland College along the birch-lined shores of Lake Superior and enrolled at Moody Bible Institute in a teeming downtown Chicago. After graduation, I worked as a pastoral resident for a year at Wisconsin's only Evangelical mega-church. I then went to Princeton Seminary, and, upon graduation, became a Presbyterian (PCUSA) minister.

All the while, I grew frustrated by my own (and the American Protestant church's) lack of spiritual maturity. Hungry for my own spiritual evolution and depth, I began to explore the long-lost treasures of meditative prayer and the contemplative, monastic practices abandoned five-hundred years ago amidst the Protestant zeal for change.

Silence

It is difficult to know exactly when I became a contemplative. My unlikely rediscovery of, and return to the contemplative way of being Christian, unfolded slowly, over several years. Reading Thomas Merton and Thomas Keating in my first years as a pastor stirred something within me that little in seminary did, connecting me to the wider inward tradition. As did my initial solo retreats at monasteries, where something very real was at work within me through the stillness and solitude of those places. At each monastery, in different ways, I witnessed in holy elders something like pure-joyful-love. I was drawn to their humble wisdom and radiant peace. No doubt, my journey into the contemplative way was a long, yet steady courtship.

I first noticed the silence. As I worked the front desk at Crowell Hall during my years as a student at Moody Bible Institute, I chose the 4:00am shift because it allowed me time to pray and study while I worked. From about 4:30am until 5:15am, I could spend time in quiet prayer. But many mornings, given my fatigue, I felt as if I wasn't praying correctly – at least not in the intercessory method I was trained in.

On occasional mornings something different happened. I ceased praying words from my guided, intercessory prayer list, but prayed wordlessly in my heart: deeply quiet and still, accompanied by a warming sensation in my solar-plexus area. It was only years later that I discovered that what I had stumbled upon during those early morning hours at Crowell Hall, was actually the ancient prayer practice of *hesychia* – what John Cassian (360 – 435 CE) called Pure Prayer – the prayer of the heart, often associated with the Jesus Prayer.[2]

Suffering

In addition to the unexpected discovery of meditative prayer in the silence, my spiritual journey and maturing seemed to require some suffering. My suffering began to crack me open deeper to myself and to the love of God; a felt presence that I had often resisted in all my busyness in the name of ministry. But then my pain became greater than I could handle on my own. I could no longer fake it. Unknown to anyone else but me, I was falling apart as a man and as a minister.

Through the eventual brokenness that unfolded in my life (including a divorce), I intuited a need to grow deeper, spiritually and psychologically, realizing how non-integrated I was – spirit, soul and body. I returned to silent prayer, both on my own at home and with others during retreats at monasteries. I also began a twice weekly yoga practice, which helped me sink down from my head and get into my body.

This contemplative way continues to deliver me into the night-then-light rhythm of God's loving silence. While it may have been suffering that first opened the door, it was silence that greeted me with open arms once the door opened. And that silence led me into a stillness that heals and renews in profoundly precise and graceful ways, such that another word for the silence and stillness has become for me the *Presence*, which I name Christ.

Slowly

Looking back now, I see that slowly, through it all, I was being drawn into the contemplative dimension. Its influences not only inspired me to remain a Christian, but also gave me a new, yet ancient way of being a *practicing* Christian. The contemplative dimension gently began to answer my *how* questions:

- How can I abide with God in Christ? (John 15.4).
- How can I cultivate the mind of Christ within me? (1 Corinthians 2.16).
- How can I become a participant in the divine nature? (2 Peter 1.4).
- How can I die to self and live to God? (Galatians 2.20).

Apart from daily meditative prayer and selected monastic practices, nothing provided a satisfying answer to these and many other *how* questions. While my consenting to faith in the living Jesus Christ on that late August morning in the Adirondack mountains surely saved my life, it is my ongoing infusion through the practices of the contemplative dimension of Christianity that *is still saving* me from myself and evolving me toward love. There is still much to be healed and transformed within me. And so too the church. It is a process that theologians call *sanctification*, and Father Thomas Keating calls the Divine Therapy.

I call it *the rhythms of silence singing love into the still space of grace within me.* Perhaps I'm not the only one who needs this song. Perhaps, through the pages of this book, we will partake in its harmonies and dissonances together.[3] And perhaps, you too will see the need to step out of the shadow of the Reformation that too often has kept your head separated from your heart and spirit, and feel the light of love again hiding in plain sight, beyond *sola scriptura,* within the silence and stillness of contemplative experience.

Shadows

In the centuries before the Great Schism divided the Eastern Orthodox community from the Western Church in 1054 CE, the contemplative dimension of Christianity was held in sacred trust by the church through an extensive network of monastic communities ranging from the deserts of Egypt and Syria to the British Isles. These were silent communities bearing living witness to the contemplative path.[4] Centuries later, the Reformation officially purged the church of virtually all of its contact with those important contemplative and monastic treasures and traits.[5] Yet, ever so gently, over the last fifty years or so, some of those treasures have returned to the wider ecumenical church, to help Christians be Christians today.

This contemplative renewal is vital because, while the shadow of preachers may cast long and wide, the shadow of silence and the contemplative practices casts deep. We discover that silence is the "*shadow of the almighty*" (Psalm 91.1); the unending Presence of love that simply *is* and calls us to be and become.

The rediscovery of the contemplative way beyond the shadow of the Reformation is a gift for such a time as ours, encumbered as it is with unprecedented social stressors. This contemplative dimension is a primary way, right now, in our era of doing and undoing, to help transform our lives and churches one degree more toward the love and wholeness of our Christ-intended destiny.

Shifts

This book is about the promise of the contemplative dimension of Christianity, particularly its gifts of meditative prayer and monastic spiritual practices. This isn't a call to return to monasticism – but rather to bring the best aspects of monasticism back into the church. It is about remembering, and re-accessing select contemplative and monastic practices which can help our life, ministry and church flourish.

The Church and the entire human family are entering an axial moment allowing us to assess the spiritual vitality of our past and present. As we glance backward into church history, it reminds us that there have often been massive cultural shifts every five-hundred years or so, that call us to evaluate and evolve our way of being and doing.

Many intuit we are going through such an adjustment right now, and I humbly propose that it is the rediscovery of the contemplative dimension that can be a harmonious, ecumenical waltz deeper into love, and an integral way forward in faith for many of us who had begun to suspect its fatal fracturing.

Saints

The future is for mystics, Karl Rahner said. If that is true, the future will be contemplative.[6] I recognize this preferred future is not for everyone. I was reminded of this by my friend and contemplative-mystic Bernadette Roberts. Sensing my intentions for this book, Bernadette wrote to me an unexpected note. She cautioned me, saying: "*Peter, not everyone can be a contemplative. But everyone can become a Saint.*" I would only add that not everyone *wants* to become a contemplative either!

I think her counsel is a wise corrective to the notion that somehow contemplatives are more special or advanced. This is a myth that needs to be equally countered just as much as the myth that the church *doesn't* need contemplatives anymore. My wish for the contemplative evolution of Christianity, arises from a love for the Church and a hope for her continued flourishing. I sense this journey is even more important, in this season of immense ecclesiastical and cultural challenge and change. May this book help the church and her leaders rediscover and integrate meditative prayer and the riches of the pre-Reformation monastic traditions within the wider Church.

Part One:

Realizing the Problems

"Deep calls to deep at the thunder of your storm…"

– Psalm 65.7b

"It was this storm of silence shook out his ghost.
We sleep; he only wakes…
Moves the dark to wholeness…"[1]

– Wendell Berry

"You silence…the tumult of the peoples."

– Psalm 65.7

"Life is but a walking shadow, a poor player that struts and frets his hour upon the stage and is heard no more. It is a tale told by an idiot, full of sound and fury, signifying nothing."[2]

– William Shakespeare

Chapter One /

Realizing

1 · *The Storm of Silence*

The storm of silence arrives to gently awaken and inspire us to listen for something new. The storm of silence helps us notice and cease our busy striving. The storm of silence helps us remember and return to the necessary condition for our spiritual growth: being present to the Presence.

We need the storm of silence. It helps get our attention. It levels our ego-projects and humbles us to sit in stillness so to listen and remember how good it is to simply *be,* even if for a moment. As the storm of silence sweeps over us, leading us into a stillness of surrender, we become participants in the Spirit of God's transformation process. A grace-filled presence and action that can renew our families, churches, communities and world.

Yet, paradoxically, we must *do* something. Contemplative Christianity invites us to *do* certain practices so to *be* – deeper, wiser, more loving and peaceful. The quality of contemplative doing is a *consenting*. It is a consent that opens us more fully to the presence and action of the Spirit of God.

As a primer for what follows in this book, I will let the words of Thomas Merton point the initial way forward on our journey. Merton writes:

> "The contemplative is...simply [one] who has risked [one's] mind in the desert beyond language and beyond ideas where God is encountered in the nakedness of pure trust, that is to say in the surrender of our poverty and incompleteness in order no longer to clench our minds in a cramp upon themselves...The contemplative has nothing to tell you except to reassure you and say that if you dare to penetrate your own silence and dare to advance without fear into the solitude of your own heart,...you will truly recover the light and the capacity to understand what is beyond words and beyond explanations..."[1]

For many of us, we have likely tried everything else on the spiritual journey: programs, new curriculum, bestselling books, new preachers – so why not take a moment to let the silence try you and transform the storms of life into stillness?

2 · *Axial Moment for a New Monasticism*

The Protestant era turned five-hundred years old on October 31, 2017.[2] While the first five-hundred-year milestone of the Reformation sets an important stage for the pages that follow, this is *not* a book about the Reformation, or really, even a book about the history of the Protestant church. It is a book about *how* the Protestant church can move beyond the shadow of the Reformation, evolving forward by going deeper.[3] This is a book *not* about the *past,* but a book *for* the *present and future.*

The Reformation widely left behind (perhaps unintentionally) essential aspects of the spiritual life that had been carefully cultivated, embedded and handed on, generation by generation, within the monastic ethos.[4] In the wake of the Reformation era, most Protestants increasingly lost touch with those key foundational monastic practices.[5] Reformation era historian Lewis Spitz notes that the Protestant church "entered the Reformation with its spiritual power sadly diminished."[6] In response, efforts by a few sought to revive something of what was lost.

We see in the subsequent centuries following the Reformation, indications of a hunger for a reclamation of certain aspects of monastic wisdom and spiritual practices. For example, the rise of the Puritans, Methodism, Quakerism, American revivalism, and, much later, Bonhoeffer's call to discipleship in community, to name a few, indicate the presence of such a spiritual hunger.

Each of these historical movements was a movement to restore the centrality of prayer and the cultivation of what might be called God-devotion, or a kind of rule of life.[7] But this ran counter to the Reformation era preacher's emphasis that the primary means of grace is not *how* we live the Christian life – whether ascetical or contemplative – but *who* we trust for our salvation. No doubt the Reformers sought to remedy the corruption they saw in the church, including its monasteries, by rediscovering the power of the Gospel, but it seems they also disconnected from a deep source of practical wisdom.[8]

In the wake of such a widespread reform movement, Monasteries became easy targets of criticism. In many monasteries, landed wealth and spiritual laxity were widespread. It is easy to understand why the Reformers railed against the worldliness of the monasteries. For instance, not only did Martin Luther see evidence of monastic excess first-hand, he also found little comfort for his soul as a monk.

This, among other reasons, inspired Luther's critique of the monasteries and the system they represented.[9] The Reformers also perceived the blatant dualism underpinning the ideas and practices infusing monastic asceticism. In contrast, the Reformers replaced this often-negative focus on the body, with a recovery of the goodness of creation, including the joys of marriage and family life. One Reformation era preacher inveighed against the apparent paltry monastic spirituality with the phrase, "The walls don't make a monastery! It must be within the heart!"[10]

Many monastic orders recognized the crisis and made repeated attempts toward reform. The Lateran Council (1512 – 1517 CE), just prior to Luther's protest, heard the general abbot of the Augustinian order, Egidio da Viterbo, call for an inward spiritual renewal with external effects.[11] In other words: clean up the monastic house!

Despite the Reformer's overall disconnection from the monastic and contemplative aspects of Christian tradition, their view of monasticism's future value was not a conclusive case. Just eight years before his death, Luther seems to defend and encourage the continuation of some expression of monastic community. His statement reveals the complex and shifting views about monasticism, even during the Reformation era:

> "I should especially like to see the rural monasteries and those that have been endowed, stay to take care of noble persons and poor ministers. Nor have I proposed anything else from the beginning. From such monasteries suitable men can then be chosen for the church, the state, and economic life."[12]

Other Reformers were open minded to a theologically renewed form of monasticism continuing, as evidenced in the Wittenberg Articles written in 1536 CE:

> "If certain men who are capable of living a life under a rule prefer to pass their lives in the cloister, we do not reprove them so long as their doctrine and worship remain pure and they consider the practices of monastic life as things indifferent. We are convinced that numerous authentic Christians of sound spirituality have lived exemplary lives in monasteries. It is even to be wished that such cloisters should exist, occupied by learned and devout men, where the study of Christian doctrine can be pursued for the greater good of the Church. These might then be a place where young people are instructed not only in doctrine but also in the ordered devotional life."[13]

Sadly, since then, the last five-hundred years of Protestant community did not take up the encouragement of the Wittenberg divines, and as a result, the children of the Reformation and her churches up to the present moment have largely missed out on treasures of contemplative patterns of prayer, study and worship.[14]

Nevertheless, some monasteries survived the Lutheran Reformation, transforming themselves from Roman Catholic to Lutheran virtually seamlessly. Of note, was the Möllenbeck monastery, near Rintein, Germany. History remembers one Möllenbeck monk in particular, Conrad Hoyer, who in 1623 published a brief defense for continuing the monastic life among Protestant Evangelicals.[15]

Likewise, in the decades and centuries following the Reformation, small monastic-like spiritual communities sprung up throughout Europe and the New World, most famous of which was the Protestant monastic community in Germany that emerged under the leadership of Count Nikolaus Ludwig von Zinzendorf (1700 – 1760 CE), known as the Herrnhut community, meaning the community of "the Lord's watch".[16] In the modern era, Germany also witnessed stalwart Protestants such as Karl Barth and Dietrich Bonhoeffer demonstrate the ongoing need for cultivating spiritual community.[17]

Reading the Reformers' theological writings of protest and revision, it is evident that silence, meditative prayer and other monastic practices, were by and large avoided as remedies to the human condition.[18] In their place, arose a heavy emphasis on belief and the adherence to correct doctrine.

This avoidance was all the more regrettable, because so much of the contemplative dimension and the monastic practices that weave throughout the contemplative tradition, are keenly able to help us spiritually be healed and flourish.

Increasingly, for many in the great ongoing conversation that is church history, it turns out that the rediscovery of this lost contemplative tradition has become a powerful connection-point to and with the emerging generation today.[19] With that in mind, the rediscovery of such monastic ideals and treasures can support the local church and her leaders with deep spiritual flourishing. And that is what the remainder of this book is about.[20]

Understanding this is an important consideration in light of the current shifts of belief and practice of the Spiritual but Not Religious (SBNR), or the Nones, who often claim no communal faith-identity, and often transcend doctrine and dogma in favor of inner and communal experience. So, it has turned out that aspects of

Christianity's pre-Reformation era spirituality deeply resonate with and for the SBNR and Nones. In particular, the experiential turn toward inwardness – in both spiritual practices and one's sense of self. We can see the appeal of earlier Christian contemplative practices to the SBNR's and Nones, especially when the contemplative is wedded with social justice.

This, in part, begins to explain the resurgence of Millennials attracted to the New-Monasticism movement.[21] And not only that, how the rediscovery of the contemplative dimension dove-tails with current leading edge of consciousness studies – revealing a convergence that should not be avoided by the church and her leaders.

3 · *Convergence*

The convergence of meditative prayer and contemplative, monastic practices with neuroscience and consciousness studies is a powerful nexus, charting useful connection points for our being and doing Christian community in the post-Modern, post-Reformation, globally-interconnected era of Presence.[22] In particular, I have in mind an intuition that, the ancient contemplative stream of Christianity can help inform questions asked by a new generation of bio-tech savvy inquirers, such as:

What is consciousness?

How does consciousness relate to, or differ from the soul or human spirit?

What is the self?

What is the soul and how does it relate to our mind?

Can Artificial Intelligence ever replace humanity?
Can AI have a soul?

How should the church and theologians prepare theologically
for contact with other advanced, alien life in the universe?

Some of these questions have been with us as long as humankind has been looking "up" into the heavens, asking questions about our mysterious existence in the universe(s) above and within. Yet these questions have taken on a more nuanced nature in the new light provided by technological advances such as Functional Magnetic Resonance Imaging (fMRI) and 3-D brain scans, not to mention the mind-expanding images gleamed from the Hubble Telescope.[23]

While this book doesn't specifically answer these questions, we will explore adjacent territory. The fact that there is now occurring a beautiful convergence of philosophy, consciousness studies, neuroscience, and biology, *and spirituality* suggests a new golden age of human inquiry, perhaps even reaching ancient fruit long inaccessible on the "tree of knowledge".

One way this convergence can be seen is in the accessible work of Jon Kabat-Zinn and his mindfulness-based stress reduction program at the University of Massachusetts Medical School. Kabat-Zinn's program has influenced a generation of doctors, scholars and practitioners on the important physiological benefits of daily meditative prayer.[24] What Kabat-Zinn and others call mindfulness, is closely linked to what the Christian heritage calls meditation. Equally insightful is the work of Richard J. Davidson, who serves as the Director of the Waisman Laboratory for Brain Imaging and Behavior, and the Center for Investigating Healthy Minds at the University of Wisconsin-Madison.[25]

While there are differences between Christian meditation and mindfulness methods, there is also much in common. For example, the physiological benefits of being still, quiet and resting in meditation for brief periods of time once or twice a day.

The contemplative convergence is even impacting the field of education and leadership. Groundbreaking work on the impact of contemplative meditation upon students is emerging on a wider scale, especially through the work of Parker Palmer and Mirabi Bush.[26]

It turns out that the once forsaken contemplative dimension has returned from its Protestant neglect, empowering a robust conversation across the academic disciplines – amazing and thrilling for the Church, which for too long has retreated from the public square of science and education.

And, it turns out, that our very own Christian spirituality and contemplative practices are a means back to the table of humble wondering in the public square about the ongoing mystery and blessing of being human.

Contemplative renewal is not just intellectual. The mind is not just our physical brain. The mind is an aperture of our being; the matrix of the self. The mind is the expression and experience of integrating the Spirit to our spirit; the Mind of Christ to our consciousness and conscience, *embodied* and experienced as a complex bio-spiritual organism: mind, heart and body. The promise of meditative prayer is not *just* spiritual anymore. It is also biological; indeed physical. Positive biological and social implications are now being articulated in clear, scientific language for human well-being and happiness.

For those willing to learn from the convergence, perhaps such a significant confluence might also lead the church toward a destiny-shaping crossroads.[27] A crossroads of consequence: one way leading forward to the flourishing of a global inter-spiritual community; perhaps the other way, leading to the dead-end of mythic religion – with its predictable fears, divisions and violence; a tried and worn *religious* way, that many of the millennial generation, and therefore the future, have already concluded is no longer viable.[28]

Notice the opportunity of this convergence and avoid concluding that a contemplative renewal of Christianity is just new age spirituality infiltrating the church. Quite the contrary. This new way forward is both ancient *and* orthodox.

The contemplative convergence is occurring just as both the Christian church and the global community are realizing how much we need every bit of wisdom we can bundle together and practically apply to our mostly unworkable, current ways of being and doing, as seven billion of us live together on this precious planet with decreasing resources and increasing stressors.

As the world culture lurches from one crisis to another, those of us discovering that as we practice contemplative prayer (whether in a mindfulness or heartfullness method) we are moored in an unshakable depth. We practice not to change the world-system; we practice so to keep the world-system from changing us. We practice so to love – God, self and others.

Perhaps unprecedented times of confusion and conflict are a gift to us. The ongoing confluence of spiritual, cultural and technological upheaval calls forth a new vision. One that has not been widely tried within mainstream Protestant Christianity; yet a vision that paradoxically inspired the Reformation![29] A vision that embodies the one necessary, but seemingly missing ingredient – rediscovering the silence and stillness of meditative prayer and monastic practices, and receiving the gifts of wisdom and love that often soon emerge from the silence and within the rhythm of contemplative practices. As to *how* this can occur, we now turn.

4 · *How*

While there is great diversity of style among our Christian churches, the contemplative dimension of Christianity accessed through meditative prayer and monastic practices can unite us. The practices can ease our anxiety. They can renew us just as we are seemingly reaching our limits. The practices can transform our lives, connecting us deeper than words and doctrines, returning us to a simpler way of *being* with God and one another.

The joy that arises through the silence of our surrender to simply be with God through a specific kind of doing connects us to our common life in Christ and helps us journey forward together.

If this contemplative vision captures your imagination, I invite you to read the following lines slowly. Let the words sink in. Then read it again. Unlike Luther's ninety-five, for me, there is only this one necessary understanding:

The renewal of meditative prayer and monastic spiritual practices is the primary hope for the present evolution and future fecundity of Christian community.

How is that? Because:

Meditative prayer is the royal road for how we can access and experience the fullness of interior life, love, wisdom and joy that Jesus promised (John 10.10; John 15.11), *and the monastic practices are the time-tested gold-standard for cultivating one's personal spiritual life in community.*

As we look to consider such a vision within and among different forms of Christianity, a renewal in a local faith community might look like this:

- Shifting the focus from programs to practices.
- Shifting the focus from Sunday worship to a liturgical life together.
- Centering everything in the grace of meditative prayer.

We will explore each of these further in Part Three. For now, it is enough to say that these practices will cultivate such a fertile ground in your life and congregation that the Spirit of God will birth new fruitfulness, creativity and an outward focused love through a simple-but-not-easy attention to your inward life. That, in one brief paragraph, is the practical uptake of this book.

So, think of this book as a manual and map that pairs the imperative of mediation (prayer, *ora*) with the invitation to key monastic spiritual practices (work, *labora*) in a practical way. Thus, this book will not only be a map that describes the territory, it will also be a practical manual to show you *how* to travel towards the forsaken depth-dimension of the Christian tradition(s). In other words, don't just study the map; take the journey![30]

The journey is our ongoing evolution into the "*full stature of Christ*" (Ephesians 4.13). And it begins with the first essential how: meditative prayer.

How #1: Meditative Prayer

It may be helpful to define terms, especially since we are dealing with two very similar and often interchangeable words: *meditation* and *contemplation.* In Chapter Three we will explore these words in depth, but for now we might say that *meditation is the method that can bring a person to experience the inner state of contemplation.*

Meditative forms of prayer are the royal way to realizing the royal rule in our life, which is love. The contemplative tradition is diverse, alive and life-giving, and as a result, meditative prayer practices have both ancient foundations as well as very adaptive, modern expressions.

Meditation usually involves a method of focusing the mind to deal with the typical barrage of thoughts we experience when we quiet down and rest in the silence, so to lead us to the gift of contemplation – which is, in a sense, "mindless" – if understood as a non-discursive grace given by the Spirit of God. Simply put, meditation is the means. Contemplation is the end. Contemplation is first and foremost a grace. Contemplation is never a technique.

In the Christian tradition, meditative prayer seeks to cultivate an overall *heartfullness*. A meditative focusing method helps us sink our attention and intention deeper than the mental chatter of the mind. As we sink beneath the surface of this mental chatter, we consent to the presence and action of the Spirit of God. There, we may discover that God's presence, love and wisdom are always here and available to us, despite what contemplative Martin Laird calls, the "cocktail party" of chatter and distraction we become aware of in our mind and body as we get quiet.[31]

One spiritual impact of meditative prayer in our lives and communities is that it tends to connect us *experientially* to wisdom and love, dynamics which are the divine energies in which we grow and flourish – whether we know it or not. Furthermore, a practical result of meditative methods is that they help us to sustain a healthy balance and sense of well-being in the midst of our life activity and day-to-day responsibilities. In sum, meditative prayer can birth in us a grounded, joyful disposition that we may simply call the contemplative state.

Meditative prayer is also the heart-center of a cluster of interconnected monastic spiritual practices. When meditative prayer is paired with such practices, our lives and our faith communities will most certainly be on the contemplative path – and the transformative journey into love. A journey where anything is possible with God, and everything flourishes – just not in the way you might think, or on your time schedule!

How #2: Monastic Practices

When meditative prayer is *also* paired with the monastic spiritual practices (practices not necessarily limited to monasteries) something very special can happen to and within our life and faith communities.

By practices, I mean habits of *doing* that shape *being*. Practices are a patterned way of life, traditionally described as *a rule of life.* A meaningful and recent template for a contemplative rule of life can be seen in Brother Rodger's *The Rule of Taizé,* which provides a more modern and contemplative update to the more well-known *St. Benedict's Rule.*[32]

The importance of monastic practices, or a rule of life, stands upon the shoulders of several interrelated ideas:

We become what we do.

We can by God's grace, change.

When we can't do, we can ask for help.

The contemplative tradition wisely sums up these ideas with the simple maxim, *action sequitur esse*, "action follows being."[33] Or, as another wisdom teacher expresses it, *our being draws our life.*[34] Increasingly, monasteries provide the wider church with a compelling model for how to shape, form and develop our being, and in so doing, help us to see what is possible through the rhythms of being a *practicing* Christian community.

No community is perfect. All living systems are in process and subject to the forces of entropy. Yet, monasticism, long forsaken by the Protestant impulse, has again returned to help us, and perhaps we them.[35]

The menu of monastic, contemplative practices we will explore in this book is not exhaustive. In what follows, we will focus on seven core monastic practices that I believe can help deepen our spiritual lives and flourish the church.[36]

In Chapter Six we will linger at each, but for now, here is a list of the seven monastic practices for Protestant rediscovery:

Lectio Divina

Prayer of the Hours

Self-Observation

Silence

Simplicity

Solitude

Stillness

These practices can change and develop our being by grace and work. Grace is a word we use to describe the experience of being given the help we need without deserving that help or doing anything for it. For many, grace is the experiential basis of our spiritual life. Something happened to us that we can't really explain, but it changed our life for the good.[37] And not only happened, but also continues to happen.

An example of such a transforming grace is the sacrament of communion. The Eucharist conveys the presence of Christ. Beauty is also another example of grace. It comes to us and changes us, like the beauty of a mountain sunrise. There is nothing we do to create that situation. We just get to receive it and be blessed by it as a grace. Grace comes to us in many ways. Perhaps the sweetest graces are the ones we least expect or deserve.

Effort, or work, are words we use to describe the conscious choices we make. The word "work" describes *doing* certain things as well as *not doing* certain things. Work requires efforts, choices and acts of will. For example, if we want to change the fact that our body is out of shape, we have to do certain things, such as increase our metabolic heart rate. We also have to *not* do certain things, such as not overeat or snack on donuts. All the more, when we are seeking to change our inner thoughts or desires.

The point is that when our *doing* shifts, our being *can* change simultaneously. When our *being* evolves, our entire life can change. When our life changes our community is impacted. When our community is impacted for the good, our world can change.

That's true in part because systems are comprised of parts and parts shape the whole. Families are shaped by individuals. When one person changes, the whole system can shift. We each matter. Our presence is important. Each person's impact is unique. We should not discount the effect our individual and group *doing* can have on our individual and communal *being*. The impact our being can have in the world is not *just* a concept. The world is a living organism comprised of individual beings influenced by the *way(s)* of being of others.

The call to partake in the wisdom of spiritual practices comes from a very early place within the Christian tradition. Take for example this injunction, from one of the early desert fathers,

> "Take flight every day! At least for a moment, which may be brief, as long as it is intense. A 'spiritual exercise' every day – either alone, or in the company of someone who also wishes to better oneself...Try to get rid of your own passions, vanities, and the itch for talk about your own name. Avoid backbiting. Get rid of pity and hatred. Love all...become eternal by transcending yourself. This work on yourself is necessary..."[38]

This counsel sounds very similar to the saying attributed to the fifth century monk, Abba Arsenius, who in a mid-life spiritual crisis, cried out to God for help, and then heard this compelling imperative back: "Flee, be silent, pray always."[39] It also echoes St. Paul's call to early Christians to live in a different way. In the Letter to the Ephesians we hear an urgency to the invitation:

> *You were taught to put away your former way of life, your old self, corrupt and deluded by its lusts, and to be renewed in the*

> *spirit of your minds, and to clothe yourselves with the new self, created according to the likeness of God in true righteousness and holiness. So then, putting away falsehood, let all of us speak the truth to our neighbors, for we are members of one another. Be angry but do not sin; do not let the sun go down on your anger, and do not make room for the devil. Thieves must give up stealing; rather let them labor and work honestly with their own hands, so as to have something to share with the needy. Let no evil talk come out of your mouths, but only what is useful for building up, as there is need, so that your words may give grace to those who hear. And do not grieve the Holy Spirit of God, with which you were marked with a seal for the day of redemption. Put away from you all bitterness and wrath and anger and wrangling and slander, together with all malice, and be kind to one another, tender-hearted, forgiving one another, as God in Christ has forgiven you"* (Ephesians 4.22-32).

Much of this wisdom is a call to *work!* While the passage doesn't explicate *how* we get this way, it does clearly call us to work and act and be in a whole new way. To be and do life in a different way – the Christ way. To be by doing. If the church of the future is to be different, we are invited to learn from the past. And the wisdom of the fathers invites us to change our way of being by doing a few key practices. And the monastic practices answer the missing *how* question.

The point is that flourishing just doesn't happen on its own. We participate in the experience. In the New Testament, the word for flourishing occurs in 2 Thessalonians 1.3. The Greek word used there is ὑπεραυξάνει (hyper-auxanei), translated variously, as ever-growing or exceedingly increasing. We can detect a familiar word in the root stem; the English word hyper. As in, hyper-drive. Or hyper-active. In the case of 2 Thessalonians 1.3, the word literally means hyper-growth. Overflowing growth. Flourishing. Notice that their faith flourishes and their love is full. Both convey ongoing development and movement in depth and breadth.

Our ever-growing, flourishing faith may not always feel like we are growing. There are seasons where no fruit or growth is seemingly visible, and yet the roots are nevertheless strengthening in silence and stillness, hidden to our perception. These may also be seasons of intense pruning, where the edge of suffering seems to cut away all that which is false within us. Suffering may even temporarily take away our sense of God's felt presence.

Nevertheless, flourishing is something we get to participate in, partly because we become what we do. If we give our attention to the practices that nurture our flourishing – we will flourish. Perhaps not in the way we think, but in unexpected ways. Perhaps not in the timeframe we expect, but in timely ways. Inward ways. Ways of the Spirit, whose fruit are unmistakable: love, joy, peace, patience, kindness, goodness, gentleness, self-control, and such. And to help us flourish, we partake in new ways of being and becoming to which, we now briefly turn.

5 · *Become*

Neither the present nor the future of Christianity needs to be driven by becoming any more *mega*, or shallower. It is time for a return to spiritual depth in our faith communities. The way forward is not more biblical literalism. Not more moralism. Not more social justice. The much-needed answer for our moment is *depth.*

While I am all for the basics, or what C.S. Lewis called *mere* Christianity, it turns out that there are also seasons for deepening in the church. Today, it seems we suffer from an overemphasis on the veneer and an avoidance of depth. Gratefully, the remedy for what ails us *now*, is the pairing of contemplative prayer with select monastic practices.

Depth is the unique gift-set of the contemplative way of being Christian. In fact, there is a strong case to be made for Christianity becoming *less* successful not more. This reveals the contrast between the self-emptying (*kenosis*) way of being and the me-expansion (*mega*) way of doing.[40] When our worship (*doxa*) is grounded in emptying (*kenosis*) it doesn't really matter how many people are attending worship, or how many satellite campuses or staff members we have in our church.

From the contemplative vantage point, we discover that perhaps the heart of worship isn't the strength of sound, but the surrender of silence. In the case of our church life, the invitation to be fruitful and multiply may have nothing to do with *quantity*, but everything to do with *quality*. In the silence, we are invited to expand in wisdom. Partake in love. And be transformed into both.

Jesus, Lord of the church and shepherd of our souls, two-thousand years ago bore witness to the impulse of divine love: *that we would be known by our love,* not our largesse (John 13.35). The poet Novalis summarized it this way: "If our life is as precarious as it is, it is so in order that we should love and need another…to love is always to feel the opening; to hold the wound always open."[41]

This wound of love both releases our constrictions and heals our repressions – especially the unconscious material that we may not be aware is impacting our life and limiting our flourishing. The wound of love is not here to torture us, but to help us flourish. Admittedly, at first, the process seems like a kind of suffering. A cursory review of the classic writings of the contemplative tradition reveals that such revered saints as John of the Cross, Teresa of Ávila and Frances de Sales all bore witness to the transformative possibilities hidden within such suffering.[42]

We have room to grow in fulfilling Jesus' wish for us to be known by our love. The invitation is to *not* just *do* loving things, but *also become love* itself. Becoming love is the destination. From a contemplative perspective, it seems becoming love is the point of the entire Gospel of Jesus Christ.

It is important to remember and reclaim that the intention of the becoming process is to transform us *"from one degree of glory to another"* (2 Corinthians 3.18). From the glory of being *merely* human, into the glory of the union of our human nature with the divine nature. It is easy to forget that becoming love is what being human is for. Becoming love is what doing life is for.

In ancient times, this was called *theosis.* And without this mysterious horizon to move deeper toward day by day through the silence and stillness, and the graces of meditative prayer; without this filament of nothingness that is everything holding onto us as we wander through the dark nights and silent storms of our undoing; without this turbulent river of living-life leading us to the headwaters of love, I daresay we are all left busily and noisily bestriding the stage of time, forgetting the reason we came to the show in the first place.

Perhaps we have had enough sound and fury for a while. Perhaps, now we seek something more, something deeper, entering the light of the inward night of silence to receive the wound of love, crying out in the darkness:

Yes! My God! Yes, to the coming storm of silence,
and from there into the Everything of love itself.

Chapter Two /

Needing

1 · *A Collective Dark Night*

It is not news that the mainline Protestant Christian churches in North America, Great Brittan, Europe, Scandinavia, and Australia are in severe decline. The era of Christendom is over.[1] The era of spirituality ascends.[2] Nor is it news that our culture as we know it, indeed our very way of life, is red-lining in every measurable statistic.[3]

We are living in a time of consequential change and pervasive anxiety. We seem aimed at an invisible edge of no return. We are confronted with the triad forces of the decline of Christianity, the rise of spirituality, and the turbulence of seven billion plus people on planet earth seeking to thrive amidst a seemingly fixed supply of natural resources. As these massive shifts of human consciousness and behavior are woven together, there is no question that we are facing what feels like both a collapse of innocence and a plunge into the unknown.

Whatever future awaits us as a global community, it is most certainly *not* a time for the end of faith; rather, its necessary evolution! With that in mind, it is appropriate to recall the language of the "dark night", poetically articulated so memorably by John of the Cross (1542 – 1591 CE).

The "dark night" is widely understood in Christian spirituality as describing aspects of the spiritual journey that involve the stripping away of the "false" self through the severe mercy of what has traditionally been called the process of purgation (or purification).[4] Contemplative Thomas Keating helpfully updated the word purgation with the phrase "unloading of the unconscious,"[5] which brings the purpose of the process into clearer focus: our healing and development as individuals and as a species, a process Keating describes as the divine therapy.

When the pattern and wisdom of the dark night process is applied to the Western Christian church, especially the Protestant American mainline churches, it becomes clear that we are in the midst of a dark night for the important purpose of our further evolution.[6]

If it is true that the church is in a dark night, we would not be surprised to discover that our churches are marked with an increasing sense of dryness, fruitlessness and weariness. Some refer to this as God's judgement, but what if instead of judgement we take the therapeutic, developmental view that the Spirit of God is undoing us to unfold us further into the divine image and likeness?

Both John of the Cross and Thomas Keating put a nuanced, sustainable and psychological fine point to the spiritual process of healing and transformation that occurs through a communal dark night. It is *not* that being in a dark night is bad. Nor should it be sped through with a reckless abandon to reform the church, or purify it in the name of "righteousness."

If we can see the dark night as an essential step on our human journey of development, we can cease to react to such seasons of purgation with fear and start to respond to them with humility and gratitude.

Why? Because fear keeps us from evolving and unfolding further into God's love. Remember, that "*perfect love casts out fear*" (1 John 4.18). Love first empties us to then fill us with itself. The emptying process is a transformative one; a purgative one. Among Protestants, an often-overlooked aspect to that above referenced passage of scripture is the word *perfect.* This is a word that hints toward the developmental perspective of our ongoing spiritual unfolding – what we might even call our evolution.[7]

However, for some, through an increased theological dialog with Eastern Orthodoxy, the Western church is slowly realizing that the purpose of life is *not just* to be saved by faith (either by Christ's faithfulness, or our own faith in Christ).[8] We are saved by faith so that the likeness of God can be restored in us.

In a word, the Christlikeness made visible in and through Jesus is meant to be ours too. Christlikeness is another way of saying that the purpose of our union with God in Christ by the Spirit through faith, is to perfect us in love not *just* save us from sin and hell, or evacuate us to heaven.

Recall that the etymological root of the Greek word "save" (σώσω), is deeply related to embodied health and wholeness – body, soul and spirit. To be made *holy* is to become more *whole*: less fragmented, more solid, more present to the other in the moment. Holiness is about an increasing gravity of presence set apart for and in the glory of God. A weightiness of being that emerges not from perfection, but from our ongoing growth into wholeness in contrast to our devolution into fragmentation.

Literally the Hebrew word for glory is *kabad,* and means heavy. What is it that creates the heaviness? It is the Spirit of God birthing love, wisdom and goodness within us in the sacrament of the present moment. Love, wisdom and goodness are three core aspects of human wholeness. When Christians speak of the process of being saved, or of being perfected, they are speaking of the journey into relational wholeness. And this wholeness gives a density of being.

Gratefully, divine love births in us a holy longing from within the dark night. Love, which is literally the presence of Christ hidden in the darkness, feeds us. Thus, perhaps our communal dark night as a Protestant church family in a seemingly post-Christian culture is a gift for our ongoing fecundity. The dark night isn't a regression into a new cultural dark age. It is, rather, more akin to the temporary darkness of noontime Golgotha. A passing shadow of darkness that gives way to the surprise of resurrection light.

2 · *System Stressors*

We are, at this very moment, embedded in multiple, nested, unfolding living systems: *cosmos, solar system, earth, soul, mind, body*. It is increasingly clear that there is a patterned, even mirrored order to all of these living systems. We are interconnected within them, shaped by them and in a certain mysterious way, also influencing and shaping them by our thoughts, feelings and behavior. Wholes within wholes. What scholars refer to as *holons,* and what Ilia Delio and others describe as quantum entanglement.[9]

In the early twentieth century, we discovered quantum interconnectedness in an expanding universe. As a result, we have a deeper language that beautifully conveys the intuition of the interrelatedness of the nested living systems we find ourselves embedded within.[10]

This leads us straight into facing the facts about our social system(s). The characteristics of our social system(s) are red-lining humankind and the biosphere in multiple ways.[11]

In biological systems, stressors are expressions of dynamics occurring within the body that may or may not be helpful or useful. Therefore, stressors, like emotions, can be good communicators, but they often don't tell the whole story. Stressors become present to alert us either that something is lacking in the system, or that something is *too* prevalent.

While there are many characteristics that could be charted, we will explore six interrelated dynamics: *noisy, crowded, busy, stressed, electrified, evolving*. These characteristics alert many of us to our sense of imbalance and disconnectedness from well-being, peace and joy. In a word, we are experiencing non-wholeness. Left unchecked, these characteristics, and the dynamics that feed these characteristics, deplete us.

My point in reviewing these dynamics is not to focus on the negative. Rather, to focus our attention on a practical, contemplative treatment plan. A way to be amidst the tumult and increasing, inevitable anxiety. To do that, I'll first explore these key characteristics in the system; then beginning with Chapter Three, we will develop the contemplative treatment plan.

Noisy

I am writing this chapter in a quiet room at the Zephyr Point Conference Center on the shores of Lake Tahoe. The lake looks like an aqua jewel nestled in a ring of golden mountains. At this moment, all I can hear is the gentle cascade of waves rising onto the rocky shore. And then, sometimes also the wind, as it whirs through the tall fir trees that line the lake, like silent kings and queens of this sacred realm.

My peaceful moment in this majestic place is in loud contrast to the crowds and noise I just experienced at the Las Vegas airport, where I boarded a packed plane to get to this retreat center. Not only was the airport overcrowded, it was also noisy. The chimes of the slot machines. The overhead announcements. The vacuum cleaner. The music seeping out from the teenager's earphones sitting nearby turned up for everyone else to also hear. And, of course the revving jet engines.

I was later intrigued to learn that the English word noise is derived from the Latin root *nausea*! Our lives are immersed in noise, and sometimes it is only in the absence of noise, like at this Lake Tahoe retreat center, that we realize how noisy our world and lives have become.

Noise is normal, nor is it going away. The issue is how we deal with it. The contemplative model invites us to remember and rediscover that meditative prayer and monastic practices help us to live *in the midst of the noise*. The peaceful center holds us as the world of noise spins around our daily life. A friend once told me that on the first day she commuted into a large urban center for a new job, she turned to the person sitting next to her on the commuter train and said, "It feels crazy here!" The stranger sitting beside her nodded and replied, "Yes, you have to bring your sanity with you." One of the ways we can do that is by daily sitting in the silence of meditative prayer.

The English word *silence* emerges from several language streams. The Gothic verb *anasilan,* described the sound of wind dying down, and the Latin *desinere* meant to stop. Such linguistic sources suggest that the word silence has something to do with ceasing and stillness, as in the quiet that arises *after* being active. Thus, while silence is not the opposite of sound, silence is the opposite of noise.[12]

Early church theologian Irenaeus' intuition was that God's first language was silence. It turns out Irenaeus was cosmologically correct. In a study done in 2005, Mark Whittle, an astronomy professor at the University of Virginia, analyzed the sound of the big bang explosion and concluded that the creative explosion that occurred nearly fourteen billion years ago wasn't really a loud explosion at all. It was a completely silent event because the initial expansion was pure energy moving outward in a perfectly balanced sphere, like an unhindered ripple from a single rock thrown into a still pond.

In Whittle's view, "there were no compression waves, no sound, just quiet, brilliant, live expansion."[13] But the silence didn't last long. Whittle concludes that the big bang was "a moment of silence followed by a rapidly descending scream which builds to a deep roar and ends in a deafening hiss."[14] Similarly, contemplative theologian Raimon Pannikar (1918 – 2010 CE) intuited in meditative prayer that "silence is a kind of property of Being prior to Being."[15] So, it is not far-fetched to say that the universe emerged from silence.

It is difficult to measure how detrimental noise is to our spiritual life, indeed to our being. Noise hinders creativity, interferes with higher brain functioning and limits the ability of the body to recharge, be at ease and simply relax. Add to that, noise is often used as a means to avoid discovering ourselves more deeply. Reducing noise in our lives is a choice. Indeed, for many, a spiritual practice.[16]

Crowded

During the twentieth century, a brief yet tumultuous one hundred years, the human population on planet earth quadrupled! Compare that to the fact that while it took 200,000 thousand years for our species to reach the one billion mark, it only took the first thirteen years of the twenty-first century to add one billion more people to the population. Another stressor, and a noise of a different kind. By 2040, we will add another two billion people, notching the global population to nine billion by the middle of the century. Most of that growth will occur in developing countries, and one-hundred percent of that growth will occur in cities. By 2025, thirty-seven mega cities with populations exceeding ten million will mark our planet.[17]

The economic and ecological impacts of such compounding population growth are widely explored and commented upon.[18] Yet, less discussed, but equally important is what this massive growth will mean for the spiritual life of all of us who share this planet as home. In particular, how will this growth impact human stress and anxiety levels in such population dense megacities? Human population growth isn't inherently negative. In fact, it can be natural and wonderful: the flourishing of human life and love in all its many splendid diversity is surely one of the reasons we were seeded here on planet earth.

However, the spiritual challenge of human growth comes in the fact that the population boom is occurring in already densely crowded megacities.[19] While there are many positive aspects to urban life, population density also brings with it increasing traffic, pollution, noise, congestion, and crime – all intensifying the need for interior solitude and silence for one's wellbeing.

Crowdedness is not going away. The question is, how we will deal with it? Meditative prayer and contemplative, monastic practices can help us to live in the midst of the crowds, centered and connected with our deepest self and with the love of God. A peaceful center will hold us as the world crowds around us.

One of the ways we can grow in our peacefulness in the midst of the crowds is by practicing interior solitude, that primary monastic practice. Being still creates a place of beauty or quiet, and a way to be with God.

Most of us need to actively find or create such a place of solitude. I went to college in downtown Chicago, and lived there four years, from 1991 to 1995. At the time, Chicago's population was 2.8 million. It felt like it. At dusk, from the twentieth floor of my dorm, I often watched the sunset peeking through the urban canyons of nearby buildings. While I loved the city nightscape, I also noted how much I appreciated visiting my family in Wisconsin. When I did visit, one of the first things I delighted in was walking down their country road, cresting the hill and watching the sunset over the stretching farm fields.

I so enjoyed living in Chicago, but quickly discovered what living in a population dense urban city meant for me: it caused me to regularly pay attention to how I was feeling and to be proactive about taking time away from the city crowds, even if that meant just going to a park or finding a quiet nook in a café.

Busy

The monks of New Melleray, a Trappist monastery nestled in the rolling fields and forests just west of Dubuque, Iowa dug deep into the wisdom of Psalm 46.10: "*be still and know…*" These monks found the inner meaning of these words illuminating the familiar line into their community motto: "*be empty and see.*" For two years, I was a member of the New Melleray Associates. The strongest impression I have of the ethos of the monks was their unhurried sense of time. It was as if they lived by a different schedule, a slower one.

I am sure the monks had their appointed tasks. No doubt when the bell rang calling them to prayer, it often interrupted their work, nevertheless, the overall sense I had of the community of monks, was that they were present amidst their busyness. They possessed their tasks; their tasks did not possess them. Perhaps because they were inhabited by the larger sweep of time that is the *Prayer of the Hours*. Day by day, season by season, their lives were formed by the slow and simple rhythms of worship and prayer.

Presence. It is a gift we give ourselves. To be in this and every moment as completely as we can. It is also our gift to others. Those we encounter in passing and those we live with. Presence mostly evades us when we are busy because busyness has a way of keeping us from being in the *Thisness* of the moment with ourselves or toward others.

When I have felt caught in the patterns of busyness, I notice that I can take my irritation out on myself, berating myself internally for not being more disciplined with my time or boundaries. For saying yes to too many things. For not taking time for the practices that sustain me with clarity and peace amidst my life-tasks and work schedule. It is a compounding problem. My busyness impacts my time and schedule. When I'm busy, I tend to stay up too late cramming tasks in. As I do that, I tend to sleep in, missing the precious morning hours for meditation, prayer, and exercise.

Our busyness keeps us on the treadmill, often unaware of the toll it is taking on our body, and most importantly on our being, until we try to get off the treadmill of life without falling. Our dismounts from busyness can often be clumsy affairs. When we realize it, we often don't have the emotional reserves to do much except fall. When we do fall, hopefully there are loving people in our life who can support us and encourage us to spend a little time daily in the silence and stillness of meditative prayer.

Stressed

Stress is a capricious tool. Like a vampire, stress sabotages the very heart of our being and body, draining us of vital forces. Stress is the primary physiological and emotional signal that there is something out of balance with our way of life. Stress is also a biological reaction designed to warn and protect us. The stress response in our bodies initiates a cascade of biological events that left unchecked, can contribute to disease.

The word stress was borrowed from the field of physics. Stress describes the force that produces strain on a physical body. Stress is our body-mind response to a growling dog charging toward us; or the gnawing fear of losing a job.

Many are living in a time of hyper-stress. There is so much that is novel, unpredictable, threatening and out of control in our world civilization today. Many of us are just barely hanging on, pushed to financial, emotional and physical limits, often cutoff from the presence and support of family and friends, perhaps only connected by means of social media and screens.

When we recognize how prevalent the stressors are and how we can improve our response to the stressors, we are then ready to explore how meditative prayer and monastic practices can help us respond to stress in much healthier ways. It turns out that experiencing a stressor doesn't doom us to a life of stress.

The more important factor is how we perceive and handle that stress. Our reaction to stress often determines whether or not we will actually become stressed. Perception and stress management become key components to our ongoing wellness – body, mind, soul. Meditative prayer and basic monastic practices are key tools to help us perceive and manage such stress more effectively.[20] Such practices help us connect with the "*the peace of God, which surpasses all understanding*" (Philippians 4.7).

Electrified

As I write this, I am watching a website that tracks in real time current mobile connections. The ticker number is growing faster than my eye can perceive, changing every 1/100th of a second. The number on my screen now says: 8,764,573,635 and counting! That is 8.7 billion. The annual revenue from these devices is listed at 1.05 trillion.[21]

Mobile devices have transformed human connectivity, relating and communicating. We are living in the age of mediated presence. Ironically, we live in a mediated era where we can be present to one another on a screen, even if we are separated by continents, and yet we may never personally meet or interact with our neighbor who lives across the street. Our schedules, communication, commerce, banking, and even our transportation is often occurring through cloud-based applications all dependent upon the internet.

Yet, we are also now dependent upon something more powerful than the internet. Sustaining the entire system is the life-giving blood of electricity, flowing through our homes, neighborhoods, cities, nations and crowded planet. More than any other utility, electricity enables our modern lifestyle. Our food, water, gasoline, transportation, communication, defense and entertainment systems are all dependent upon electricity. If and when the electrical grid goes down, so too does our way of life.

While electricity is an untold blessing that has transformed human history, industry, economy, and has enhanced our quality of life in every dimension, our electrified lifestyle also brings with it the recognition that we are dependent upon a resource that few of us actually own, make or control. The point isn't to negate the gift of electricity, but more to draw attention to our vulnerability and dependence upon this utility.

Evolving

The truth of evolutionary development is perhaps the most important discovery of the modern era.[22] The record of the earth bears witness, layer by layer, to the span of the ages – the time and physical substance in which biological life emerged and evolved. Applied, to human development, we have now discovered that there is also a spectrum of development in human consciousness. Culture, technology and especially religion are key expressions on the spectrum of consciousness.

Similar to how a trained biologist can locate a particular species on the spectrum of evolutionary development, and a trained geologist can identify the chronological time of a certain layer of rock, so too can a developmental psychologist identify a particular expression of a level of consciousness identifying the ways human consciousness is expanding and evolving,[23] as particular epochs of time mark momentous leaps forward in human consciousness.

A popularized way of speaking of these epochs was introduced by the German philosopher Karl Jaspers, who coined the term *axial age*, in the sense of a pivotal age characterizing the period of ancient history during about the eighth to third centuries of the first millennium BCE. During this time, according to Jaspers' axial age concept, new ways of thinking simultaneously appeared in Persia, India, China and the Greco-Roman world.[24]

The concept was introduced in Jasper's 1949 book, *The Origin and Goal of History*. There, Jaspers claimed that the axial age should be viewed as an objective, empirical fact of history, independent of religious considerations. He identified a number of key thinkers as having had a profound influence on future philosophies and religions, as well as characteristics of civilization common to each era from which those thinkers emerged.

The axial age was the time when all the classics were written – from the Hebrew prophets, to Plato and Aristotle, to Confucius, to the Bhagavad-Gita, and the Buddhist Pali Canon.

When we ask Charles Taylor's beguilingly simple question, "When do the first classics appear?",[25] we must look to the first millennium axial period for the answer. Recently, scholars such as Karen Armstrong, Robert N. Bellah, and Phyllis Tickle re-introduced the idea of the axial age to help explain both what has happened historically in the field of religion, but also to help articulate what might be happening *at the present time*, as we move through what may be *another* axial age in the forward development of human consciousness.[26]

It is one thing for scholars to identify the strata of human and cultural development in the past, such as they have done with the axial age for the middle centuries of the first millennium BCE, but it is quite another to claim that we might be entering into a new axial age. In a lucid essay on the future of transcendence, scholar Richard Madsen intuited that any new era or age,

> "would be characterized by new movements within the great Axial traditions toward ecumenical openness. This would be arrived at not through some superficial syncretism but through an intellectual and moral commitment to the deepest roots of a tradition. But how would one distinguish reactionary, parochial clinging to tradition from a progressive, transcendent springing out of tradition? The only way would be through the fruits of the enterprise."[27]

The contemplative dimension is such a resourcement. Its value is further strengthened by the way all the ecumenical religious axial age religions are able to share in the practice of silence. It is a common truth that it is more difficult to disagree with one another when we are *not* talking. That is the power of silence.

Madsen goes on to describe how he discerns new beginnings in the different religious traditions, and points to the Taizé community as representative of such a positive development within Christianity:

> "such movements usually occur at the margins of their respective institutionalized religious traditions. They reach across doctrinal religious boundaries to create networks of concerns, cross-national and cross-class affiliations of unlikely bedfellows. It is such movements that Jaspers seemed to think were the potential fabric of authentic world community."[28]

Perhaps we also see something new in the groundbreaking synthesis of evolutionary development with human consciousness. The popular work of transpersonal philosopher Ken Wilber, is a primary instance of this. While not perfect, or by any means the last word on the subject, Wilber's model is very user-friendly and comprehensive, applicable to the full range of human interests.

For our purposes here, as well as in my own spiritual development, I have resonated with the writings of two Christian practioners who have applied Wilber's model of human development to their understanding of the church and their own spiritual journeys: Paul Smith and Jim Marion. I deeply believe these writers deserve deeper consideration by the entire Christian community today. Their models help articulate so much of our difficulties and also point to future possibilities.[29]

Though there are other cultural, political, financial and environmental stressors in the system, these six stressors, pose unique challenges to how we do Christian community and worship. My intent isn't to criticize, but rather to encourage thoughtful pondering of the issues.

As we consider the implications of a possible new axial age, we are called to understand more clearly how the contemplative dimension of Christianity could help us respond to very prevalent and ordinary stressors occurring in our lives. The contemplative remedy for these stressors begins with a willingness to reconsider and reconnect with the depth dimension – an evolutionary (personal, church, global) movement deeper than any ephemeral cultural or social moment. To this endeavor, we now turn.

3 · Explore

Sensing a need to respond spiritually to these stressful symptoms, the Protestant Christian community has begun to seriously explore the contemplative dimension – what I like to call the depth-dimension.

For example, the writings and teachings of contemplatives Thomas Merton, Henri Nouwen, George Maloney, and Thomas Keating have significantly shaped several generations of spiritual leaders and teachers, Protestant and Roman Catholic alike. Their impact seems to have shaped mainstream modern Christian writers such as Ruth Haley Barton, Joan Chittister, Richard Foster, Meg Funk, Ken Gire, Brian McLaren, Kathleen Norris, Eugene Peterson, Phyllis Tickle, Dallas Willard and Phillip Yancey, to name a few luminaries.

In addition to the enduring contemplative impact of Merton, Nouwen, Maloney and Keating, Franciscan author Richard Rohr and his Center for Contemplation and Action have graciously expanded the contemplative influence into mainstream Christianity. Rohr's influence and partnerships are significant, connecting the contemplative dimension with wider circles of church life through his Albuquerque wisdom school. Rohr's conversations with such Christian thought leaders as Rob Bell, Cynthia Bourgeault, and Ilia Delio have also helped many identify unworkable patterns in their own spiritual journeys and expand toward the contemplative depths.

These explorations have influenced the American Protestant church in several ways. First, in the early 2000's the New Monasticism movement began to impact the Protestant Christian community, combining the contemplative insights of monastic daily spiritual practices, prayer and liturgy with social justice. Author and practitioner Jonathan Wilson-Hartgrove has personified this movement. His work is also connected with the Emergent conversation, and the shift toward orthopraxis – that is, spiritual practices as articulated by Dorothy Butler-Bass and others.[30]

This is not just a recent phenomenon. The new monasticism movement can be located in the immediate decades following World-War II, with leaders such as Brother Roger (1920 – 2008), founder of the Taizé community, or Chiara Lubich (1920 – 2008), founder of the Focolare community. In Protestant circles, new monasticism traces inspiration back to Dietrich Bonhoeffer (1906 – 1945), whose book, *The Cost of Discipleship* called a new generation of Christians into intentional spiritual community and faith practices that place a more particular focus on the invitation to become imitators of God.[31]

More recently Richard Foster and Dallas Willard's (1934 – 2013) *Renovaré* movement was an expression of this depth-desire, with its focus on spiritual development and spiritual formation. Not only has the *Renovaré* movement spawned its own spiritual formation study bible, it has also created a spiritual formation program for lay people in conjunction with Fuller Theological Seminary.

But perhaps most surprising, is Willow Creek's *Reveal Study*. Founded in 1975 by pastor Bill Hybles, Willow Creek is arguably the nation's first and most prominent seeker-sensitive mega-church. However, after decades of focusing on numerical growth and outreach, their internal Reveal Study indicated that their congregation was hungry for spiritual growth – for the dimension of depth.[32] What was most sorrowful to me, was the admission by Hybles that he had misread the *church's* spiritual maturity.[33] So, Hybles admits,

> "I wound up not teaching on the spiritual practices very often. Decades later, I found out, primarily through the Reveal study, that I should not have been dissuaded by the kind of feedback I was getting. I should have done a major series on the classic spiritual disciplines every single year. You can strip away almost every other thing the church does. But at the core of the core of the core, growing people into Christ followers is all about helping them engage God's Word and inspiring them to invite God to be at the center of their lives. I did not emphasize that as much in the early days as I do now. It's a deep regret I carry."[34]

Thankfully, at places like Willow Creek, the contemplative explorations continue. With Willow Creek launching a Sunday evening worship community called The Practice. The new worship launch creatively seeks to embody the ancient spiritual practices that have marked the contemplative dimension of Christianity for centuries. While not formally a contemplative service, it is clearly a significant nod to the emerging hunger for spiritual depth.[35]

While these explorations are important, and a starting point for many, now is the time for the Protestant Christian community to move beyond a first-date with the contemplative way and sink into the depths and blessings waiting for us in complete betrothal. For this to happen, it is necessary, now more than ever, to shift priorities toward a renewed being by doing, a hybrid along the lines of this potent idea:

our being is transformed by our doing.

Salvation should no longer be viewed as *just* about believing the right information (i.e. that Jesus died for your sins). Yes, we believe, but *we believe to become something*: a love that loves.

Surely the gift of Christianity is beyond mere believing information encoded as doctrine or dogma. In her book, *Christianity after Religion,* Diana Butler-Bass recently showed the shift of priorities occurring within Christian communities by contrasting the different order of three simple verbs.[36] She argues that the older, previous model of Christian priorities was this:

Believe. Behave. Belong.

In contrast, Bass urges a reversal of the verbs:

Belong. Behave. Believe.

This shift of priority represented by these words is a further reason our understanding and experience of salvation must mature to incorporate transformation in community. When our salvation message is based on *belief* alone (i.e. mental faith), it pits one belief against another: I believe this. You believe that. The result is that we often fight. The contemplative dimension, through meditative prayer and the monastic practices, invites us to ponder this template of order:

Do. Be. Become.

And…

Be. Do. Become.

And simply…

Be…until there is no more you to be.

By a clarity born of experience, we recognize that the way forward is not more entrenchment of knowledge or beliefs about someone (Jesus) or something (human nature and sin). The way forward for faith is about practices that truly transform us into love as individuals and as a community through the inward re-formation of our thoughts, emotions and actions into the image of Christ.

In other words, the transformation through the *"renewal of our minds"* (Romans 12.2); where mind represents the totality of our being. Meditative prayer paired with the monastic spiritual practices energize just such a renewal. Paired, prayer and practice function as the exquisite and precise process and grace of sanctification. In such practices, grace comes close and personal into our lives.

This shift into the contemplative way of being can also harmonize our inter-religious dialog in a world-community too often fractured by faith and singed by old religious fears rearing up with new violence. Sitting in the silence of contemplative prayer has a way of nurturing intimacy with others, even those we disagree with. The silence of meditative prayer is how we can experience and access the peace that surpasses understanding and return to God's first language, understood by all.

4 · *Reconnect with Depth*

Ironically, the impulse toward inward authority that funded much of the Reformer's rejection of ecclesiastical authority, was made possible in the first place by the mystical and contemplative streams bubbling up throughout Europe in the four centuries prior to the Reformation.[37] Mystics such as Meister Eckhart and the anonymous author of the *Theologica Germanica* bear witness to this contemplative inspiration and connection.[38] In fact, scholars often refer to the Reformation as the birth of Western secularization – a movement toward modern ideals of the autonomous, inward self.[39]

Throughout the last five centuries, important attempts were made to regain that inner depth. Four in particular mark Protestantism's historical development: Pietism, Romanticism, Revivalism and Pentecostalism.[40] I am confident history will also record a further renewal movement: the *Contemplative*.

Philosophically, you might say we are rebalancing our intellectual capital, shifting away from Plato and moving towards Aristotle. It is a dance the church has been doing for two centuries.[41] Perhaps the path of contemplation will find a third way forward, evolving us beyond the classical tensions and dualities between doing or being; form or idea; Aristotle or Plato.

Our thesis is that as the Protestant movement slowly disconnected from the Roman Catholic mainstream flow, we mostly lost touch, at least structurally, with the living waters of spiritual community cultivated over a thousand years of monastic spiritual development.[42] Despite the many blessings the Reformation era brought Western civilization, the Protestant community and its pastors have been playing spiritual catch-up ever since, seeking prayer and practices that can help direct and sustain a vibrancy of inner life, both for individuals and communities.[43]

As Western Christianity lost touch with the inner, depth-dimension during the sixteenth through nineteenth centuries, the quiet spiritual practices of silence, solitude and stillness, were increasingly replaced with *thinking* about God, accessed through logic and creed.[44]

Against this background, thankfully, meditative prayer and the monastic-contemplative spiritual practices are returning to our awareness. Slowly, the wider Christian community is reconnecting with its own spiritual headwaters from within its tradition. Surprisingly, significant parts of Luther's and Calvin's writings attend to such contemplative, even mystical intimations.[45] As Luther wrote,

> "But faith must be taught correctly, namely, that by it you are so cemented to Christ that He and you are as one person, which cannot be separated but remains attached to Him forever and declares: 'I am as Christ.' And Christ, in turn, says: 'I am as that sinner who is attached to me, and I to Christ. For by faith we are joined together into one flesh and one bone.'"[46]

And Calvin added:

> "I confess that we are deprived of this utterly incomparable good until Christ is made ours. Therefore, that joining together of Head and members, that indwelling of Christ in our hearts – in short, that mystical union…"[47]

In one sermon Calvin affirms that, "Christ must present Himself to us and invite us into such a relationship that truly we are united to Him, that he dwells in us in such a way that everything that belongs to Him is ours."[48]

These are just two examples that indicate long-forgotten contemplative seeds. Hidden within the immense gifts of the Protestant movement, there are such treasures as these that are resurfacing in the present generation.

The contemplative dimension isn't a new phenomenon, but a dimension foundational to the Judeo-Christian and Protestant experience, because Jesus grounds all spiritual life in contemplation's biblical synonyms such as *abiding* (John 15.4) and *flourishing* (John 15.8; cf. 2 Thessalonians 1.3).

The hope is that more of us understand that the *depth of our being* is formed by our doing and undoing in the silence. Such an understanding is rooted in the wisdom that one's being is the result of one's attention and surrender to the ever-deepening light, life and love of God.

Understanding this, faith communities no longer need to be measured by how many attend worship, rather, a deepening surrender to be a "*participant in the divine nature*" (2 Peter 1.4), empty vessels increasingly filled with the presence of wisdom becoming love. Or, in St. Paul's words, "*it is no longer I who live, but it is Christ who lives in me*" (Galatians 2.20).

As spiritual leaders move toward embodying this vision of wisdom-love, I suspect that in five-hundred years, in the year 2517, denominations will have lost their schismatic nature and have returned to that early unified church model, comprised of the core founding Protestant communities, such as Episcopalians, Presbyterians, Methodists and Baptists.

Or, perhaps by the sheer grace of the Spirit, a Global Catholic Church, will emerge reunited in Christ as one family. For such a miracle to occur, it would require a wide-spread life-giving engagement with the spiritual practices that shape us in the depths of Divine hiddenness and love. Perhaps in prior eras, such a resourcement of spiritual practices would have been called revival.

Part Two:

Rediscovering the Pathway

"We must close our eyes and invoke a new manner of seeing…A wakefulness that is the birthright of us all, though few put it to use." [1]

– Plotinus

"For neither the inspiration of the prophets, nor the immersion in God of the mystics, nor the contemplation of God in the mirror of the creation by the sages is equivalent to the new experience of the "vision" of God – the "beatific vision" of Christian theology. For this "vision" takes place in the domain of essence transcending all substance; it is not a fusion, but an encounter in the domain of essence, in which the human personality (the consciousness of self) remains not only intact and without impediment, but also becomes "that which it is", i.e. becomes truly itself – such as the Thought of God has conceived it for all eternity." [2]

– Valentine Tomberg

Chapter Three /

Defining

1 · *Inwardness*

Contemplative. It is more than a spiritual adjective or boutique brand of Christianity. It is a universal invitation. To attend to the quantum beauty of the image of God entangled with our being – body, soul and spirit – to all beings. In a word, it is the timeless draw of humankind toward *inwardness.*[1] Yet an inwardness connected to an *everywhereness.*[2] It is an inwardness grounded in a practical grace that frees and empowers us to both be and do from a deeper wholeness. Indeed, an inwardness formed with an authenticity and a strength that we may not otherwise experience on our own without stepping into a contemplative environment of silence, stillness and solitude.

By inwardness, I don't mean to suggest that all a human needs to do is turn inward to find God. It is more accurate to say that this is the inwardness of being in God's presence, versus the presence of God being in us. This allows us to acknowledge the mystery of our participation in the divine life and love – which is ultimately the mystery of the Trinity – without collapsing into the error of somehow thinking our experience of the divine presence within is containing or limiting God. Perhaps this is what the Psalmist is seeking to convey with the soaring affirmation, "*How lovely is your dwelling place, O Lord...My soul longs, indeed faints for the courts of the Lord*" (Psalm 84.1-2).

To be contemplative is to say yes to the inward presence and action of the Spirit of God. This inwardness helps us attend to the presence of love hidden in the present moment, and the ground of our being. Contemplation is, at its heart, a participation in the presence of love that births wisdom, kindness, mercy and understanding in us.

A continuity of inwardness weaves thorough the centuries of Christian faith in experiential and practical spirituality. St. Augustine, perhaps the father of Western Christian theology, sets the tone for such a theologically, inward, contemplative disposition, with his poignant confession in the wake of his own experience of the Presence of Trinitarian love: "My mind, in the flash of a trembling glance, came to Absolute being – That Which Is."[3]

Whatever glory Augustine may have experienced or sought to convey with these words, certainly today, we can extend Augustine the grace of recognizing the limitations of the word "mind." We intuit that what he meant by his flashes of insight, was a kind of trans-self-discovery akin to what intimate lovers experience wordlessly, gazing eye to eye and face to face in the silence. That Which Is, is Love, loving the Beloved, and quickening the Loved more into Love.

It turns out that this kind of knowing is more like a *seeing* than a becoming. The seeing is a way of expressing the happening. When words are needed to express the ineffable experience, it is by their shape, intelligence and influence that we and others are helped to remember that which we and everyone *already is*: love. We become what we already are.[4] We are born with love pre-installed.

The words merely point us toward a more profound awareness of the experience. Words, especially the long-ago-words of the saints and scriptures, invite us to personally plunge into the journey ourselves. Perhaps as we plunge, we often realize that we will never fully get the Mystery of God because the Mystery has already gotten us! In a real sense, we are plunged into It!

While the contemplative dimension of Christianity is activated by the grace of the Spirit of God, the contemplative dimension is also often accessed by a path of practices. These practices gently yet profoundly help us remember our deepest possibility, by leading us to what Jesus called "*the one necessary thing*" (Luke 10.42). Whatever else this one, essential is, it certainly intends to nurture in us our most real and developed life in Christ. In a word, by the Spirit of God, this one necessary dynamic, helps us *flourish.* We do so, by consenting; by being still in the silence to the Reality of Its Presence.[5]

The contemplative dimension of integral, inward union is a human birthright. It is the state of being that every human is created for. So, in a certain sense, this is one reason I suggest that a meaningful synonym for the word contemplative might be *inward.* This both demythologizes and democratizes the oft polarizing word contemplative and opens its meaning up to all sorts of inward, human experiences – from singing your infant to sleep with a lullaby in the quiet shade of the porch swing; to sitting in the stillness of an autumn forest attentively watching the empty space among the trees from a deer stand, completely present to the moment.

Yes, all of this and more is the contemplative way of being, indeed of being human. Little by little, as we journey more deeply on the contemplative path into divine love and grace, we become the *most real*-I in relation to That Which Is Most Real.

2 · *Outwardness*

The famous contrast between Mary and Martha that Jesus outlines in the Gospel of Luke Chapter Ten, has often been mistakenly used to segment out the contemplative in contrast to the active. The essential point of the story is that inwardness and outwardness belong together. They supplement each other. Think of inwardness and outwardness as the base and treble clef of the symphony of our spiritual life.

In Jesus' teaching to Martha, he uses the phrase "better part" (Luke 10.42). This is instructive not so much because it qualifies the contemplative way as being the *better* part, but that it clearly acknowledges that the contemplative way is *just one part* of the whole – which is the union of the contemplative and active.

Perhaps the incorporation of the contemplative dimension helps us see things differently. We are here to love the world *as* the world – as parts within the whole become more deeply aware of each other as each other – embodied humans in the ever-evolving cosmos that is becoming love.

The key is remembering the deep interrelatedness of inward and outward, action and contemplation. This harmonization is a contemplative grace. The union of inwardness and outwardness is a healthy foundation for all life and ministry and is the safest place to enter the wounded world with the love of Christ and the justice of mercy. A union cultivated by consenting more and more to the Center, to which we now turn.

3 · *Centeredness: Defining Meditation and Contemplation*

The word most commonly used in the Christian tradition to describe contemplation is the word *meditation,* from the Latin *meditare.* The root *stare in medio*, which literally means "to remain in the center." The word contemplation suggests the same. Experientially, the temple is our heart, the depth and center of our being.[6] Contemplation is the gift of being with God in our heart, beyond words and engagement with thoughts, in the grace of silent stillness.

In current cultural usage, the words meditation and contemplation seem to have become virtual synonyms. But it wasn't always that way. In the unfolding centuries of Christian faith, theology and experience, there were deep and unique distinctions in how the words meditation and contemplation were used, especially between different traditions, East and West.[7]

In the Eastern and Asian traditions such as Hinduism and Buddhism, the word contemplation was more related to discursive or mental reasoning.[8] A kind of analytical discourse progressing from one thought to another. This was also the classical Greek concept of contemplation. Such notions of contemplation are still retained in Western English when we say things like "contemplate your options," or on an aesthetic level, "let's contemplate the meaning of this beautiful painting."

In contrast, by and large in the West, the word meditate was more often used to describe what the East called contemplation. In the West, meditation meant a kind of reflective, mental activity. In Christianity, mental meditation was encouraged to cultivate a devotional depth and imaginative connection with Jesus and the biblical stories, such as meditating on the Passion of Christ.[9]

We can see this approach to mental meditation, using thoughts and words in the practice of *lectio divina.* In the second step of the process, one is invited to ponder the meaning of a biblical text with the mind and imagination. The traditional term for this is discursive meditation, wherein the mind or imagination is actively involved in picturing or sensing our interior relationship to and with God, or even a biblical story.

In the East, non-discursive, wordless prayer was called meditation. In the West, contemplation.[10] More simply stated, the idea and practice of contemplation was the Western equivalent to Eastern meditation. In Christianity, the word and activity of contemplation described the practice and experience of the "gaze of faith," or "pure prayer," or even "a silent love" and "union" – experiences the Eastern world would call meditation.[11]

In our common usage today, neither the word meditation nor the word contemplation is about philosophical or speculative thinking. At the most, we might say something like, "Let me meditate on that," or "I'll contemplate my options." But these phrases are clearly understood to be referring to a kind of intellectual pondering and not referring to silent, wordless prayer. One anonymous author of the spiritual life brilliantly describes the process from concentration to meditation to contemplation like this:

> "Meditation is therefore the honest and courageous effort of the 'lower self' to think together with the 'higher self' in divine light. And just as *concentration* necessarily precedes meditation, so does the latter lead sooner or later to *contemplation*, i.e. a transition is made from consideration and discourse to the immobility and complete silence of supernatural communion, where one no longer thinks *something* from a distance, but where this Thing itself is present and reveals itself. Contemplation is the union of the thinker with reality. Here one does not arrive at a 'conclusion', but one receives – or undergoes – the *imprint* of Reality."[12]

By the words contemplation or meditation, I don't mean an intellectual focusing on something until an insight is gained. Nor by contemplation do I mean a kind of philosophical state of mental rumination. While the words meditation and contemplation have a long history associated with such aspects of mental, discursive thought and inspiration, for our purposes here, both meditation and contemplation have less to do with rational thinking (philosophical or otherwise), and everything to do with the intuitive experience of knowing and being known by Love in silence.

In Christianity, and especially in the *lectio divina* tradition, meditation was a step in the process toward the potential grace of contemplation.[13] Notice how Francis De Sales (1567 – 1622 CE) describes the transition from meditation to contemplation. In his book *Treatise on the Love of God,* De Sales defines contemplation as "a loving, simple, and fixed attention of the mind on divine things."[14] And then he goes on to say that,

> "prayer is called meditation until it has produced the honey of devotion; after that it changes into contemplation...Thus, as bees draw nectar from the flowers, we meditate to gather the love of God, but, having gathered it, we contemplate God and are attentive to [God's] goodness because of the sweetness that love makes us find in it."[15]

Etymological Origins of Contemplation

It is useful to recall that the English word *contemplative* comes from the Greek word *theoria* (Θεωρία). When the Greek *theoria* was translated into Latin, the word *contemplatio* was used. The English word contemplation comes from the Latin *contemplatio.* The Greek term *theoria* covered a range of meanings such as to look at, reflect, meditate, investigate, and even to be present at a spectacle, such as a play or sporting event. All this points to the fact that contemplation means much more than just thinking about something deeply.

Furthermore, the Latin *contemplatio* derived from *templum*, which meant a set-apart sacred space for the offering of worship and divining into matters, which is one reason why the English word temple continues to be used to describe places of sacred worship or reverence. It is useful to notice a few linguistic and phonetic components within the Latin and Greek roots of our English word *contemplate.* I offer this further pondering in a spirit of playfulness:

Latin
Con = with, for

Template = pattern, model, measure

Temple = sacred space

Temp = time, measurement

Tem = to cut

La = the sixth tone in the musical scale, and also the root in the French, turned English phrase, "Ooh-la-la!," meaning literally "Oh, there, there!" Or, "La-La land," referring to a state of dreaminess, or someone who appears to be completely out of touch with reality.

Ate = English verb for ingesting into one's body and being a substance of influence

Greek

On = being

Emp = passion, feeling

Emerging from this word collage, an impression of time, space, harmony, influence, existence and feeling arises.

Blending it all together, one can say that to contemplate certainly means more than just thinking about something. Thus, my definition of contemplation is:

> *The experience of being held by a center of infinite space in and beyond time into the order and pathos of beauty, truth and goodness felt so deeply it feeds your soul and very being so that you can't help but grow, develop and flourish.*

Theological developments

Beyond etymological origins, in practice, *contemplation is simply the awareness and perception of God as our center amidst the circumference and seasons of life.* Contemplation is the ever-deepening awareness that God is the Being of our being; the Love of our loving; the Seeing of our seeing; the Knower of our knowing.[16]

Contemplation is the realm of faith, so it is inevitable that contemplation transcends most descriptions. As St. John of the Cross says, "Who can describe the understanding God gives to loving souls in whom God dwells? And who can express the experience God imparts to them? Who could ever explain the desire God gives them? Certainly no one can. Not even the very souls through whom God passes."[17]

And yet John of the Cross also seeks to describe contemplation as "none other than a secret, peaceful and loving infusion of God which, if the soul allows it to happen, enflames it in the spirit of love."[18] Is this not what St. Paul expressed as well, in a deep state of prayer? *"I pray that you may have the power to comprehend, with all the saints, what is the breadth and length and height and depth, and to know the love of Christ that surpasses knowledge, so that you may be filled with all the fullness of God"* (Ephesians 3.18-19).

For Christians, the divine mystery of contemplation can only be known by a revelation, and the condition for this revelation is purity of *nous,* the spiritual eye (or mind) that Jesus speaks of in Matthew 6.22-34, which according to Origen, Evagrius, and other church fathers and mothers, can be cultivated through specific spiritual practices *(praxis).*[19] The practical take away from this is that the essence of theology is contemplative prayer.

John Cassian (c.360 – c.435 CE) was one of the first Christian theologians and monastics to write about contemplation.[20] He wrote that contemplation is "when God shall be all our love."[21] Cassian experienced contemplation as the most subline prayer, ineffable, and transcending "all human sense." For Cassian contemplative prayer was *not,*

> "Characterized by any sound of the voice, or movement of tongue, or any pronunciation of words. The mind illumined by that infusion of heavenly light, does not describe it in human or limited language, but…ineffably utters it to God, producing such things in that brief moment of time, that returned to itself, it cannot easily speak about them [later]."[22]

Expanding on this silent method of prayer, Cassian comments on Jesus' prayer in solitude (Matthew 6.6 and Luke 5.16), encouraging us that when,

> "we pray within our room, when we remove our heart completely from the din of all thoughts and anxieties, and in some secrete and intimate way, we disclose our prayers to the Lord. We pray with closed doors, when with sealed lips and in deep silence we pray, not to the searcher of words, but the searcher of hearts. We pray in secret when with fervent heart and mind we lay open our petitions to God alone."[23]

Nearly a thousand years after Cassian, a distinction began to be made between different kinds of contemplation: acquired, active, and ordinary, which were then set in contrast to infused, passive and extraordinary. The primary distinction between these forms of contemplation was that some were discursive, meaning with words (discursive), actively engaging the mind and imagination. Whereas others were not, meaning wordless (non-discursive). We can see this particularly in the writings of Saint Teresa of Ávila and Saint John of the Cross, who both began to further distinguish contemplative prayer over against meditative prayer (i.e. mental prayer).

John of the Cross describes God calling one into the non-discursive, wordless, passive form of prayer, which John described as the "prayer of loving attention," which aptly describes the essence of contemplation itself. John follows Thomas Aquinas in this, who also says that contemplation is "spiritual vision." Aquinas (following Gregory the Great) spoke of contemplation as a loving gaze directed toward the transcendent divine reality. A vision not really induced by human activity, but inspired, infused, bestowed as a divine principle, or what we might call, grace.[24]

In one of the clearest theological descriptions of contemplation anywhere, John of the Cross develops the notion of love, not-knowing and the pure divine grace that is the source and protection of one's experience in contemplation:

> "Contemplation [is called] secret since, as we mentioned, contemplation is the mystical theology which theologians call secret wisdom and which St. Thomas says is communicated and infused in the soul through love. This communication is secret and dark to the work of the intellect and the other faculties. Insofar as these faculties do not acquire it but the Holy Spirit infuses it and puts it in order in the soul…the soul neither knows nor understands how this comes to pass and thus calls it secret. Indeed, not only does the soul fail to understand, but no one understands, not even the devil, since the Master who teaches the soul dwells within it substantially where neither the devil, the natural senses, nor the intellect can reach."[25]

John of the Cross' succinct definition also points us to this experience of being love. He says that contemplation, "is a science of love; it is an infused, loving knowledge of God."[26] He goes on to say that the difference between meditation and contemplation is like, "the difference between working, and enjoyment of the fruit of our work; between receiving a gift, and profiting by it; between the toil of traveling and the rest of a journey's end."[27]

Unfortunately, it was at John of the Cross' time in history when contemplation also became even less ordinary and more exclusive. This occurred, thanks in part, to both his own, and especially Teresa of Ávila's writings, which paired her understanding of infused, passive contemplative prayer, with what Teresa described as the higher states of the mystical life.

Teresa contributed a great deal to our understanding of the dynamic process of contemplation. In particular, Teresa mapped out the two primary categories of contemplation mentioned earlier, which Teresa called:

Acquired contemplation

And

Infused contemplation[28]

For Teresa, acquired contemplation was an intuitive knowing. Commenting on Teresa's definitions, Saint Frances De Sales described acquired contemplation as "a loving, simple and permanent attentiveness of the mind to divine things." Teresa also taught that infused, or higher contemplation (also called intuitive, passive or extraordinary), was a very rare, supernatural gift by which a person's mind and will become totally centered on God. Thus, for centuries, this kind of wordless prayer and unitive experience was referred to as "mystical prayer" or "infused prayer." And thought to be reserved for only "advanced" souls.

In time, such distinctions limited contemplation to the privileged few. Thankfully, these distinctions have receded, and contemplation is now viewed as more of an ordinary gift of God's grace available and open to *anyone* who might ask, seek and knock for the blessing to be opened to them also.

Still, combine such special levels of contemplation with the presumed "superiority" of the monastic climate, it is no wonder that contemplative Christianity is often viewed as a form of spiritual snobbery at worst, and quiet escapism at best.[29] This, despite the fact, that centuries prior to Teresa, both St. Augustine and St. Gregory taught that every Christian should practice both lives – the active and the contemplative. This spilt contributed to the founding of uniquely orientated monastic orders: the contemplative, such as the Cistercians and Camaldolese, and the active, such as the Franciscans and Jesuits.[30]

Contemplation is the desire hidden within all things that turns us toward love. Contemplation is life itself, growing toward the light of wisdom. We are seeds, created to grow and develop in body, mind and spirit, and the field of this growth is consciousness; plowed asunder and tilled with tenderness by the furrowing of contemplative practices.

Moving into the insights of modern times, notice also how the *Catechism of the Catholic Church*, defines contemplation as "a form of wordless prayer in which mind and heart focus on God's greatness and goodness in affective, loving adoration; to look on Jesus and the mysteries of his life with faith and love."[31] Richard Rohr similarly summarizes contemplative prayer as "receiving the moment in its present wholeness and un-wholeness."[32]

For many, the word contemplative may seem outdated. My aim is to give it a facelift. In my view, contemplation is *the* leading-edge way to help the Christian church turn the corner from Christendom to the spiritual but not religious mood that marks much of post-Modernity. As a part of the face lift, consider two more modern helpful definitions focusing on the development of the concept of contemplation. First, from Thomas Merton, in the mid-twentieth century:

> "In the strict sense of the word, contemplation is a supernatural love and knowledge of God, simple and obscure, infused by [God] into the summit of the soul, giving the soul a direct and experimental contact with God. Mystical contemplation is an intuition of God born of pure love. It is a gift of God that absolutely transcends all the natural capacities of the soul and which no person can acquire by any effort of their own. But God gives it to the soul in proportion as it is clan and emptied of all affections for things outside of God...But the thing that must be stressed is that *contemplation is itself a development and a perfection of pure love.* The person who loves God realizes that the greatest joy, the perfection of beatitude is to love God and renounce all things for the sake of God alone – or for the sake of love alone because God is love. Contemplation is an intellectual experience of the fact that God is infinite Love, and that God has given Godself to us, and that from henceforth, love is all that matters."[33]

And, from Daniel P. Barbezat and Mirabai Bush, in the early twenty-first century,

> "The word *contemplation* derives from *contemplari,* to "gaze attentively," but the word was originally linked to the act of cutting out or creating a space, as in "to mark out a space for observation." The word *temple* comes from this definition: a place reserved or cut out for observance...Introspection is inward (*intro*) looking (*specere*) – the mental act of attending carefully to what is occurring within, often in response to an activity, theory, or text...From the Stoic practices *meletai,* and the prophetic Kabbalah practices of Abraham ben Samuel Abulafia, to the "noble connection" of Sufi practice through the *Exercitia spiritualia* of Ignatius of Loyola right up to modern programs of mindfulness-based stressed reduction, internal reflection and

> the cultivation of awareness have been important aspects of both religious and secular attempts to deep and enrich experience and meaning. Although the specific practices are very different in the various traditions, two aspects of meditation are common among them: a deep focus and the intention of developing insight."[34]

Furthermore, theologian Josef Sudbrack wisely highlights six aspects of contemplation in one of the most thorough and brief modern summaries available in English, which I have taken the liberty to elaborate upon. Contemplation is:[35]

1. The primacy of love: *in the self's encounter with God/Other through a self-forgetting.*

2. Darkness and suffering: *the encounter transcends the self, allowing the other to become the center of attention. This encounter often occurs through a specific path of asceticism or self-denial.*

3. Given as a grace: *the journey toward encounter is an ascent of the soul, but a given one. It is all grace. Only God gives the gift of encountering God beyond the self.*

4. Historical: *the experience of encounter occurs in time and history with hope for its future consummation.*

5. Contemplative and Active: *the transcending of self is interwoven with action for the other in love.*

6. Trinitarian: *the experience of divine encounter is a participation in Trinitarian love.*

And finally, contemplative theologian Raimon Panikkar also joins in with the stunning affirmation that, contemplation is,

> "that activity which situates us in an open space from which we can observe and contribute to the course of the universe; or as the Gita will say, that activity that delights in the well-being of all beings, or that maintains the world in cohesion."[36]

Cohesion! What a brilliant image! One that is most certainly another way of saying what Jesus invited us to experience too: the quality of "*abiding*" (John 15.4). Union is intimated by the word cohesion. In contemplation, we discover again and again that underneath all the surface fragmentation and division of life, we are held together by a force of love making contact with each of us, inwardly in the silence, so to hold us as we grow. Jesus invited us to experience it as the quality of "*abiding*" (John 15.4).[37]

As we have looked at definitions, keep in mind one caution: don't confuse contemplation with mysticism. While similar, they are distinct. In the Christian tradition(s), the word contemplation is older than the word mysticism.[38] By and large, the terms mystical theology and mysticism in general as we now think of it, came into usage after the Reformation and Enlightenment.

Contemplation points us more toward a practice of meditative prayer rather than the general term mysticism, which conveys an overall mystical experience. Admittedly, different words often get in the way of describing the same experience. Yet, it is fair and probably important to say, following the counsel of Bernadette Roberts, that one could easily be a contemplative *without* being a mystic, but it would be rare to find a Christian mystic who wasn't first also a contemplative.

Thankfully, beyond words, doctrines and definitions, each of our spiritual journeys is evolving and unfolding, and created to deepen – to which we now will explore.

Chapter Four /

Deepening

1· *A Brief Tour of Foundational Contemplatives*

There are many contemplatives we might view as foundational contributors *prior to* the Reformation, yet for the sake of brevity, I will limit our survey to just seven theological thinkers and contemplatives, as a primer to help reacquaint the Protestant church with these key pre-Reformation era resources.

Unfortunately, they are all men. There are significant pre-Reformation women mystics and contemplatives, yet surveying them here would take us beyond the bounds of this chapter. Women such as Hildegard of Bingen (1098 – 1179 CE), Hadewijch (d. 1248 CE), Marguerite Porete (1250 – 1310 CE) and Mechthild of Magdeburg (1207 – 1282 CE) deserve our deeper attention and study, unfortunately just not here.[1]

Also, left out here are all the writers *during* the Reformation up to the *present.* That list would certainly include such beacons of inspiration as Teresa of Ávila, John of the Cross, Theophan the Recluse, Thomas Merton, and Bernadette Roberts, just to name a few.

Nevertheless, we begin our tour early in the third century of the Common Era in Northern Egypt in the intellectually and spiritually vibrant city of Alexandria, with the father of Christian mystics.

Origen (c. 184 – c. 254 CE)

Origen's many contributions to Christian theology have long been overshadowed by his ecclesial condemnation at the Second Council of Constantinople in 553 CE. Yet, Origen is undoubtedly the father of Christian mystical theology and a vital voice to help us remember and return to the treasures of the contemplative Christian dimension.

In many ways, Origen is a bridge between the classical Greek philosophy of Plato and Plotinus and the creative emergence of a more mature, individuated Christian theology.

Among his most significant spiritual work, as it relates to the contemplative tradition, is Origen's *Commentary on the Song of Songs.* Two selections from his *Commentary on the Song of Songs* reveal his enduring impact, with themes such as the "dart of love" and the "stages of knowing." Twelve centuries later history will witness Origen's enduring influence of the image of a dart of love showing up in the anonymous author of the *Cloud of Unknowing,* and later, in the stages of knowing with such contemplative classics as Theresa of Ávila's, *The Interior Castle.*

We begin with Origen's image of God's love as a wounding dart that leads to the image of the burning heart:

> "Indeed, the soul is led by a heavenly love and desire when once the beauty and glory of the Word of God has been perceived, it falls in love with God's splendor and by this receives from God some dart and wound of love...And the soul will receive from God the saving wound and will burn with the blessed fire of God's love..."[2]

And now notice Origen's explanation of the different modes of knowing culminating in the contemplative, or what the Greeks called, the *enoptic* way – the way of inward seeing, literally, *in-seeing*:

> "There are three general disciplines by which one attains knowledge of the universe. The Greeks call them ethics, physics, and enoptics; and we give them the terms moral, natural, and contemplative...The moral discipline is defined as the one by which an honorable manner of life is equipped and habits conducive to virtue are prepare? The natural discipline is defined as the consideration of the nature of each individual thing, according to which nothing in life happens contrary to nature...The contemplative discipline is defined as that by which we transcend visible things and contemplate something of divine and heavenly things and gaze at them with the mind alone, since they transcend corporeal appearance..."[3]

In this small selection from Origen's vast literary legacy, we see key themes that, over the centuries, infused the work of other contemplative Christian writers. In particular, the theme of a seeing that transcends visible things and contemplates heavenly things, through the mind alone. This resonated with philosophical, classical contemplation: a way of inward seeing and perceiving. A kind of mental prayer that may give way toward the depths of what we would today call the prayer of the heart: a wordless prayer of intimacy, where we both know and are known. Thus, for Origen, the gift of the contemplative dimension was to invite the soul deeper into the experience of divine union.

From Origen, we skip forward a century, and turn our attention to one of monasticism's founding fathers, Evagrius Ponticus.

Evagrius Ponticus (346 – 399 CE)

Like Origen, Evagrius' influence on the monastic tradition is unparalleled. Evagrius is famous for compiling the writings and sayings of the Desert Fathers. Not only was he a student of Origen, Evagrius also further developed a coherent mystical and contemplative theology. His enduring impact upon the formation of Western monasticism continues through his writings, *Praktikos* and *Chapters on Prayer.*

As it relates to the contemplative tradition, Evagrius urges that prayer be *unceasing*. His spiritual command is based upon St. Paul's exhortation in 1 Thessalonians 5.17 to *"pray always."* On ceaseless prayer, Evagrius is echoing the teaching of both Athanasius' *Life of Antony* (*Vita Antoni*), and the wisdom *Sayings of the Desert Fathers* (*Apophthegmata Patrum*). While Evagrius raises the importance of the practice, he leaves the reader wondering how ceaseless prayer is to be done. What was the *method* by which a monk or Christian could pray *ceaselessly*?

As best I can tell, a method of praying ceaselessly only emerged *after* Evagrius, in fifth century Palestine, with the repetition of a short prayer sentence such as, "Lord Jesus Christ, Son of God, have mercy on me."[4] Modern contemplative Basil Pennington also points out that to the best of his knowledge, methods of meditative prayer were not written down, but were taught orally, spiritual "father" to spiritual "son."[5]

If a method of prayer had been widely practiced in Egypt, we would expect to find it described in the earliest sources (e.g. Athanasius's *Life of Antony,* the *Apophthegmata,* Palladius's *Lausiac History,* and the writings of Pachomius), but the practice is not found therein.[6] Evagrius does not instruct on the specific practice of unceasing prayer, but insists that it be cultivated. In time, this unwritten method of meditative prayer grounded in the gospel texts, would in later centuries widely become known as the Jesus Prayer, especially in Byzantine, Greek and Russian Orthodox spirituality.

Evagrius also urges that true prayer is to be *imageless*. This is in part, because he believed that any image of God was idolatrous. Prayer must seek total transcendence, to the extent that it was possible while still using words. This is perhaps one reason why silence would become so important in the development of imageless prayer. Notice Evagrius' logic:

> "When you pray, do not try to represent the divine in yourself, do not let any specific form be imprinted on your mind. Instead, approach the Immaterial immaterially, and then you will understand."[7]

The deepening of prayer for Evagrius meant moving from *imageless* prayer to *wordless* prayer. What better way to *not* generate a mental image than by *not* using words? Thus, constant, imageless, wordless prayer led to what Evagrius called pure prayer, or true prayer, or even spiritual prayer. Such prayer was "an ascent of the mind to God."[8] And what does Evagrius mean by "mind"? Reading Evagrius, stay alert for an answer that echoes with Plato. Here is how historian William Harmless explains it:

> "Notice that here and elsewhere Evagrius uses the word "mind" (*nous*) to describe what in us prays. For most people today, the word "mind" implies the faculty of logic, of thinking, of rational deduction. But in the Greek tradition, the mind, the *nous,* is our intuitive side...For Evagrius, the way the mind knows God is not a matter of logic, of thinking; it is a direct intuition. As he once put it, 'for knowledge of God, one needs not a debater's soul, but a seer's soul.' In the Eastern theological tradition, the mind, the *nous*, is the highest dimension of the human person. It is the image of God within us..."[9]

We might say Evagrius believed that prayer is less something one does and more something one *is*.[10] Evagrius writes, "Just as when we are asleep we do not know that we sleep, so neither when we are contemplating do we know that we have passed into contemplation."[11] For Evagrius, this is not ecstatic prayer (*ekstasis*), leaving oneself. Rather, it is *katastasis*, returning to one's true, most real state of being – the very state we were created for.

However, Evagrius believed that such a contemplative state was not for everyone. One indication of this fact is that Evagrius believed that serious ascetic preparation was called for, requiring the advanced state of passionlessness (*apatheia*).

Like the Platonists, and his teacher Origen, Evagrius taught that ascetic practice (*praktike)* can lead to mystical knowledge (*gnostike*), which can then lead to contemplation (*theoria*).[12] While Evagrius's writings are profound and important,

Evagrius is lesser known than his intellectual successor – John Cassian, to whom we now turn.

John Cassian (360 – 435 CE)

Like Evagrius, Cassian's influence on the monastic movement was foundational. Scholar William Harmless wisely summarizes both the contrast and connection between Evagrius and Cassian: "Cassian inherited from Evagrius the view that 'pure prayer' is unceasing, imageless, and wordless. Evagrius never says precisely how, practically speaking, such prayer might be done, but Cassian (in the voice of Abba Isaac) does."[13]

Whereas Evagrius was imprecise regarding method, Cassian was not. There is no question about the issues at stake. It was the same in Cassian's time as in ours. What are we to do with our thoughts as we seek to pray unceasingly? The mind is unstable and easily distracted – resulting in our experience of thoughts. While trying to focus on a brief text, Cassian discovered the normal human experience with thoughts. Cassian realized, as meditative practioners often do, that the mind is,

> "Ever on the move, forever wandering, it is tossed along through all the body of Scripture, unable to settle on anything, unable to reject anything or to hold on to anything, powerless to arrive at any full and judicious study, a dilettante and speedy taster of spiritual ideas rather than their creator and possessor. And so the mind is always on the move, and at the time of assembly it is pulled, like a drunk, in every direction…it seems to be a victim of chance."[14]

Cassian's solution to this problem of mental chatter and distraction was a method of prayer that involved taking a sentence of scripture and repeating it with every breath. He urged Psalm 70.1: "*O God, come to my assistance; O Lord, make haste to help me.*" This method allowed the monk to pray without ceasing, without using images, and to pray in a way that drives other thoughts away.

Cassian grounded this method in the monastic tradition. He says, "Just as this [method] was handed down to us by a few of the oldest fathers who were left, so also we pass it on to none but the most exceptional, who truly desire it." [15] Here we see two aspects: first, that an oral tradition existed that handed down a certain kind of meditative method. And second, that the method was only given to those who were most mature or advanced in their spiritual formation. Harmless summarizes Cassian's method this way:

> "In terms of method, Cassian is recommending monologistic prayer (literally, 'one-word prayer'), a sort of Christian mantra. The classic form of Christian monologistic prayer would appear later, in fifth-century Palestine, in the so-called Jesus Prayer – the unceasing repetition of the name of Jesus sometimes accompanied with a petition for mercy."[16]

Notice that the prayer consists in saying a brief sentence. Thus, in a sense this is still not pure, contemplative prayer. This brief word or sentence-based method of prayer was essential for the life of the monk, but it was also not the summit (or depth) of prayer. It is understood that this method of prayer could lead a monk to wordless prayer – the state of contemplation.

Thus, the mantra-like prayer was not an end-in-itself. Rather, it was a way-station on the journey toward a deeper experience of prayer. Sprinkled throughout Cassian's *Conferences*, Cassian hints at this kind of deeper, wordless prayer.

In Conference Ten, Cassian links the developmental spectrum of *lectio divina,* the slow, prayerful reading of scripture, with the goal of interior, wordless experience. This helps us see more clearly the developmental movement from *lectio,* text-based meditation, toward a wordless, infused prayer – what we would today describe as contemplation or contemplative prayer:

> "We shall penetrate its meaning not through the written text but with experience leading the way. So it is that our mind will arrive at that incorruptible prayer to which, in the previous discussion, as far as the Lord deigned to grant it, the conference was ordered and directed. This is not only not laid hold of by the sight of some image, but it cannot even be grasped by any word or phrase. Rather, once the mind's attentiveness has been set ablaze, it is called forth in an unspeakable ecstasy of heart and with an insatiable gladness of spirit, and the mind, having transcended all feelings and visible matter, pours it out to God with unutterable groans and sighs."[17]

Such an experience, in later centuries, would probably be called a mystical state, a revelation, or even an ecstasy. In Cassian's view, this was less about an exterior ecstasy, and more a *katastasis*. A coming to one's true state. Today, we might say it was, simply, a special grace.[18]

Our brief review leads to an additional important passage from Cassian, who with beautiful clarity, establishes a theological foundation strong enough to carry the load of many future centuries of contemplative experience:

> "Yet sometimes the mind which advances to that true disposition of purity and has already begun to be rooted in it, conceiving all of these at one and the same time and rushing through them all like a kind of ungraspable and devouring flame, pours out to God wordless prayers of the purest vigor. These the Spirit itself makes to God as [the Spirit] intervenes with unutterable groans, unbeknownst to us, conceiving at that moment and pouring forth in wordless prayer such great things that they not only – would say – cannot pass through the mouth but are unable even to be remembered by the mind later on."[19]

A brief survey of Cassian would be incomplete without exploring one other important passage. Here, Cassian discusses the meaning of Jesus' teaching on the Lord's Prayer, particularly the invitation to *"go into the secret room, close the door and pray to the Father who is in secret"* (Matthew 6.6):

> "We pray with the door shut when, with closed lips and in total silence, we pray to the searcher not of voices but of hearts. We pray in secret when, intent in heart and mind alone, we offer our petitions to God alone."[20]

Insights from Cassian's *Conferences* were foundational for the intellectual and practical development of the theology and method of Centering Prayer in later centuries, as a distant family member in the beautiful lineage of spiritual gifts given by the love of God.

Having said that, it is important to see Cassian speaking about prayer as a mental and emotional petition to God in the silence and stillness of one's being. What Cassian teaches is not technically contemplative prayer, as we would understand it today (as in Centering Prayer). Nevertheless, the early outlines of the then still developing contemplative, interior tradition for both prayer, worship and spiritual leadership, are clearly evident in seed form.

We conclude our brief survey of John Cassian connecting meditative prayer with Cassian's teaching on purity of heart. As Jesus insists, we are "*to be perfect, even as your heavenly Father is perfect*" (Matthew 5.48). Cassian saw that there were degrees of perfection: the highest is divine love, modeled within the life of the Trinity – the love of the Son for the Father. The next highest is the love for God of those in heaven, who enjoy direct contemplation of God. The next highest are those who are sanctified by grace in this life and love God with their whole heart, preferring nothing else to God.

> "The whole purpose of the monk and the perfection of his heart is directed toward a continual and uninterrupted perseverance in prayer. In so far as it is possible for human frailty, he strives for immovable tranquility of mind and perpetual purity. For this reason, we tirelessly seek and continually practice both bodily labor and contrition of heart: between the two there is a reciprocal and indissoluble bond. For since the entire edifice of the virtues is directed toward the perfection of prayer, the whole structure will not be firm and durable, unless all the parts are brought together and help fast by this keystone."[21]

Commenting on the four types of prayer listed in 1 Timothy 2.1 (supplications, prayers, intercessions and thanksgiving), Cassian adds his own fifth category of prayer, which he calls "fiery prayer," where in a flash of exhilaration, one's prayer transcends speech, thought and imagination.

While Cassian deserves more attention, we will conclude our brief survey with a reference from Columba Steward, who summarizes the significance of Cassian's teaching on prayer for us very well:

> "For Cassian, both fiery prayer and imageless prayer are ascents from multiplicity, words, and images to a realm of spiritual experience marked by a profound apophaticisim. This apophaticisim does not exclude feeling, but it is feeling expressed as energy and exuberance. Cassian's ease in working in both registers of spiritual experience – the *apophatic* and the *kataphatic* would become the norm in both east and west."[22]

Augustine (354 – 430 CE)

Our fourth stop on this brief contemplative-influencer tour is St. Augustine of Hippo. Like Origen, Augustine was significantly inspired and intellectually shaped by the writings of Plotinus. We can see this clearly in his *Confessions.* In memorable passages of rich beauty and wisdom, Augustine presents himself seeking the ecstasy that Plotinus describes in his *On the Contemplative Life.* The ecstasy, or beatific vision, is a result of the mind's ascent to union with God, or the highest Reality. Such an integration of Platonic ideas with Augustine's spiritual journey was impactful to Augustine's faith development, as well as on the future of Christian mystical theology.[23]

Augustine maintained that there was a contemplative element (faith) and a practical element (morals) in every Christian's life.[24] Augustine believed that the goal of every Christian life is the vision of God, i.e. contemplation *(theoria)* and that contemplation is the fruit and reward of a life lived seeking God. Infused with faith, Augustine came to believe and experience that contemplation – as in a kind of meditative prayer – is a foretaste of heaven on earth. Notice how Augustine speaks of contemplation as a prayer to the living God:

> "Warned by these writings that I must return to myself, I entered under your guidance the innermost places of my being; but only because you had become my helper was I able to do so. I entered, then, and with the vision of my spirit, such as it was, I saw the incomputable light far above my spiritual ken [range of insight], transcending my mind: not this common light which every physical eye can see, nor any light of the same order but greater, as though this common light were shining much more powerfully, far more brightly, and so extensively as to fill the universe. The light I saw was not this common light at all, but something different, utterly different, from all these things. Nor was it higher than my mind in the sense that oil floats on water or the sky is above the earth; it was exalted because this very light made me, and I was below it because by it I was made. Anyone who knows truth knows I, and whoever knows it knows eternity. Love knows it. O eternal Truth, true Love, and beloved Eternity, you are my God, and for you I sigh day and night. As I first began to know you, you lifted me up and showed me that while that which I might see exists indeed, I was not yet capable of seeing it. Your rays beamed intensely upon me, beating back my feeble gaze, and I trembled with love and dread. I knew myself to be far away from you in a region of unlikeness, and I seemed to hear your voice from on high: 'I am the food of the mature; grow then, and you will eat me. You will not change me into yourself like bodily food: you will be changed into me.'[25]

And, similarly, here is Augustine's famous "tremulous glance" experience:

> "I proceeded further and came to the power of discursive reason…And then my mind attained to *That Which Is*, in the flash of one tremulous glance. Then indeed did I perceive your invisible reality through created things, but to keep my gaze there

> was beyond my strength. I was forced back through weakness and returned to my familiar surroundings, bearing with me only a loving memory, one that yearned for something of which I had caught the fragrance, but could not yet feast upon."[26]

From these historic quotations we can begin to see the significant mark Augustine has made on the spiritual and theological ethos of Christianity. Tracing Augustine's thinking and experience of the contemplative is especially useful, since the Reformers drew so heavily from him in their efforts to reform the church. So, likewise it seems wise and harmonious that, in our wish for a contemplative reformation, we again re-access Augustine. A lineage that also leads us forward one century to Gregory. Though separated in time from Augustine, Gregory is deeply connected in spirit.

Gregory the Great (c. 540 – 604 CE)

Using Augustine's focus, Gregory the Great developed the classic definition of the contemplative life as a life devoted exclusively to the love of God. Augustine also influenced St. Gregory in his teaching that we may know God by first loving God.[27] Gregory the Great's love-mysticism centered on the term *contemplatio*, understood broadly as attentiveness toward God.[28]

For Gregory, humankind was created contemplative by nature, but humankind lost this precious gift through Adam's sin. Christ restored the possibility of our turning toward the divine un-circumscribable light, though imperfectly in this life. Compunction joined with desire was the fire of contemplative progress. Gregory put it this way,

> "Hearts are wounded so that they might be healed...The soul struck by the darts of his love...burns with desire for contemplation...She has been brought back to health by a blow, called back to the safety of deep restfulness by the disturbance of his love. When the wounded mind begins to pant for God, despising all of the offerings of this world, it stretches itself by desire toward the homeland above."[29]

Prior to Gregory, that passage was commented on with mystical insight by both Origen and Gregory of Nyssa. The wound of love unites the pain of compunction with the reward of loving contemplation. Columba Steward describes how in Gregory's *Homilies on Ezekiel*, Gregory "depicts a cyclical pattern of compunction, self-transcendence through being 'suspended' in contemplation, and then a feeling of being pushed back down (a *reverberatio*) into the mundane reality of life in the secular world"[30]

Interestingly, while Gregory's homilies lack the platonic language inherited from the classical Western philosophers, they do focus on biblical themes, and especially the theme of light as it relates to contemplation. In this way, Gregory's role is something of a stabilizing bridge between two eras – the decline of the Roman Empire and emergence of the Middle Ages, an era that witnessed the rise of the monastery, and later the Holy Roman Empire.

Gregory modeled an ever-deepening spirituality grounded in theological understanding, shaping one's inner life. For him, true theology was a kind of contemplation. A mode of seeing the invisible and incomprehensible. He was inspired by Moses, who entered the cloud of Divine Presence and communed with God, as if face-to-face. Therein, Moses was transformed by God's glory. While Moses did not see God, since God is hidden, Moses did experience God's presence. To this, Gregory says that,

> "the true vision and the true knowledge of what we seek consists precisely in *not* seeing, in an awareness that our goal transcends all knowledge and is everywhere cut off from us by the darkness of incomprehensibility. Thus that profound evangelist, John, who penetrated into this luminous darkness, tells us that 'no one has seen God at any time, teaching us this by negation that none – indeed no created intellect – can attain a knowledge of God."[31]

From Gregory, we advance nearly half a millennium. During these centuries, the West slipped into the "dark ages." At the turn of the second millennium, something novel was unfolding in Paris, through the teaching of a community that would come to be known as the Victorines – a new light dawning in what would become the heart of intellectual Europe, and of course, the birth of the university, through the matrix of an evolving monastery.

Hugh of St. Victor (1096 – 1141 CE) and *Richard of St. Victor* (d. 1173 CE)

Both Hugh and Richard of St Victor (Victorines) are less known than other foundational contemplatives, such as Meister Eckhart (c. 1260 – c. 1328), yet they were just as creative in their theological development and mystical theology.[32] For example, Hugh of St. Victor conceived of the contemplative journey in four stages, with each stage divided in several divisions:

First, *awakening*, in three divisions: with fear, grief and love.

Second, *purgation*, where we flee from concupiscence (disordered desires), occurring in three divisions: with patience, mercy and compunction.

Third, *illumination*, where we flee from ignorance, in three divisions: with cognition, meditation and contemplation.

Fourth, *union*, where we flee nothing, but move toward a deepening advance in virtue, in three divisions: with temperance, prudence and fortitude.

His addition to the earlier Pseudo-Dionysius in threefold path (purgation, illumination and union) brings a new starting point: awakening.[33] With the Victorines, it appears we are reaching something of the zenith of theological development, nearing the cusp of the Renaissance and the Reformation. With the Victorines, we also begin to see the fusion of contemplation and knowing applied to a scholastic-monastic community.[34] As such, a unique characteristic of the Victorines came with the rise of the first European universities in the twelfth and early thirteenth centuries, where academic endeavors blended into aspects of the contemplative life.

For example, the Abbey of St. Victor became a place where theologians such as Hugh and Richard incorporated scholasticism with contemplation to simultaneously sharpen and deepen the mind and the quest for further knowledge of God, world and self.[35] We can see this incorporation in Richard's six degrees of contemplation, moving downward in depth, from the surface senses, to the depth of intuition:

6th Degree:
Sense experience

5th Degree:
Imagination

4th Degree:
Knowledge through Reason with images

3rd Degree:
Knowledge through reason without images

2nd Degree:
Understanding that transcends reason

1st Degree:
Intuitive knowing in a unique way – contemplation

Through understanding, we apprehend the invisible, spiritual realities that are otherwise inaccessible to reason.[36] For the Victorines, the goal of contemplation is never separated from the deeper spiritual journey into the love of God and the humility of Christ.

The process of transformation by divine love is beautifully presented in Richard's treatise, *On the Four Degrees of Charity.* In the fourth degree, the soul is not only reborn in the image and likeness of God, but is also conformed to the humility and servanthood of Christ. Through this inner reformation, an individual may become a fearless guide, qualified to help others on their own journeys of spiritual transformation. So, we see that in the Christian understanding, contemplation isn't meant to lead to superiority and inflation, but rather to wisdom, love, humility and service.

As we draw our brief survey to a conclusion, it is important to mention one towering figure in the contemplative-mystical Christian tradition: Meister Eckhart (c. 1260 – c. 1328 CE). Eckhart is a short step from the Victorines. While Eckhart's writings were officially condemned by Pope John XXII in 1329 CE, Eckhart's mysticism and apophatic theology left an enduring impact on the Rhineland Mystics. Chief among them were: Hildegard of Bingen (1098 – 1179 CE); Johannes Tauler (c. 1300 – 1361 CE); Henry Suso (c. 1295 – 1366 CE); Mechthild of Magdeburg (c. 1207 – c. 1294 CE); and Nicholas of Cusa (1401 – 1464 CE).

Combined, the influence of Eckhart and these Rhineland mystics and teachers is incomprehensible. In their absence, our understanding of the spiritual journey and contemplative dimension in the history of Christianity, would be diminished. In addition to their Christ-centered, contemplative writings, these celebrated mystics also set the stage for the Reformation era themes of spiritual inwardness and personal experience.

It has also become increasingly clear that Eckhart's influence endures to us today, especially noticeable in the fourteenth century anonymous author of *The Cloud of Unknowing,* which, centuries later in the twentieth century, would deeply imprint the development of Centering Prayer.

In the wake of these spiritual luminaries, the living contemplative tradition continued to flow forward. Through them we understand the contemplative dimension is not new or foreign to Christian orthodoxy, but has been and remains *essential* to it.

2 · *A Brief Word on Mysticism*

Mysticism is a deep and sometimes murky river. Some fear the very word mysticism, because as some humorously note, it begins in mist, ends in schism, and has I at the center.[37] Some even fear mentioning the subject. Yet, sometimes this mysterious river has a flourishing flow. The river of mysticism has meandered throughout every century of Christian history and experience, even now, reaching our present bend in the river of time.[38] Over the years, many have attempted to dam the river's flow, to no avail. Others have sought to chart its headwaters, or even exploit its hidden powers.[39]

In talking about mysticism, my intention here is to provide more of a lightning-strike reminder that the essence of Christian experience is and always will be mystical, and therefore, experiential.[40] This essence is, in part, accessed through the contemplative dimension – such as meditative prayer and some monastic practices, and in an essential way, in the Eucharist.

While the heart of Christianity is mystical, it would not be correct to say that mysticism is Christianity. Yet, as noted previously, Karl Rahner quipped that the "Christian of the future will be a mystic or he or she will not exist at all."[41] How is that?

One answer to that question, is rooted in the theological vision of Jesus, whose farewell prayer recorded in the Gospel of John models the essence of Christian mysticism:

> *"Father, I ask not only on behalf of these, but also on behalf of those who will believe in me through their word, that they may all be one. As you, Father, are in me and I am in you, may they also be in us, so that the world may believe that you have sent me. The glory that you have given me I have given them, so that they may be one, as we are one, I in them and you in me, that they may become completely one, so that the world may know that you have sent me and have loved them even as you have loved me. Father, I desire that those also, whom you have given me, may be with me where I am, to see my glory, which you have given me because you loved me before the foundation of the world"* (John 17.20-24).

Or, from a different biblical angle, what word *but* mystical describes this sample from the first-century Pauline Epistle to the Ephesians:

> *"For this reason, I bow my knees before the Father, from whom every family in heaven and on earth takes its name. I pray that, according to the riches of his glory, he may grant that you may be strengthened in your inner being with power through his Spirit, and that Christ may dwell in your hearts through faith, as you are being rooted and grounded in love. I pray that you may have the power to comprehend, with all the saints, what is the breadth and length and height and depth, and to know the love of Christ that surpasses knowledge, so that you may be filled with all the fullness of God. Now to him who by the power at work within us is able to accomplish abundantly far more than all we can ask or imagine, to him be glory in the church and in Christ Jesus to all generations, forever and ever. Amen"* (Ephesians 3.14-21).

So much of the story of contemplative Christianity – past *and* future – is woven together with the history of mysticism. In fact, one is hard pressed to separate the two. Yet the contemplative dimension of Christianity is not necessarily mystical. One does not need to be a mystic to be a contemplative, though it would be difficult to be a mystic without also being a contemplative. What we observe in the historical study of mysticism is that every century has provided the church with fresh expressions of Christian mysticism. Sometimes the river of mysticism has diminished to a trickle, whereas other eras saw the mystical river gushing.

In our era, the modern renewal of mysticism came thanks in part to the work of William James (1842 – 1910 CE) and Evelyn Underhill (1875 – 1941 CE), bringing a renaissance of mysticism studies slowly unfolding throughout the twentieth century.[42] As a result, Christianity began to recover the important role mystical experiences and theology have played throughout church history.[43]

On a scholarly level, the pioneering work of Bernard McGinn has helped birth the modern resourcement of the Christian mystical tradition in academia.[44] In his monumental series, *The Presence of God: A History of Western Christian Mysticism,* the church has been given a *magnum opus* of historical and spiritual insight that will inspire and inform pastors and scholars for decades to come.[45]

Defining Mysticism

As we look briefly at mysticism, let's first begin with a general definition.[46] Prior to the mid-eighteenth century, the English term mysticism did not exist. Instead, the term "mystical theology" was used.[47] Mystical theology signified a range of experiences and interpretations, and also encompassed spiritual practices, contemplation and aspects of asceticism.[48]

The English term "mystic" or "mysticism" comes from the Greek *mystikos,* meaning "to close," especially related to the closing of one's eyes. The term was used in pre-Christian writings such as with the Mystery cults, whose secret rites were kept hidden except to initiates. Early Christian interpreters such as Clement and Origen took up the term *mystikos* to describe their biblical interpretations of God and Christ.[49]

Even St. Paul uses the term to speak of the "*mystery of iniquity*" in Second Thessalonians 2.7, and extensively in the second chapter of First Corinthians. Notice the juxtaposition of mystery and the revelation of wisdom by the Spirit:

> *"When I came to you, brothers and sisters, I did not come proclaiming the* ***mystery*** *of God to you in lofty words or* ***wisdom****. For I decided to know nothing among you except Jesus Christ, and him crucified. And I came to you in weakness and in fear and in much trembling. My speech and my proclamation were not with plausible words of wisdom, but with a demonstration of the Spirit and of power, so that your faith might rest not on human wisdom but on the power of God. Yet among the mature we do speak wisdom, though it is not a wisdom of this age or of the rulers of this age, who are doomed to perish. But we speak* ***God's wisdom, secret and hidden,*** *which God decreed before the ages for our glory. None of the rulers of this age understood this; for if they had, they would not have crucified the Lord of glory. But, as it is written, "What no eye has seen, nor ear heard, nor the human heart conceived, what God has prepared for those who love him" – these things God has revealed to us through the Spirit; for the Spirit searches everything, even the depths of God.* (1 Corinthians 2. 1-10, emphasis added).

This Pauline passage is perhaps the summation of Christian mysticism in the New Testament. Paired with Jesus' upper room discourse recorded in the Gospel of

John chapters fourteen through seventeen, we begin to build a deeper understanding of the range in which the Christian tradition resonates with the mystical-contemplative dimension.[50]

But, let's move to a more specific definition. Bernard McGinn has famously defined mysticism as "a special consciousness of the presence of God that by definition exceeds description and results in a transformation of the subject who receives it." [51] Similarly, David B. Perrin views the core of mysticism as "the radical surrender of self to the loving embrace of the other who is at the foundation of all life, the One to whom we owe our very existence."[52]

In a complimentary definition, Robert Forman uses the term "innate mysticism," because it implies that mystical awareness and experience is a human capacity, perhaps even essential to our flourishing.[53] With these definitions we begin to see a beautiful picture coming into focus, that helps us see mystical experience more clearly.

Mystical Experiences

And what about descriptions of mystical experiences from contemplative Christian mystics? Among the classic contemplative Christian mystics, most immediately think of Meister Eckhart and the Spanish Mystics: John of the Cross and his friend Teresa of Ávila. We also are reminded of Pseudo-Dionysius, who sums up the Neo-Platonic influence on Christian mysticism with this mystical paradox: "Into this Dark beyond all light, we pray to come and, unseeing and unknowing, to see and to know That Which is beyond seeing and beyond knowing precisely by not seeing, by not knowing."[54] St. John of the Cross developed this Dionysian theme further:

> "When God himself visits [the soul]…it is in total darkness and in concealment from the enemy that the soul receives these spiritual favors of God. The reason for this is that, as his Majesty dwells substantially in the soul, where neither angel nor devil can attain to an understanding of that which comes to pass...These communications, since the Lord Himself works them, are wholly divine and sovereign, for they are substantial touches of Divine union between the soul and God."[55]

While there is a robust treasure house of well-known historical examples of mystics, there are many lesser known mystics who build on those principles. Many, like Margaret Porete, used language that often got them into trouble with church authorities.[56] Perhaps that was because they were so rarely understood, and in the absence of understanding, fear arose.

Historian William Franke suggests that, "mystic writers press language to the limits and expose its utter inadequacy in order to direct readers' gazes beyond language toward some 'deeper,' 'greater,' 'other,' 'reality' or 'experience' of the 'divine'…"[57] In part, language is pressed because what can we say about the unsayable? All language, in some sense, fails in the presence of ultimate reality – source of all order, language and knowledge in the first place.[58] Such is the inspiration of the apophatic – way of unknowing and negation – latent within Christian mysticism.[59]

From the unsayable and unknowable, it is easy to notice the similarity of *dark* and *light* themes in the thought of many other Christian mystics. Take for example the fourteenth century mystic John Ruusbroec (c. 1293 – 1381 CE), who writes that,

> "All those who are raised up above their created being into a contemplative life are one with this divine brightness and are that brightness itself. And they see, feel and find, even by means of this Divine Light, that, as regards their uncreated nature, they are that same simple ground from which the brightness without limit shines forth in a godlike manner, and which according to the simplicity of the essence remains in everlasting, mode-less simplicity."[60]

Lest you think mystics are mere relics of the past, look at three clear and gracefully disruptive teaching of twenty first century Christian mystics, among them Bernadette Roberts. Her life, teachings and witness are the $E = mc^2$ of mystical theology and Christian spirituality in modern times.

In her, *The Path to No-Self* and *The Experience of No-Self,* Roberts brilliantly and winsomely charts a rarely traveled path beyond the unitive mystical experience into what she calls the "No-Self" condition. This is essential reading for anyone interested in both exploring and experiencing more of the Christian spiritual journey, and the mystery of God.[61]

Few in the history of humankind could have written this clear guidance and instruction for others still on the spiritual journey. Notice the deep connections with the mystical tradition and the new ideas and experiences Bernadette is revealing in these paragraphs from her book, *The Experience of No-Self*:

> "In closing this account, I feel a beginning has been made by clearing the ground for much more that remains to be said. As stated initially, this writing stems from the failure to find this movement beyond self in the classical contemplative literature, and though I am no longer concerned for myself, I am concerned for those who may come to a similar end when they discover that their traditional path has suddenly disappeared. Having made this journey I now see clearly, that a dimension unmistakably exists beyond anything that could be described as the self's union with God – be it called spiritual marriage, transforming union, or whatever the terminology one may care to use. For the contemplative to regard such a union as the final or ultimate consummation of his [her] life is a grave mistake. He is setting his sight at a midway point which, I now see, is too low, too close-in, and too narrow. At this point he may even be so centered in God that he is still subject to the illusion of self's deification, wherein his only feat is to unwittingly shortchange God. Whenever possible, it is best to get beyond such a point, even when letting go means surrendering this union with all its experiences and ensuing qualities of strength, love, certitude, and much more; for as long as there is any feeling, knowledge, or inkling that any self remains, be it a divine self, true self, or even an empirical self, we have not gone far enough. Of our own accord we cannot cross the line into the unknown, only God knows if we are ready for such a step, only he can take us across and see us through. In fact, self never crossed the line, it simply ceases to be; for if the truth be known, only Christ dies and only Christ rises. Though we may never fully understand this mystery, it is vitally important to realize that such a step exists, that others have taken it, and to be prepared so there will be no illusions about what lies beyond self. For us to give our self to God is, as Eckhart says, to give Him absolutely nothing; but for God to take the self, is for Him to take absolutely everything. Though John of the Cross stresses the giving over the taking, and Meister Eckhart stresses the taking over the giving, the fact remains that no matter how we evaluate this exchange, these are two different movements, two different contemplative experiences. Where the first movement of our life culminates in the union of self and God, the second movement culminates in no union – no self, and no God for that self. The reason for this is that in order to come upon God as he is in Himself – and not as he is in our self – there must be no self. There is no other way."[62]

Note the deep connection between the contemplative and the mystical paths, and the ongoing unfolding of our knowledge about spiritual realities and the human condition. In such mystics as Bernadette, we have a living witness into the pantheon of saints and mystics.

Along with Bernadette Roberts, Eastern Orthodox author Catherine de Hueck Doherty speaks of the nothingness beyond such as a birth-moment that leads one into a deeper kind of prayer, similar to what St. Paul speaks of in Romans where the Spirit intercedes within us "*with sighs too deep for words*" (Romans 8.26). Doherty beautifully describes this experience with profound clarity, and concludes our brief exploration of mysticism nicely:

> "There comes a moment in this movement toward nothingness which seems to be a moment of nonexistence. It appears idiotic, positively idiotic to say such a thing. But it is true. It is a moment in which you are nonexistent as far as being a person is concerned. Everything has disappeared. You are not even cognizant that 'you are.' You are only cognizant of darkness. Whether you are in depths or heights is unimportant; you are not even cognizant of that. But there is a moment of nonexistence out of which you come. And when you come out, prayer begins…Now it is a very strange prayer. It is a prayer that is no prayer, because it takes place in an interiorized passivity. It has no connection with what you are doing – walking, sleeping, whatever. In you now there is a tremendous change. Prayer now begins to make sense because you don't pray; God prays in you. This is where true liberation enters. Up till now, freedom has been operating. You've submitted yourself to God of your own free will. Now [God] takes over, and that's where true liberation begins."[63]

While the role mysticism plays in the contemplative dimension of Christianity is important, it is *not* central to the primary invitation of contemplation, which is that we begin a daily meditative prayer practice.[64] It is to this foundational role and practice of daily centering prayer to which we now turn.

Chapter Five /

Centering

1 · *The Center Is Everywhere; the Circumference Nowhere*

Occasionally, we may get glimpses of the divine light possible here and now. When we do, it is a beautiful grace, with glimpses that may come by way of the chinks of contemplation. The chink or crack is a thin place where the light gets through. While the phrase is made famous by a Leonard Cohen verse, it was revealed earlier to the prophet Ezekiel who describes the Heavenly Temple as having an inner chamber with slanting window light (Ezekiel 41.16).

In his *Homily on Ezekiel,* Gregory the Great (d. 604) comments on this verse suggesting that, "in the slanting windows, the part through which the light enters is narrow, but the interior part that receives the light is wide, because the minds of those contemplating, although they see only a bit of the True Light in tenuous fashion, are still enlarged in themselves…" Gregory's analogy, when applied to our interior spiritual life, reminds us that it is the light that is doing the work – we are the space for the light.

The light enters us through the narrow, interior silence that is contemplation. The practice that allows us to attend to that light is one that is practical, that takes a short amount of time each day (twenty minutes, twice a day), and is a center for us, a narrow space in our life, that lets the light, life and love of God in.

I agree with Bernard McGinn, who commenting on Gregory's interpretation, suggests that a more current image for this intersection of our mind with the light – the sanctuary with the Presence, the timeless with time, infinite with finite – is the word *center,* which can be conceived of either spatially or temporally.[1] It is the *center* that comes to us. Center comes to circumference and helps us in our lifelong journey toward and into the wholeness of God's peace, love and wisdom. In a word, into Christ, which is the Center.[2]

The word center calls to mind the Hermetic definition of God in the mysterious, *Book of Twenty-Four Philosophers.* One of the most enduring maxims therein describes God as "the infinite sphere whose center is everywhere and whose circumference is nowhere."[3] Curiously, Meister Eckhart references this ancient axiom, inviting us to "deal with how the center, that is the least of God, fills all things and how its breadth is nowhere comprehensible. Hence, it is not to be sought in any place, but rather far above all and beyond all."[4]

Both the mystic and the contemplative; the lay person and the clergy, in one way or another seek for the center as a source of strength and stability. The grace and goodness of God is that the center comes to us. The center holds us as we grow. This shifts the perspective and invites us to simply give our attention to the center, which is our life-source. The "farnearness" that mystic Marguerite Porete speaks of.[5] I love the way theologian Grover Zinn sums this up referring to the theological insight of Hugh of St. Victor, who taught that the Christian contemplative,

> "Seeks the stable center. The quest begins by asking, 'Why is the human heart restless?' The answer...is that a divisive love of the world leads to restlessness. One must recover a unified love of God and seek the stable historical, cosmic, and contemplative center represented by Christ, the creative, sustaining, contemplative, and judging Word [of God]."[6]

I trust that it is clear that Christ is the center and that our attention and consent to that center will only be enhanced by a meditative practice. The method of Centering Prayer is just such a practice. It helps us daily die to self and give our attention and intention to the divine center. In a sense, that is where the name for Centering Prayer comes from. Not only does Centering Prayer help us get centered, it is a practice of and by the center, which is Christ.

2 · *Where Did Centering Prayer Come from?*

While there are several methods of contemplative prayer available to us today, in what follows, we will explore the method of Centering Prayer. The reason I focus solely on Centering Prayer here is because it is the method I have practiced for almost twenty years, and because I believe it is the most theologically grounded and psychologically developed of all the modern methods of contemplative prayer. There are many resources available that describe the method of Centering Prayer, some of which I list in the Bibliography. So, for now, I will only briefly touch on some of the important aspects of the method of Centering Prayer, particularly as it relates to locating it within the Christian tradition.

Thomas Keating has helpfully and honestly reflected on the eclectic background of the Centering Prayer method. In an essay entitled, *"A Traditional Blend: The Contemplative Sources of Centering Prayer,"* Keating uses the analogy of blending herb teas to describe the foundational sources of the Centering Prayer method. What is so helpful about Keating's essay is that it confirms a fact I had suspected for some time: that there is no *one* source of the Centering Prayer method. In fact, prior to the method developed by Keating, Menninger and Pennington, (and John Main's similar method), as best I can tell, there was no *written method* of meditative, non-discursive, wordless prayer in the Christian tradition.

Consider Keating's insightful description of the "blend" informing the method of Centering Prayer. Let's understand that he is waxing eloquent here, and not listing these authors in any order of chronology or rank of importance:

> "The conceptual background of centering prayer restates in contemporary terms the apophatic tradition of the desert fathers and mothers, Pseudo-Dionysius, the Hesychasts of the Eastern Orthodox tradition, and blends significant elements from Saint John of the Cross, especially his teaching on the dark nights of the sense and spirit, and his lengthy advice for the passage from discursive meditation (devout reflections) to contemplation. In addition, centering prayer incorporates Saint Francis de Sale's spirit of gentleness; Jean-Pierre de Caussade's attitude of total self-abandonment to God; the clarity of the spiritual discernment of the Venerable Francis Paul Liebermann; the theology of humility and of personal love of Christ of Saint Bernard of Clairvaux, William of Saint-Thierry, and other medieval Cistercians; the mysticism of Saint Gregory of

> Nyssa, Saint Gregory the Great, and the Rhineland mystics; the boundless confidence in God of Saint Thérèse of Lisieux, along with her extraordinary insight into the Gospel of Jesus Christ; the charm, humanity, humor and wisdom of Saint Teresa of Ávila; the liberty of spirit of Saint Philip Neri; and the salty wisdom of the fourth-century desert fathers and mothers. In short, centering prayer is a blending of the finest elements of the Christian contemplative tradition with an eye to reducing contemporary obstacles to contemplation, especially the tendency to over-activism, that is, to put too much confidence in our own efforts, or over-intellectualism, which is too much dependency on concepts in our efforts to approach God."[7]

From Keating's overview, I believe we can isolate six main blends, so to speak, all graciously infusing the lineage of Centering Prayer:

The apophatic: both in its theological and philosophical expressions; particularly inherited from the Neo-Platonists, and uniquely developed by Origen, Augustine, Pseudo-Dionysius, *The Cloud of Unknowing,* and nearly a thousand years later, by John of the Cross.

The hesychastic: desert monastic spirituality and its ascetical expressions, but especially the cultivation of *the Jesus Prayer*, the prayer of the heart, or the fiery prayer, as the Philokalia describes it.

The mystical: traditionally described as mystical theology or mystical union, flowing from the theologies of devotional love that culminated in the bridal mysticism of union found in Saint Teresa of Ávila and others.

The Trinitarian: the method of Centering Prayer is deeply shaped by an awareness of the indwelling Trinity, and other Trinitarian presuppositions which ground Centering Prayer in relationship, orientating us toward a heartfullness of love not just the enlightenment of mindfulness.

The interreligious: the simplicity of various Eastern methods of meditation, and their availability to Western monastics after Vatican II, broadened and deepened the Christian contemplative tradition toward a simple meditative prayer method, that we now know and practice as Centering Prayer.

The psychological: infused with the wisdom of depth psychology, developmental psychology and the reality of repressions buried within the unconscious, Centering Prayer dove-tails with the overall spiritual journey of human development, providing opportunities for a gentle inner healing. The process of healing supports human flourishing. In this way,

> it is a particularly important upgrade to the outdated psychological language found in the writings of John of the Cross, as well as the developmental model of Teresa of Ávila. The divine therapy of Centering Prayer is a needed evolution of the classic threefold pattern of spiritual development heavily influenced by Neo-Platonism: purgation (*catharsis*), illumination (*photismos*) and union (*henosis*).

What Father Thomas Keating is saying isn't new. But he and others have placed it in such a simple four-fold method, it is hard to avoid recognizing the yet-to-be-fully-acknowledged genius of Keating's gift to the world. This evolution is what the Spirit does.

William Meninger, a fellow monk with Thomas Keating and Basil Pennington, explored the history of Christian methods of prayer. From this survey, Meninger incorporated the following influences:

- John Cassian's teaching on a prayer sentence, such as that inspired by Psalm 70.2, repeated silently to oneself so to "turn it into a salutary way over and over in your spirit to lift yourself upward to the most sublime sights."[8]

- Pseudo-Dionysius' apophatic, mystical theology applied to prayer, where one moves through that which is sayable and knowable about God, to what is unknowable and unsayable in a oneness with the indescribable, which is, literally, a prayer of wordless silence.

- *The Cloud of Unknowing*'s invitation to pierce the darkness of our unknowing with a dart of prayer and longing – a one-word dart of prayer.

- *Lectio Divina's* invitation to rest in God after a process of preparation in relationship to the reading and meditation upon scripture. Evagrius described the goal this way, "Happy is the soul that attains to perfect formlessness at the time of prayer…that becomes free of all matter and is stripped of all at the time of prayer...that attains to complete unconsciousness of all sensible experience at the time of prayer."[9]

Meninger distilled these primary monastic and contemplative aspects into what he called "The Prayer of the Cloud" and began teaching this method to retreatants at Spencer Abbey in Massachusetts. In 1976, Menninger's colleague, Basil Pennington, was invited to lead a series of retreats for Roman Catholic monastic superiors. During that retreat, Pennington remembers that the group chose to rename Meninger's method, *Centering Prayer.*

How to pray

Thomas Keating and Contemplative Outreach have created a simple four-fold path, which Keating refers to as guidelines not rules. These guidelines are the essential *"how to"* of Centering Prayer. (If you are interested in learning more about each of the guidelines, please explore them at ContemplativeOutreach.org).

> ***Guideline #1:*** *Choose a sacred word as the symbol of your intention to consent to God's presence and action within.*
>
> ***Guideline #2:*** *Sitting comfortably and with eyes closed, settle briefly and silently introduce the sacred word as the symbol of your consent to God's presence and action within.*
>
> ***Guideline #3:*** *When engaged with your thoughts, return ever so gently to your sacred word.*
>
> ***Guideline #4:*** *At the end of the prayer period, remain in silence with eyes closed for a couple of minutes.*

Though there is much to be said about each of these guidelines, for now, just notice that Centering Prayer is *a one-word prayer method*, technically referred to in the tradition as *monologistic* – yet the sacred word is not meant to be repeated continuously. The goal of Centering Prayer is not to repeat, mantra style. The method of Centering Prayer only uses a "sacred word" when we notice we are engaged with thoughts. When we notice, we simply return ever so gently to our sacred word.

The implicit hope is that after a period of time, perhaps around twenty minutes, we might begin to have moments where we do not need to return ever so gently to our sacred word. Why? Because we are no longer as engaged with our thoughts. That is to say, we have been embraced by the silence of God's loving center.

When to pray

When we begin to attune and frame the day using the method of Centering Prayer, we likely will meet inner resistance. Surprising aspects of ourselves arise, and beliefs come to the fore that shout, "I'm too busy." "I'm too tired." "My mind is too full of thoughts." "It is not working." All this is an opportunity to offer up our resistance to God and allow the Spirit of God to replace the resistance with acceptance. Little by little, the desire will grow in us to return to our inner room, closing the door and praying with Abba in the secret place of our heart.

For many of us the pre-dawn hours have a special quality, a presence that meets us in the stillness and silence. The morning offers a consciously chosen pause and preparation before the busyness of the day. These morning hours can be energizing, calling to all living things to prepare to receive the gift of the new moment and day.

The Gospel of Mark records two instances where Jesus rose early, even while it was still dark (Mark 1.35, 16.9; Luke 21.37-38). Even more compelling is Jesus' all-night prayer session alone on the "mountain" (Luke 6.12). What captures my imagination is the recognition that *this* long of a session in prayer probably involved intercessory, verbal prayers, but also silent surrender to the Presence of Abba in Jesus' life and inner experience.

Morning meditation tends to fill our reservoir of silence and stillness allowing us to take this reservoir of silence with us into our day, and it supports us. But many find it tends to be depleted as we encounter situations that confront our false self and frustrate our emotional, intellectual and physical programs for happiness. Just think rush hour traffic. Or a screaming three-year-old. All the peace received in our morning meditation can easily evaporate by one stressful encounter.

For this reason, practice Centering Prayer later in the day is important, perhaps before dinner, or even before returning home for the night, stopping by a local church or park on the way home from work for a twenty-minute pause in the silence. Some find it useful to take a pause during the middle of the day, perhaps at lunch time to incorporate ten or twenty minutes in the silence. Centering Prayer offers a way to pray in solitude, but also community, as some participate in group Centering Prayer to supplement a daily, personal commitment.

Yet truthfully, regarding times and gatherings, there is no *one* specific way to incorporate Centering Prayer into our life; there are multiple ways. The important thing is a commitment to prayer and each person can personalize their meditation schedule. In building a Centering Prayer practice, it is important to find a workable schedule around our life and family commitments.

What Centering Prayer does

Over the years, we may notice that a twice-daily Centering Prayer practice begins to infuse our life with an unmistakable quality of inward stillness regardless of whatever else is occurring. In a sense, the daily practice ushers us into a contemplative state that never leaves us or forsakes us.

We become the prayer. This is a grace of the practice and something that happens to some lovers: they simply and beautifully become one with whom they love, echoing Jesus' promise and wish for his disciples – including us, that we might realize that "*you are in me and I am in you*" (John 14.20 NIV).

Centering Prayer is a primary and foundational contemplative practice, because Centering Prayer provides a deep reservoir of internal peace grounded in our increased awareness of the presence of Christ. A presence that enlivens our worshiping, studying, serving, and reading of scripture – indeed our entire life and ministry.

As we have focused on aspects of meditative prayer, we now move to focus on selected contemplative, monastic practices. The hunch is that the church needs to recover not only meditative prayer, but the treasures of contemplative practices that have been given to us through the monastic tradition.

Prayer and practice have always gone together, a faithful pairing throughout Christian tradition. The recovery and pairing of meditative prayer with the contemplative, monastic practices holds rich promise as a way to replenish and flourish our lives, ministries and congregations, to which we now turn.

Chapter Six /

Practicing

"By your endurance you will gain your souls."

– Luke 21.19

"We are waiting not for a Gadot, but for another – doubtless very different – St. Benedict."[1]

– Alasdair MacIntyre

"The monastic life is a structural opportunity to be human, and in seeking God we touch the deepest desire of our heart. This is not a new theory. St. Augustine said that we seek one mystery, God, with another mystery, ourselves, because God's mystery is in us. Our mind cannot be understood even by itself, because it is made in God's image."[2]

– Brendan Freeman

1 · *A Brief Overview of Key Monastic Practices*

Spanning nearly twenty centuries, the Western and Eastern Christian monastic traditions are vast.[1] A brief survey of the writings and sayings of the early spiritual fathers and mothers, of both the Eastern and Western traditions, reveals that even a basic study of their legacy would require a lifetime of reading. No doubt, the monastic-contemplative well is not only deep, it is broad. And blessed are those who draw from it.[2]

Each monastic community is unique, and each historical era of the church contributes its own charism and shape to the flowing stream that is monasticism. For example, the diversity and uniqueness of such communities as St. Catherine's in the Saini desert can be seen in contrast to Mount Athos beside the Mediterranean Sea.

The diversity of form and practices include the Trappist and Franciscan renewal movements. The Jesuits. The Community of Taizé. On and on the roster of historical communities and names unfold, encompassing a lifetime of diverse practices and spiritual exploration.

In what follows, we will take a brief glance at one of the foundational gifts the monastic charism bequeaths to the wider church: the contemplative spiritual practices. In recent decades, Western Protestant Christianity has seen a popular uptick in interest in spiritual practices. This is important because the practices are meant to help us both forget ourselves and discover ourselves. In the depth of their embrace and engagement, we can remember God.

It is helpful to set these practices in perspective, by way of an historical example of a monastic rule of life. A rule of life is like a fusion between a daily schedule and spiritual vows. For example, Saint Romuald wrote a short and simple rule in the eleventh century that, to this day, governs and guides Romuald's enduring monastic tradition, the Camaldolese:

> "Sit in your cell as in paradise; put the whole world behind you and forget it; like a skilled angler on the lookout for a catch keep a careful eye on your thoughts. The path you follow is in the psalms – don't leave it.

> If you've come with a novice's enthusiasm and can't accomplish what you want, take every chance you can find to sing the psalms in your heart and to understand them with your head; if your mind wanders as you read don't give up but hurry back and try again.
>
> Above all realize that you are in God's presence; hold your heart there in wonder as if before your sovereign. Empty yourself completely; sit waiting, content with God's gift, like a little chick tasting and eating nothing but what its mother brings."[3]

From such a brief rule as Romulad's, we see much of what we understand as contemplative – and even what we mean by spiritual practice – coming to us through the witness and experiences of the monastic traditions.

The monastic tradition(s) are nurtured by the sayings of the desert mothers and fathers in the third and fourth centuries in Northern Egypt, made famous by the life of St. Anthony the Great. Similarly, later in the sixth century, St. Benedict of Nursia, led a monastic renewal movement at Monte Cassino in Southern Italy.

Benedict's movement would eventually imprint other monastic communities, such as the Cistercian and Trappist monastic orders. And yet, the value of the monastic practices expands beyond the monastic traditions and the walls of any one specific monastery. It is to this broad monastic values expressed as key practices that we now turn.

Among the many monastic practices, seven core contemplative/monastic practices stand out for adaptation in spiritual communities:

Lectio Divina

Prayer of the Hours

Self-Observation

Silence

Simplicity

Solitude

Stillness

A more exhaustive list might include such traditional monastic practices and values as: Fasting, Humility, Hospitality, Spiritual Direction, Stability, Stillness, Work, and the threefold classic monastic vows of Obedience, Poverty and Chastity.[4]

Summarizing the wisdom of the practices is this memorable phrase: *we keep our practice and our practice keeps us.* Yet let us not forget that the crown of all these practices is the truth and presence of the Eucharist. Not technically a spiritual practice, the Eucharist, for much of Christendom, grounds, shapes and infuses all our spiritual practices in a central and enlivening way.

We will briefly survey these seven, core contemplative, monastic practices, and then also suggest how these practices can help renew us and renew the church.[5] The practices are simply the means.

The ancient Chinese saying from the book of *Chaung Tsu* wisely summarizes this cautionary point: "When the shoe fits, the foot is forgotten." Pair that with the anonymous wisdom saying that "what we do daily, we do dully, unless we do it deeply." The practices are practices until we forget them. When that forgetting happens, the benefits of the practices often become a part of us.

Yet it is wise to begin any conversation on spiritual practices with the admonition not to confuse the means with the end, nor the method with the experience of simply being held in God's love. Practices aren't about legalism or rule-following, and no method should be made a "god."

Lectio Divina

Lectio divina is the Latin way of saying spiritual reading or sacred reading. In *Lectio divina,* the reader actually "listens" to a brief scripture or text slowly and prayerfully. This requires a kind of spiritual attentiveness, and this attentiveness can become a disposition brought to the reading.

As the text is read slowly, we ponder it, letting the listening process deepen as we listen for a word from God to us. In a phrase, we listen "with the ear of the heart." As we descend from just a mind-understanding toward a deeper heart-understanding, we often encounter an integrated and life-giving wisdom.

By way of analogy, listening slowly and quietly for God's word is like the daily practice of tending to the little weeds that creep up ever so innocently in the garden of our heart. If the word of God is at work weeding the weeds away, our inner life is protected from being smothered out by the barrage of our normal, negative thoughts and feelings.

Such negativity often seems more prolific than the weeds! *Lectio divina* is more than just sitting down to read a book. In a sense, it is more about the book reading us. To help convey what I mean by this, let's explore several key aspects involved in the process of *lectio divina:*

- An unhurried pace and a generally quiet atmosphere are very helpful to the *lectio divina* experience. The goal is to have a sufficiently long enough time to read so that we can sink into the silence of the reading. Many find the quiet hours of the morning or evening good for this kind of reading.

- Twenty minutes is a good time to plan for, although it will vary from person to person, and situation to situation. The place of our sacred reading should be somewhere we feel comfortable, but not so much so that we would be prone to fall asleep. A quiet spot in the house, church or neighborhood park might provide an ideal place to listen with the ear of the heart to sacred scripture.

- A relaxed, calm disposition and mindset will help the reader get the most out of the sacred reading. If the body feels anxious or restless, it may not be the best time. A sense of peace and a calm mind will also benefit our reading. That is not to say we wait till things are perfectly peaceful – for they rarely are. Often the reading brings the peace we are seeking.

- A peaceful interior state will help us move from the activity of reading to the disposition of prayer. To that end, it is wise to begin and conclude the reading with a brief verbal prayer, perhaps using a scripture, such as Psalm 103.1: "*Bless the Lord O my soul, and all that is within me…*", or Psalm 118.1: "*O give thanks to the Lord, for he is good; his steadfast love endures forever!*"

A common daily schedule in many monasteries provides for two to three hours of *lectio* spread throughout the day. St. Benedict's Rule supports such an emphasis, urging that "the monks be free (*vacent)* for reading."[6] The Latin verb *vacare* suggests that the monks were to be left free for God, and connects with our modern

English understanding of taking a vacation. During vacation, we are free to rest, to be quiet and to pursue what we love.

In the monastery, *Lectio* provided the time and space for the reading, repetition, and refection on the bible (or other sacred texts), and through that process, the monk experienced what we would call the contemplative gifts – such as insights and wisdom, compunction of spirit, tears, or various spiritual consolations.

The classic fourfold pattern of *lectio divina* comes to us from the late twelfth century author-monk Guigo II (d. C. 1188). In his *The Ladder of Monks,* Guigo names the four stages of the process of *lectio divina* as: *lectio* (reading), *meditatio* (meditating), *oratio* (praying) and *contemplatio* (contemplating). [7] Each step is compared to the rungs of a ladder. Here is a simplified summary of the process:

> "Reading is the careful study of the Scriptures, concentrating all one's powers on it. Meditation is the busy application of the mind to seek with the help of one's own reason for knowledge of hidden truth. Prayer is the heart's devoted turning to God to drive away evil and obtain what is good. Contemplation is when the mind is in some sort lifted up to God and held above itself, so that it tastes the joys of everlasting sweetness...Reading seeks for the sweetness of a blessed life, meditation perceives it, prayer asks for it, contemplation tastes it. Reading, as it were, puts food whole into the mouth, meditation chews it and breaks it up, prayer extracts its flavor, contemplation is the sweetness itself which gladdens and refreshens. Reading works on the outside, meditation on the pith, prayer asks for what we long for, contemplation gives us delight in the sweetness which we have found."[8]

I would daresay that most preaching preparation stops at the second step of *meditatio.* Pastors are trained to bring their analytical minds to the text, accessing its historical-critical-literal meaning by using the best linguistic tools available. That kind of reading and study provides exceptional information. It is exegetical in nature, the kind of information that commentaries are full of. The preaching event often translates the exegetical information into homiletical flair and flow.

However, in personal, private bible study that is more akin to devotional reading, many do move deeper beyond the second step of pondering the textual information. *Lectio divina* can be so enjoyable because it speaks to our hearts so deeply and gives us delight.

The steps of *lectio divina* are not air-tight. That is to say, there is always a fluidity to the process, where we interweave from one to another, in a non-linear way. It is more like the wind, coming and going; lingering and leaving. Guigo's ladder analogy is helpful at first, but then as we deepen our practice of participating in the listening for the word of God, the pattern gives way to a process of grace that can't be controlled or contained.

The practice of *lectio divina* invites us to read the text slowly. To pause frequently to listen to what is arising within. To attend to the Spirit of wisdom beyond and underneath the text, conveying its life-giving guidance in that moment. And not only guidance, most of all, it seems something of God is revealed to us in the silence.

It is not just reading the bible that feeds us in *lectio divina.* For example, one of my most treasured books is the two-volume classic, *The Spirituality of the Christian East,* by Cardinal Tomáš Josef Špidlík. I devour it. I feast on it. When I first began my spiritual journey, Špidlík's book pointed me in a very helpful direction and helped me begin a long journey of research, exploration and discovery of other similar books and ideas. Here is a quote from Cardinal Špidlík related to what I am wishing to convey:

> "Among contemplatives, one notices the symbolism of spiritual food, of eating scripture. A biblical symbolism, certainly, but one which Origen inserted into the tradition. To him, scripture and the Eucharist were intimately connected. Since scripture is one of the 'indwellings' of the divine Logos, a meditative reading of the sacred books helps, little by little, to unlock the divine secret hidden in our heart."[9]

Introducing *lectio divina* into a church community is a good place to begin implementing the contemplative, monastic spiritual practices. For Protestants, there is much crossover appeal, since the practice of *lectio* is so grounded in bible reading.[10]

Prayer of the Hours **(The Divine Office)**

Gathering alone or with others for regular periods of worship and prayer throughout the day, is a primary way that the "*soul which longs for God*" (Psalm 42.1) can be satisfied and enfolded further into love, joy and peace. Gathering for morning and evening prayer as a community of faith has long been the foundation of a deepening spiritual life – for multiple religious traditions, monks and clergy alike.

For example, the ethos of the Jewish Temple, gathering multiple times a day, had an immediate bearing on the early development of Christian worship and prayer. The Prayer of the Hours is a way of ordering the schedule of our day and life, in addition to our householder requirements of work and family. Combined with worship or Eucharist, these pauses through our day help us re-connect to the awareness of Spirit and to the grace of God hiding in every moment.

In the monastic tradition of St. Benedict's Rule, the Prayer of the Hours is a primary expression of the *opus dei* – the work of God. In the monastery, the daily office was mostly sung. What was sung? The prayers and scriptures, of which the Psalms played a primary role.[11]

The Prayer of the Hours provides the liturgical superstructure of the monastic day. Monasteries attend to the hours differently, adapting their liturgy to their unique community, context and charism. The traditional seven hours of the daily office were inspired from Psalm 119.164, where the Psalmist affirms, "*seven times a day have I praised you.*" Guided by Scripture, St. Benedict structured the daylight hours with seven offices: *Lauds, Prime, Terce, Sext, None, Vespers and Compline.* These seven periods were later broken into two categories, the major and minor (or little) hours:

The three major hours of *Matins*, *Lauds* and V*espers.*
and
The four minor hours of *Terce, Sext, None*, and *Compline.*

The Prayer of the Hours helps us order our day to the rhythm of prayer, anchoring our awareness in scripture, silence, prayer and song. The rhythm of the day helps us remember God and discover ourselves. For many church communities, an extensive liturgy of the hours will not be possible, but a moderate order of daily prayer would be very possible. While many churches build their life around programs and then worship, primarily limited to Sunday morning worship, what if instead we built the church life around a daily liturgical rhythm? To begin with, why not try a daily 7:30am Centering Prayer service, and a Friday or Sunday evening compline service at 7:00pm?

In the absence of spiritual practices and a rhythm of daily communal prayer, the church often drifts down all sorts of rabbit trails. Pastors become more event planners and program mangers than spiritual guides of wisdom and prayer. It seems that in ministry, many become worried and distracted by everything *but the one necessary thing* (i.e. Luke 10.38-42).

So, while the Prayer of the Hours is not a widespread *current* Protestant experience, it is a significant part of our Reformed heritage. Even John Calvin's Geneva was a living epicenter of daily prayer, worship and personal devotion.[12] Gratefully, the Prayer of the Hours is returning to our communal awareness as a part of the broader liturgical renewal movement among the Protestant mainline traditions, and among less mainline expressions such as through New Monasticism.[13]

Self-Observation

The practice of self-observation, or paying attention to oneself, has less to do with navel gazing and more to do with heeding Jesus' invitation to his disciples in the garden of Gethsemane to keep watch and pray so as not to fall into temptation. The Eastern Orthodox community calls this practice "*prosoche,*" which means to give our attention to our way of life. The biblical allusions to this practice are significant, including:

> *"Only be careful, and watch yourselves closely so that you do not forget the things your eyes have seen or let them fade from your heart as long as you live"* (Deuteronomy 4.9).
>
> *"Above all else, guard your heart, for everything you do flows from it"* (Proverbs 4.9).
>
> *"Keep watch over yourselves and all the flock of which the Holy Spirit has made you overseers. Be shepherds of the church of God"* (Acts 20.28).
>
> *"Pay close attention to yourself and to your teaching; persevere in these things, for as you do this you will ensure salvation both for yourself and for those who hear you"* (1 Timothy 4.16).

Self-observation is the king of several other interior practices that help us tend to our soul by honestly and non-critically watching our thoughts, feelings, sensations and the provocations or events that precede those thoughts and feelings. It is king because of the primary role it plays in all inner work.

Here is how the Sufi poet Rumi conveys the nature of self-observation: "The guard at the gate drowses. The king stays awake. You have a king inside who listens for what delights the soul. That king's wakefulness cannot be described in a poem."[14] Though primary, self-observation pairs beautifully with the practice of guarding one's heart, an inner vigilance, (*nepsis*), and the practice of stillness, called *hesychia.*

The practice of self-observation helps us see and watch our mental-emotional-physical patterns. We can begin to recognize the wisdom that we are *not* them. In many cases, *we see what we be*, and *in seeing, there is freeing*. We are freed from the tyranny of our thoughts and emotional patterns, and can recognize that since we are more than our thoughts, feelings or sensations, we need not believe them, or go along with them. Indeed, we can see and separate from what we see. We can remember who and what we really are: sons and daughters of God. We may benefit from a friend or pastor who can help us process what we see within.

In the monastic environment, the practice of inner observation was supplemented by other practices, such as the remembrance of God and fasting. These ascetical practices help us see that we are not our physical appetites and to help us remember God in more of our embodied life. All spiritual practices are intended, at their heart, to help us become more healed and real. Our reality is a remembering journey toward returning to Abba, as the prodigal son story reveals (e.g. Luke 15).

As we return our attention to Abba and the loving presence and action of the Holy Spirit within, we may discover that it is not we ourselves who are doing the returning. We are not going anywhere. It is as if God is being revealed more; as our self is being peeled open. Like water to wine, we are being transformed, *"from one degree of glory to the next"* (2 Corinthians 3.18), until *"it is no longer I, but Christ who lives in me"* (Galatians 2.19-21). The church father St. Basil summarizes the experience of self-observation with the wider range of practices in view, for our spiritual well-being and God's glory this way:

> "We should watch over our heart with all vigilance not only to avoid ever losing the thought of God or sullying the memory of his wonders by vain imaginations, but also in order to carry about the holy thoughts of God stamped upon our souls as an ineffaceable seal by continuous and pure recollection....so the Christian directs every action, small and great, according to the will of God, performing the action at the same time with care and exactitude, and keeping one's thoughts fixed upon the One who have each of us the work to do. In this way, we fulfil the saying, 'I set the Lord always in my sight; for the Lord is at my right hand, that I may not be moved' and we also observe the precept, 'whether you eat or drink or whatsoever else you do, do all to the glory of God.'"[15]

Self-observation is most useful if practiced in tandem with a spiritual director or spiritual friend. Even more ideal is to have a small group to share one's insights and struggles. The key is to remain uncritical of what we observe and confidential in what is shared. Together, we help each other see our own patterns, speech, moods, attitudes, behavior and manner of life, more honestly and clearly, so to live more freely.

Silence

Paradoxically, endless words are needed to plumb the depths of silence. For the well of silence is deep. So too is the speech of the sky, oceans and boreal forests. And yet, the silence is deeper. The poet Kathleen Riane suggests "it is not that birds speak, but men learn silence." John Muir once reflected that by going out for a walk in nature, he discovered he was really going in. A Native American poem concludes that I, "heard silence, silence."[16] Wise ones often concede that it is within our relating and in our silence apart from those we relate with that teaches us where we have room to grow. The poet Mark Strand puts it this way, "Wherever I am, I am what is missing." Silence teaches and shapes what must be spoken and discovered *about ourselves.*

If self-observation is the king of the practices, then silence is the queen. Mainly because she creates the atmosphere of the interior life of our house – the house of our heart – which is also the house of worship. St. Benedict's Rule dedicates an entire chapter to the nature of monastic silence. Benedict taught that in the monastery, silence should be the general rule, and conversation the exception. Thus, silence toward others isn't rude.

The practice of silence helps us feel comfortable in the presence of others without the need or compulsion to have to say anything with words or gestures. We can let go of the need to impress or chatter, and focus inwardly on being present and still, even in the company of others. Silence, in many ways, is the deepest expression of human intimacy. In silence, we may deeply know and be deeply known.

One learns to be silent by being silent. It is a practice that we enter slowly; each person discerning their capacity or level of attraction to the silence. Silence and conversation go together, for they are both aspects of deep, empathetic listening and presence to another. Thus, silence is balanced with presence. We don't keep the practice of silence to be anti-social or anti-relational. We practice silence in order to help us know our self and to cultivate a listening atmosphere to the mystery of God's presence as well as the presence of others in our life.

The practice of silence need not go to the extreme quietism, which views all social and verbal interactions as somehow sub-human. We wish to be fully alive and celebrate the gifts of being human – including conversation, joy and relationships. In this way, silence is a blessing when practiced in the spirit of love – for God, self and others. Basil Pennington summarized this idea with a pithy brevity I find helpful: "God is Word. God is communication. And we therefore are essentially a *listening.*"[17] The primary purpose of silence is that silence supports spiritual listening and meditative prayer. Silence is the atmosphere *most* conducive for a fruitful *hearing* of God's word and *consenting* to God's presence in meditative prayer. Silence is the womb from which the word of God is birthed in our hearts and minds. Silence is the atmosphere in which our spiritual nature is fed.

Exterior silence supports the grace of interior silence, wherein we may discover something more true and real about ourselves and about God's energy toward us. If meditative prayer is the royal road to the royal rule, then silence is the "royal" part of the phrase royal road. And meditative prayer in the silence is the road. While one may not always pray in the silence, without the silence it would be very difficult to pray, much less to be prayed by the Spirit (e.g., Romans 8.26).

Monastic wisdom conveyed the instruction to "keep the silence and the silence will teach you everything." Silence was clearly related to the practice of stability and solitude as reflected in the parallel saying, "stay in your cell and your cell will teach you everything."[18] The seventh century father Abraham of Nathpar even went so far as to say that "God is silence, and in silence is God sung and glorified by means of that psalmody and praise of which God is worthy."[19] The fourth century father St. Ephrem said that praise moves from "sound to silence…the more refined and purified it becomes, the more it takes on the character of the silent praise of the angelic beings."[20] And John Climacus says, "the one who achieves silence, has arrived at the very center of the mysteries."[21] I also like the way the modern Constitution of New Melleray Abby describes what silence does:[22]

Silence assures solitude for the monk in community.

Silence fosters mindfulness of God.

Silence fosters fraternal communion.

Silence opens the mind to the aspiration of the Holy Spirit.

Silence favors attentiveness of the heart.

Silence favors solitary prayer to God.

The monks of New Melleray simply affirm that "our deepest communion with each other is realized in our communion in silence."[23]

Thus, the monastic, contemplative tradition teaches us at least two things regarding silence. First, the atmosphere of silence nurtures a life of prayer and study. This is one reason for silence within the monastic enclosure. The sacred space honors and supports others who might be in prayer or silence themselves. Second, the essential movement from prayer and meditation toward contemplation is more possible in the silence.

Silence is not limited to actual monasteries, but can also be incorporated into our personal life and church life. For example, instead of turning on the TV, computer or radio, practice cultivating silence where we are.[24] From a human perspective, silence is one of the essential elements of our flourishing, and is the primary atmosphere that makes spiritual growth possible. Silence must be cultivated. Silence rarely just happens.[25]

Perhaps our deepest most intimate communication doesn't interrupt silence. Quaker Thomas Kelly affirms that, "words should not break silence, but continue it. For the Divine Life who was ministering through the medium of silence is the same Life that is now ministering through words."[26]

I share the intuition of past sages and saints, who believed that out from the silence of divine life and love, the word flared forth *everything* – and before this point of silence, is the concealed of the concealed, pure *possibility*; which is another word for what can happen in the silence.

Thus, silence is an atmosphere of possibility. Even if uncomfortable at first, we *can* acclimate to and in this atmosphere. It is an atmosphere necessary for spiritual depth and maturing beyond the surface level of our life. As an atmosphere, silence is a profound influence that *influences*.

Where is this atmosphere? The answer is that we enter the atmosphere of silence both in our field of conscious awareness and in our body. The atmosphere and influence of silence is experienced within our internal perception and in our body. This is one reason why meditative practices that play in the fields of silence have such positive effects on neurochemistry and physiology.

Another practical aspect of silence is that it is the primary bond of peace between diverse peoples and their religious expressions. In the silence, we can feel the presence that holds us as we grow – as human beings in community and as individuals. In the silence, we can give our attention not to what divides people as so often expressed in our wordiness and doctrines detailing right from wrong, but to what unifies everyone in the field of silence and silent awareness from which love and language are first born.

As for integrating the practice of silence into our life and church, it is useful to begin with one of the practices that incorporates silence, such as *lectio divina.* There are many other methods that incorporate silence – journaling, walking, retreat, Eucharistic adoration, worship and reading, to name a few. The miracle of silence is that it opens us to the healing, refreshing grace of God.[27] This grace may also confront us and undo us, but it is an un-doing so as not to destroy us, but to liberate us from the often-hidden aspects of our self buried in our unconscious, and sometimes unconsciously manifested in our personality in negative and unloving behavior.

Yes, what can be said of silence is endless, but the enduring truth of silence is hidden in itself. Thus, perhaps only this remains to be said: silence is the house of God whose crest is the royal rule, and whose crown is the royal way of meditative prayer. This is one reason Isaac of Nineveh, the seventh century Syrian spiritual father, said that "if you pile up on one side of the scales all the rest of spiritual efforts and practices, and on the other – silence, you will find that the latter outweighs them all."[28] Indeed, in the monastic tradition, it was common wisdom that resting with God in the silence could teach you more than going out-and-about in the world of distractions.

Simplicity

The image of a simply clad, barefoot monk captures the cultural image of a monastic who has taken a vow of poverty. While the vow of poverty is important, it is different from the practice of simplicity. The practice of simplicity is a tonic to our consumer driven desire to accumulate. It seems that in Western culture, buying and acquiring have become the reason for our existence. And our economy has structured itself around our acquisitional appetites. In contrast, notice the counterintuitive remedy of simplicity.

The practice of simplicity is a chief monastic value that supports the primary contemplative practices of solitude, stillness and silence. For example, St. Benedict's Rule gives specific guidance on simple matters of provision for the monk's basic human needs: clothes, food, sleep, possessions.

All such items are appointed with a humble awareness for human vulnerability and generosity toward the infirm, weak, sick and dying. Simplicity isn't meant to be a torture device, but it is meant to help clarify what our priorities are. As a disposition and practice, simplicity keeps our lives and environments free from the distraction of too much clutter, as well as the Western tendency to over-indulge our appetites.

Paradoxically, the practice of simplicity isn't always simple. As we move toward simplicity, we confront the dynamics of desire. Desire is often connected with the human dynamics of greed, lust, gluttony, fear and hoarding, to name a few. Scarcity is the great opposition to simplicity. The fear of scarcity is an emotional driver, and feeds the inclination to think we don't or won't have enough. Fear of scarcity makes the practice of simplicity very challenging.

In our ordinary human experience, desire is stimulated by the senses. We often feel content, until that is, we see something in the store window or online. We probably didn't even know that thing existed until we saw it. And then we think we can't live without it! We often have no idea we need something until we see it, or observe others who have it. Simplicity helps us moderate this behavior.[29]

Solitude

The practice of solitude pairs perfectly and necessarily with meditative prayer. Solitude is the intentional disposition to remove distractions from our sphere of perception and presence so to be confronted with who we are in any given moment. For it is in the solitude and stillness that we can more fully discover ourselves, and, more importantly, become more aware of the presence of God.

We are "saved" again and again as we return to our heart, where we can feel the oneness with God that Jesus wished for us (John 14.20). As noted earlier, St. Irenaeus once famously commented that God's first word is silence.[30] And in the silence and solitude of God's Being-of-Endless-Love, an eternal birth of community takes place, which we call the Universe and our human unfolding therein. As we consent to God's love in the silence, we are participating in God's life (2 Peter 1.4), and we may more clearly experience the love-miracle of Christ being "*all in all*" (Colossians 3.11).

Just as silence is more than not speaking, solitude is more than just being alone. The first monastic communities were formed by individuals withdrawing from their day-to-day life; a civic life which most likely took place in the city, perhaps with some form of extended family nearby.

The intent of withdrawing from the world and seeking increasing silence and solitude was to listen for God's word; to become ever more attentive to the Spirit of God's presence and action at deeper and deeper levels of interior perception: the place where wisdom is born of stillness.

In the early monastic tradition, the appeal of a spiritual father or mother was also part of this early Christian phenomena. Recruitment to the ascetic life of solitude was surprisingly strong. A holy teacher, dwelling in the Egyptian or Syrian deserts, could gather up to one hundred followers in a season.[31]

Whatever the historical context may have been for the pursuit of solitude, modern contemplative Thomas Merton wisely captures the current interior, spiritual meaning of withdrawal into solitude best:

> "This is the secret of monastic 'renunciation of the world' Not a denunciation, not a denigration, not a precipitous flight, a resentful withdrawal, but a liberation, a kind of permanent 'vacation' in the original sense of 'emptying.' The monk simply discards the useless and tedious baggage of vain concerns and devotes himself henceforth to the one thing really necessary – the one thing that he really wants: the quest for meaning and for love, the quest for his one identity, his secret name promised him by God (Revelation 2.17) and for the peace of Christ which the world cannot give (John 14.27)."[32]

Solitude is less a secret and more of a gift. The gift of solitude is freedom. Freedom from ourselves. Freedom from the compulsions of our culture that call for our attention. Solitude is a training ground for our interior freedom, and when this freedom unfolds, we can love the world with our whole heart. It is not a dualism. Everything belongs. It is more a matter of style. We wish to live in a way that nurtures our freedom in love. Yes, in a similar way that silence is a deep listening, so too solitude is a deep discovery of a living communion always hidden *and* available in the love of God.[33]

Stillness

The practice of stillness is referred to in the Eastern Orthodox monastic tradition as *hesychism.* The term *hesychism* comes from the Greek word *hesychia* and means quiet or still, particularly referring to interior quiet and stillness that attends to the prayer of the heart. The prayer of the heart is often a fruit of the *Jesus Prayer*. As in Centering Prayer, *hesychia* is not passivity, but more like an intentional waiting upon God. *Hesychia* is an attitude of listening-consent to God's word and presence.

We can cultivate our interior stillness toward our thoughts, appetites and passions through a hesychastic lifestyle, that is to say: through the spiritual practices, or *ascesis*, the Greek word that the English word asceticism derives from.

The purpose of this *ascesis* is to make us more receptive to God's love and grace, so to be transformed more and more into the divine likeness. In Eastern Christianity, such spiritual practices that cultivate *hesychia* are: *Proseuche* (Self-Observation or inner attentiveness); *Nepsis* (Watchfulness); *Mneme theou* (Remembering God); and *Phylaki kardia* (Guarding the heart).

The *hesychastic* practices are deeply related to the Jesus Prayer, and support the development of the Jesus Prayer, as the Jesus Prayer similarly supports these practices. The writings of the *Philokalia* wisely teach us that, "Stillness [hesychia] gives birth to ascesis, ascesis gives birth to tears, tears to fear, fear to humility, humility to the gift of wisdom, and wisdom to charity. Charity makes the soul healthy and free of passion, and then [one] may realize that [they are] not far from God."[34]

Stillness is hard to cultivate in our modern, busy life, and more challenging to practice in a congregation. Nevertheless, modeling stillness and presence in our own life as a spiritual leader will influence the congregation in subtle yet profound ways.[35]

Lectio divina, Prayer of the Hours, Self-Observation, Silence, Simplicity, Solitude and Stillness. These are some of the core contemplative practices that can help each of us grow deeper. Following the pattern of Jesus' life, such practices emerged from within the earliest Christian experiences in both solitude and in community.

Such contemplative practices can also be found in other world religions. So, there is no question that one of the primary hopes for ecumenical and inter-spiritual relationships and healing, is our shared participation in such spiritual practices. In the silence, no one can disagree. By its very nature, silence connects everyone and everything.

I acknowledge that most of us are not called to go and live in a monastery. However, all of us can bring the monastery to us by incorporating more of the contemplative, monastic practices into our daily life. However, visiting a monastery can provide a boost of encouragement to our spiritual life and explorations of the monastic, contemplative practices.[36]

So, that is a brief overview of seven, key contemplative-monastic spiritual practices. These practices can help us live into answering *how* we can grow toward Christlikeness and fulfill the profound and perplexing Gospel invitation to "*be perfect as your Heavenly Father is perfect*" (Matthew 5.48).

By perfect, I take the meaning to be more akin to the idea of *completion*, or what elsewhere the scripture refers to as reaching "*the fullness of Christ*" (Ephesians 4.13), through practicing silence, simplicity and solitude, to name a few. To put it another way, this kind of Christ-centered fullness is our primary way to flourishing, and a new being by doing.

2 · *Why Monastic Practices?*

Modern philosopher Alasdair MacIntyre provided a general catalyst for the renewal of the spiritual practices in our time. His impactful book, *After Virtue* helped continue a conversation in academic circles that has, in recent years, trickled down to the church.[37] MacIntyre discusses intentional spiritual practices that connect word and deed, faith and action, being and doing, or what some theologians call patterned activities. These are activities or practices that are meant to lead to human transformation.

MacIntyre concluded his book *After Virtue* with an enigmatic turn of phrase, suggesting that Western civilization needed a monastic renaissance. Nearly forty years after the book's publication, in a new preface to the anniversary edition of his influential book, McIntyre clarified his intentions:

> "In the last sentence of *After Virtue* I spoke of us waiting for another St. Benedict. Benedict's greatness lay in making possible a new kind of institution, that of the monastery of prayer, learning, and labor, in which and around which communities could not only survive, but flourish in a period of social and cultural darkness. The effects of Benedict's founding insights and of their institutional embodiment by those who learned from them were from the standpoint of his own age quite unpredictable. Ours too is a time of waiting for new and unpredictable possibilities of renewal."[38]

What might these new and unpredictable possibilities of renewal be? For me and many others, it is a resourcement of certain practical aspects embodied in the monastic ethos, an invitation to take aspects of the monastic ethos and way of being into our day-to-day life.

The word monk derives from the Greek word *monos*, meaning unique, alone, or solitary. The word has traditionally described someone who retreated from the world of work and family to live alone, or with a like-minded community. Monks and monasteries are not exclusive to Christianity. Monks exist in many religions, all around the world. In Christianity, monks can be both solitary hermits (anchorite) or dwell in a monastic community (eremitic). Monks also typically live under a rule of life, such as the well-known Rule of St. Benedict.[39]

A common telling of the history of the monastic tradition goes something like this: following the Christianization of official Rome in the early fourth century, Christians experienced a positive reversal of fortunes. After centuries of inconsistent treatment ranging from violent persecution to lukewarm tolerance, Christians now began to experience a new, powerful alliance between Emperor and bishop; state and church. In response, some Christians began to feel uncomfortable with the church's newfound position and wealth. Seeking a deeper life with God, many chose to move to the deserts of Egypt, Palestine and Syria to pursue a life of holiness on the margins of Empire and an emerging Christendom.[40]

Figures such as Saint Anthony the Great (251 – 356 CE) became widely popular examples of this early monastic expression of Christianity.[41] This desert lifestyle is where much of the contemplative way of being Christian first emerged. It is to this time-frame that we can look to find the headwaters of those who also chose to retreat from the world and its customary opportunities, demands and duties, including family life.[42]

Key to this retreat was a lifestyle of asceticism. The ascetical practices helped them to cultivate an interior life with God, or so they believed. When asked for biblical grounds for such a flight into solitude, the desert fathers quickly turned to the themes captured in the famous Gospel story of Mary and Martha (Luke 10.38-42), and Jesus' own wilderness journey (Luke 4).

Whatever the origins of Christian monasticism, for centuries early monasticism flourished, providing a rich soil for some of the most significant spiritual writing known within the Christian tradition(s), East and West. Overall, Western monasteries flourished until the sixteenth century, when decline set in during the post-Reformation decades.[43] Before the Reformation, the monastic life was a common and accepted part of Western and Eastern Christendom.[44] After the Reformation, at least in Protestant Europe, England and the Americas, not so much. One example will suffice. The decline and virtual extinction of the monasteries in England and Wales during the Reformation is referred to as the "dissolution of the monasteries."[45]

The dissolution was a re-appropriation of land, title and wealth from monastic estates back to the Crown. The issue was less about theological rejection of the monastic model, or even fear by the crown of disloyalty by the monasteries, but rather a convenient opportunity for the Crown to reclaim the vast landed wealth held by the monasteries. Monastic communities that traced their foundations to gifts of landed property came to an abrupt closure in the wake of surrendering their properties to the Crown, particularly during the reign of Henry VIII.

While we can understand the historical context and theological concerns motivating the dissolution of the monasteries in the wake of the Reformation in England, we cannot overstate the important role monasteries and the monastic practices played in nurturing and maturing Western Christian spirituality overall.

The consensus in the imagination of modern Protestants has been that *all* monks were slack in their spiritual life, and *all* monasteries were corrupt. Many have falsely believed that all monks had ceased living their vows. Quite the opposite. There are countless examples of monastic communities that did *not* go lax in their observances or dedication to their contemplative calling. In this, it is easy to conclude that the Reformation overreacted, charging monasticism with guilt by association, lumping the good in with those who had lost their way.

No spiritual community – monastic or church alike – is perfect. There are abundant examples of monastic abuses in the high Middle Ages. However, if there were a community seeking to diligently follow a rule of life and faithfully keeping the Prayer of the Hours, more than likely, that community was also spiritually thriving.

In my view, much of the Reformer's disdain for monasteries and their elite categorization of monks as being more spiritually important than the laity, or even the priesthood, could easily have been corrected, and in many cases, such concerns were remedied through the efforts of the Counter-Reformation following the Council of Trent (1545 – 1563 C.E.).

During the Reformation, while the external monastic forms that incubated mystical experience were cut out, the internal, personal spiritual practices that infused and birthed such experiences were not. Practices such as reading scripture, meditation upon scripture, or the life of Jesus, cultivating one's personal piety, and maintaining awareness of the presence of God in ordinary life and relationships.[46] These practices endured, even after the Reformation closed many monastic communities in Protestant Europe and England.

Thankfully, strong monastic communities continue to exist in our era as living witnesses to what is possible when brothers and sisters dwell together in unity and prayer. Obviously, no community is without its flaws and weaknesses. But, in a time where the wider Protestant church is in need of a meaningful spiritual infusion, there remains a voice from the silence crying out in the desert: make straight your path! Return to the silence and the grace of the spiritual practices. Be enlivened once again and flourish in a way that does not so closely mirror the cultural milieu of distraction and busyness![47]

Again, this is not a call for people to become monks and nuns, rather, a call to learn from the monastic ethos and incorporate key monastic spiritual practices into our personal life and congregation, so to help us survive and flourish. The vision is to become a monastery without walls. The goal is to bring more of the monastery into daily life.

One reason we need a renaissance of monastic practices in the church is because of the lack of stability in our culture and lifestyle. We are a people on the move. The easy access to airfare, automobiles, gas, and our extraordinary interstate infrastructure have created a culture of relatively cheap and easy movement. A vow of stability embraces the wisdom of remaining in one place, and being shaped by the space and rhythms of life in that space, taking time to be intentionally and consciously still.

Stability is not just the remedy for our physical movement. It is also a helpful antidote to our restlessness in relationships. In our culture today, it is both easy and acceptable to quickly end and begin friendships or relationships. But the heart of all monastic practices and vows, is a life of stability. The practice of stability provides an individual the rootedness to give one's life to worship, contemplation and service to one's community in consistent, ongoing ways.

Many spend a lifetime trying to answer the ancient questions, *"Where are you?"* (Genesis 2.9), and find great freedom in finally discovering the simple answer is always, *right here*. Wherever we go, there we are. Perhaps the real question is, *can we be at peace there?* Or do we bring with us our interior disquiet and interior wandering and lack of presence?

Humans cannot live or flourish when constantly uprooted and transplanted. What we often discover after having gone on our life-quests and journeys is that we return to where we first began and find there the treasure we were seeking in the first place. This wisdom is conveyed in multiple ways in the monastic tradition. For example, in the instruction to the monk to remain in his/her cell. For the monastic, the cell often became a purgatory and a paradise. Staying inn one place, with interior stability is the quality in us that enables us to be like *"a tree planted by living water that yields its fruit in every season"* (Psalm 1.3).

Theophan the Recluse (1815 – 1894 CE) reminds us that, "when we are in the heart, we are at home; when we are not in the heart, we are homeless."[48] Homesickness teaches us that while we may achieve stability in this life, we are also pilgrims journeying toward the next, and in many ways, our companions are not only our brothers and sisters in Christ. Our companions are also our spiritual practices.

A further insight into the importance of monastic practices comes from the Hebrew Scriptures, which often provide detailed proscriptions for holy living (e.g. Leviticus and Deuteronomy). And throughout scripture, specific spiritual practices were the way in which Christians could fulfill the biblical mandate to be holy. Take for example this passage from the Epistle of First Peter:

> *"Therefore, gird up the loins of your mind, live soberly, and set your hopes completely on the grace to be brought to you at the revelation of Jesus Christ. Like obedient children, do not act in compliance with the desires of your former ignorance, but, as he who called you is holy, be holy yourselves in every aspect of your conduct, for it is written, "Be holy because I am holy"* (1 Peter 1.13-16).

Similarly, in some of the most meaningful passages in all of John Calvin's *Institutes,* Calvin beautifully summarizes the Christian life in Book Three, chapters seven and eight, "*The Sum of the Christian Life: The Denial of Ourselves*" and "*Bearing the Cross, A Part of Self-Denial.*" Here is a small sample:

> "Even though the law of the Lord provides the finest and best-disposed method of ordering a man's life, it seemed good to the Heavenly Teacher to shape his people by an even more explicit plan to that rule which he had set forth in the law. Here, then, is the beginning of this plan: the duty of believers is 'to present their bodies to God as a living sacrifice, holy and acceptable to him,' and in this consists the lawful worship of him. From this is derived the basis of the exhortation that 'they be not conformed to the fashion of this world, but be transformed by the renewal of their minds, so that they may prove what is the will of God' Now the great thing is this: we are consecrated and dedicated to God in order that we may thereafter think, speak, meditate, and do, nothing except to his glory."[49]

For all the Protestant and Reformation doctrinal and historical emphasis on faith and grace, the intention was never to rid the church of spiritual practices altogether. Rather, to order those practices aright.

As noted earlier in chapter Four, one of the chief architects of the monastic practices and ordering practices aright was Evagrius (345 – 399 CE). Evagrius was one of the first Christian monastic teachers to codify the practices and their relationship to the passions. In his *Praktike,* Evagrius significantly shaped the future of monasticism, developing a spiritual asceticism meant to cultivate the virtues and eradicate the passions (referred to as *apatheia).* It was not a novel view or method. Evagrius shared this ideal with fellow Christian teachers such as Clement of Alexandria, Origen and Gregory of Nyssa, and the Neoplatonist Philo and Greek Stoics.

Evagrius' short answer to the question "*Why monastic practices?*" was, because we need a way to respond to the human passions. The Apostle Paul said it even more simply: "*Work out your salvation with fear and trembling*" (Philippians 2.12).

As soon as a monastic tried to become still and silent, one would quickly see that various thoughts and human passions arise, many of which were unsettling and disruptive to the one experiencing them. It is no different for us today. Evagrius classified these thoughts into eight categories, a classification that morphed down to us in the modern era as the seven deadly sins: gluttony, greed, sloth, sorrow, lust, anger, vainglory, and pride.

For Evagrius and other monastics, a significant remedy for these thoughts was the application of the spiritual practices. For every ailment there was a therapy. And in this way, those who endured through their healing process, could also show others the way to deeper wholeness in Christ. These liberated ones became the soul-doctors and spiritual fathers and mothers who could help others on their journeys with wise counsel and words. These words that were later collected, known generally as "*the sayings of the desert fathers*."

As we also reviewed in Chapter Four, the ancient voice who contributes to the wisdom of spiritual practices is John Cassian (360 – 435 CE). Cassian describes the goal of the monastic life, beginning with the disposition of the heart – which represents the totality of one's body-being: "The whole aim of the monk and the perfection of his heart consists in a continual and uninterrupted perseverance in prayer, and as far as is possible for human frailty, it is a striving for immovable tranquility of mind and lasting purity..."[50] Without the spiritual practices arrogating, nourishing and cultivating our spiritual life, we cease to grow. As a result, we justify our lifestyles of consumption. We eat what we want. We do what we want. For most of us, the only rule of life we are under is the desire of our own whims, financial limits, or personal preferences and appetites. Seemingly anything in the name of freedom. The monastic solution to this is to pick up our cross of spiritual practice(s).

In the Protestant tradition(s), we may believe we are "right" with God by faith and grace alone, but we may also be very wrong with our self, or others if we buy the policy that promises us a future heaven by simply believing the correct information that Jesus died on the cross for our sins, while disregarding our inner life, or even the health of our body. We can't "just believe in Jesus" and live however we want.

If belief or faith *alone* is the extent of what is required of us to experience or acquire the abundant, abiding life in Christ, it is no wonder the church is the way the church is. But if you hunger and thirst for the kingdom of God, and if you intuit that there is a deeper life awaiting you both here and *now* as well as then and there, this hunger can lead to an understanding and experience that we are invited by Christ to die to our self. And for that life-long journey, we will need the spiritual practices as our trusted companions.[51]

Paradoxically, it is also true that believing with our heads may be something we are asked to let go of later-on in our spiritual journeys. For many, spiritual growth only continues after a crisis of faith, wherein it is as if we are asked to let go of the content of our ideas and doctrinal beliefs, and move through a second naiveté, or what some call the cloud of unknowing – a dark night. Through the journey, we become more balanced. An integration of faith occurs – body, mind and spirit. And an intuitive, humble wisdom replaces rigid doctrinal certitude.

While we are wired to grow deeper spiritually, many of us don't know how to grow deeper on our own. Yes, there are many useful gifts for our edification produced by the main-stream Christian media-machine. Wonderfully helpful for a time, they ultimately keep us coming back for more, and as a result, sometimes the Christian sub-culture looks uncannily similar to what our Western culture does best: it creates consumers. I'd like to see more practitioners than consumers.

Five-hundred years ago well intended reformers closed the monasteries, isolating the church off from many positive aspects of the monastic expression of

Christian spirituality, community and worship. Our era is the ideal time for us to widely return to the monastics for help with our church dilemmas and desires for deeper spiritual growth. The monastic, intentional ethos of God-devotion grounded in spiritual practices, can and will transform the wider church toward deeper growth and continued flourishing.

This flourishing begins in changing our behavior, our practices. And, beyond our own doing, there is the mystery of God's grace *undoing* us. Such is the essence of what is conveyed in the following beautiful phrase from Galatians: "*The only thing that counts is faith working through love*" (Galatians 5.6). By working, I easily read the word *practicing.*

Spiritual practices are vital for our development. Yet development is not necessarily contingent upon our spiritual practices. Development is often the fusion of grace and practice. And in this alchemy, there is always a space for divine grace, which transcends human accounting (e.g. Matthew 20.1-16), and always takes the initiative, wooing us deeper into the divine dance of possibilities.[52]

Part Three:

Recovering the Possibilities

"These things God has revealed to us through the Spirit, for the Spirit searches everything, even the depths of God..."

– 1 Corinthians 2.10

"Peter began to say to Jesus, 'We have given up everything and followed you.'"

– Mark 10.28

Chapter Seven /

Becoming

1 · *Becoming a Contemplative: the Spiritual Journey*

The intent of this chapter is to provide you with a practical roadmap to recover the contemplative experience(s) of God's presence in your personal life, as well as in your faith community. We will do so by pairing meditative prayer with select contemplative practices. In previous chapters, we have rediscovered and explored the foundations and particularities of both meditative prayer and monastic practices, now we seek to integrate that valuable information in practical ways for individuals and communities.

The Spiritual Journey

Father Thomas Keating is widely known for his role in the development and teaching of the method of Centering Prayer. What is less known about Father Keating, and yet perhaps will be his most enduring impact, is the way he updated the classical terminology of the spiritual journey for the modern era.[1]

For much of Christian history, the spiritual journey was built around a triad of developmental phases: *purgation, illumination, and union.* Keating dovetailed this traditional schema and adapted them to the modern era, with its focus on psychological awareness.

While Keating's famous book and introduction to Centering Prayer, *Open Mind, Open Heart,* is an international bestseller, perhaps his most enduring contribution to our understanding of the spiritual journey and the contemplative experience is his DVD series, *"The Spiritual Journey,"*[2] transcribed into book form, *Invitation to Love: The Way of Christian Contemplation*. Though the book is a blessing, nothing compares to the recorded, personal presence of Father Keating's teaching. And the DVD resource, though somewhat dated, is something I have used in every church I served to help introduce the contemplative Christian journey to the congregation.

In this video series, we discover Keating's foundational ideas related to the human spiritual journey, and their relationship to the contemplative dimension of Christianity, and the method of Centering Prayer in particular.

Programs for Happiness and the False Self

For Keating, when Jesus said "repent", to his first disciples (Mark 1.15), "he was calling them to change the direction they were looking for happiness."[3] It follows then, that another definition of sin, is looking for happiness in the wrong direction.

This makes sense theologically, since the Greek word for sin (*harmatia*) comes from the discipline of archery, literally meaning, to miss the mark. In Keating's helpful psychological updating, to stop "looking for happiness in the wrong direction" is to repent (*metanoia*), which in this context, means *change the direction you are looking for happiness*. By *wrong*, I take Keating to mean *fruitless*, ultimately unsatisfying, and not leading to a flourishing life or a fruitful church.

Jesus also demonstrates this truth. Rather than giving into the temptations he confronted in the wilderness immediately following his baptism (Luke chapters 3-4), Jesus transforms the temptations into opportunities for spiritual growth. In beginning his ministry this way, Jesus provided a model for our own lives and ministries. We are invited to follow the Jesus way as we confront the human condition and our overwhelming needs, demands and addictions for security, power and affection.

In part, the Jesus way was to remember truth in the face of temptation. Or, to put it another way, "*to have the mind of Christ*" (Philippians 2.5-11) by "*letting the word of God dwell richly...*" in us (Colossians 3.16). To have the mind of Christ is to remember God amidst the attraction to satisfy our appetites on our own terms. As we emerge into the world as vulnerable infants and grow into childhood, adolescence and adulthood, we normally begin to develop programs for providing for our own happiness (blessings) apart from God. Articulated by psychologist Abraham Maslow, and summarized by Father Keating, they are:

Survival and security

Affection and esteem

Power and control

Now notice the similar pattern to Jesus' temptations, as recorded in the Gospel according to Luke, chapter four:

Turn stone into bread =
The temptation to take care of our self apart from God.

Jump off the tallest building in Jerusalem =
The temptation to show off and gain fame.

Bow down and receive power over the kingdoms =
The temptation to take power.

In the biblical context, it is useful to recall that another word for happiness is blessing. This brings to mind the wisdom of the Westminster Confession, which taught that the chief end of humankind is to love God and enjoy God forever. This idea of enjoyment is closely connected with our pursuit of happiness. However, we often overlook the giver and focus on the gifts. Perhaps this hearkens back to the much-loved Psalm: "*Happy are those...whose delight is in the law of the Lord, and on this Word they meditate day and night. They are like flourishing trees planted by streams of water, fruitful in every season. In all they do, they prosper*" (Psalm 1.1-3, my translation).

The trouble with many of these programs for happiness is that, in large part, their motivations and energy is often buried in our unconscious – invisible to our awareness, except for the external behavior these programs and desires energize. From the contemplative perspective, this is important because in the classical model of spiritual development, this is the phase called *purgation;* the discovery, confrontation and uncovering of our forgetfulness and falleness on the psycho-spiritual level.[4]

It can be overwhelming to see oneself as we really are, and in that moment of honesty, we are given the grace and desire to repent – to literally change the way we are living and pursuing happiness. In most cases we are innocent of these programs and preferences, since they were laid down in our unconscious mind, psyche and body very early on in our life. Perhaps in some cases, even in the womb, or, let the reader understand, from a prior life (e.g. the "sins of the fathers").

The good news is that the grace of God's presence and action in the silence and stillness of prayer has a way of unloading the unconscious and healing us from the inside, little by little. In this way, over time, the method of Centering Prayer is a kind of a restructuring of our consciousness, which is a very precise way of updating the word sanctification. These programs for happiness, woven into the fabric of our life and personality, can become dynamic within us. They construct and shape what Keating calls our false self system.

The false self (i.e. sin = our sense of separation from God), along with its programs for happiness, also form what Keating calls the "human condition." Thus, it is not that anyone is really bad, it is more accurate to say that we are all simply suffering from a *bad case of the human condition*! The root problem is so simple it is shocking: "We have come to full reflective self-consciousness without the experience of intimacy with God."[5] This is Theology 101 in a sentence. We trust that the dismantling of our programs for happiness will lessen the influence of our false self, opening the space for grace to bring about the "*new creation*" in us (e.g., 2 Corinthians 5.17-21).

It is the false self that God's love is freeing us from, birthing the new person in its place. Over time, the grace of God working through our daily consent to God's presence and action, begins to heal and transform our programs for happiness, and in so doing, releases us from the unconscious compulsion to the false self – leading us into the freedom of being sons and daughters of God, and heirs of Christ.

Unloading of the Unconscious and the Divine Therapy

The method of Centering Prayer is a gentle practice, yet our spiritual journey might get worse before it gets better! That's because, when the light of the Spirit shines in the unconscious, with its hidden programs for happiness, the self does not go away quietly.

The light that is let into the unconscious by the presence and action of the Holy Spirit as we consent in the silence and stillness, has a powerful healing effect. Curiously, we may not know that it is happening until *after* the fact. Indeed, the fruit of the prayer often shows up in our life much later: we are more patient, where we used to be irritable. We are more kind, where we used to have a quick temper. We discover new insights in our scripture reading, where we used to feel dry and barren in our understanding. These and other examples demonstrate that we can't control the effect of our prayer, and most of all, we don't work for results. We simply consent to the ongoing presence and action of the Holy Spirit, which does the heavy lifting for our interior healing, on our behalf.

As a part of this process, an unloading of the unconscious occurs. This might feel like a front-loader, excavating memories or buried feelings. Powerful sensations might occur – emotionally or physically. For example, it is not unusual to experience tears or sensations in the body. This is the subtle movement of energy being released and healed.

The importance of the unloading of the unconscious is based on this truth: *that which is in us must first come up in order to come out.* We often don't need to know or understand the content of the unloading – it might have an energetic, emotional charge, or it might be related to a memory or a thought, or a body sensation, or even a past trauma. We just need to recognize the process is a kind of unloading coming up into our awareness. We are invited to let it go with tears or confession to another. Mercifully, that which once was hidden or repressed, most likely contributed in some measure to our suffering, but graciously, is now being released and healed.

Another wise principle is that *seeing is freeing.* By that I mean once you see an insight or a pattern of behavior at work in you, it begins to be freed from you. Our seeing enables a deeper way of being, in part because that which sees is the seeing of the Spirit. This is an aspect of the divine therapy: the totality of our being is not only refreshed in the silence and stillness of consent, it is also healed in hidden ways that we may not understand, or even be aware of. Contemplative Bernadette Roberts says that just seeing it undercuts that which is seen.[6] In other words, its power over us and in us begins to be undone.

The divine therapy is occurring beneath our level of awareness in the depths of intimacy that is possible in the silence. This is one reason why Father Keating says that "contemplative prayer is the world in which God can do anything."[7] Indeed, the purpose of the divine therapy is to "enable us to become who we really are."[8] We enter into this world of new possibilities by changing the direction we are looking for happiness and consenting to God's presence and action. As we do so, we will discover what Jesus meant when he invited us into the inner room (Matthew 6.6).[9]

The Divine Therapy begins to heal us, and this healing and wholeness radiates outward into our relationships. We may begin to experience a deep joy and happiness for no reason. We may begin to feel the lightness of being that Jesus promised when he invited all who were weary and burdened to come to him (Matthew 11.28). In sum, this is the invitation to rest and be renewed in the presence of God.

Perhaps for the first time we will feel free, grounded in the love of God. A love that strengthens us with a sense of fearlessness and joy. We know who we are and *whose* we are because, in part, we experience both the divine indwelling and remember our deep core of goodness; which are two foundational ideas conveyed in the treasure-house of Keating's practical theology and pastoral teachings.

There is no one way to become a contemplative. It is always a fruit of the grace of God working in our lives. However, in reviewing the historical tradition of Christian spirituality, a very clear pattern emerges: contemplatives become contemplatives by practicing some method of contemplative prayer.

All around the world pastors and lay people alike, have discovered the difference contemplative prayer makes in life, family and ministry – and though most don't start out their journey with the goal of becoming a contemplative, many discover that having taken the journey, they have become a contemplative.

One further practice can serve you becoming a contemplative and that is spiritual reading. It is a bit of an expansion of what we discussed earlier around the practice of *lectio divina.* In what follows, we will briefly expand *lectio divina* into the value of reading other spiritual classics within the contemplative tradition.

2 ·*Spiritual Reading*

In Chapter Six, we briefly looked at the ancient practice of *lectio divina.* But I'd like to expand on that, highlighting the nourishing partnership reading and prayer play when they are paired together.

When paired with meditative prayer, *lectio divina* is like the contrast between first looking at a black and white photo and then looking at a color photo. Meditative prayer reveals the deep color spectrum of scripture – helping us see deeper than the surface meaning.

Lectio divina is not just for the slow, prayerful reading of a short passage of scripture. It is also a way of reading any spiritual text. Many bring the practice of *lectio divina*, in addition to Scripture, to the readings in the classics of the contemplative Christian tradition. Monasteries provide a lovely model of this idea: during meals, in order to help limit aimless conversation, a designated reader reads aloud a selection appropriate in content and length to the monks, providing spiritual nourishment along with the physical nourishment of the meal.

This model might inspire appointing times during the week for "family reading time", or a house-hold reading hour, as reading out loud to another person has great value. Equally valuable is cultivating the skill of listening to another read out loud.

Reading the classics of Western and Eastern Spirituality also may ground our mind and soul in the living tradition, providing fresh inspiration for the present moment, rooted in the wisdom of the past. Since the tradition is vast and extends over two thousand years, it can be overwhelming knowing where to begin, so here are some classics of contemplative spirituality to start with:

Pseudo-Dionysius
Mystical Theology

Evagrius Ponticus
The Praktikos

John Cassian
The Conferences

Marguerite Porete
The Mirror of Simple Souls

John of the Cross
Spiritual Canticle
Dark Night of the Soul
Ascent of Mount Carmel

Theresa of Avilla
The Interior Castle

Various
The *Philokalia*

Anonymous
The *Cloud of Unknowing*

Meister Eckhart
On Detachment

Thomas Merton
New Seeds of Contemplation
The Inner Experience

Above all, we wish to cultivate the mind of Christ. Through the lens of contemplative reading our perception of ideas, experiences and relationships begins to expand.

This contemplative lens helps us not only read the text, *but also opens us to being read by the Holy Spirit through the text.* We become more intuitive in approach. Less dualistic. We listen with the ear of the heart and move deeper than mere intellectual objectivity that so often makes a scripture passage something to be analyzed rather than a means to see ourselves more honestly and our God more clearly.

3 · *Replenishing the Center*

Without question, a twice-daily practice of Centering Prayer, paired with a daily practice of *lectio divina* will replenish our being, providing fertile ground for on-going spiritual growth and flourishing. Yet, there is another dimension that can help us as individuals and communities of faith, flourish spiritually: a regular practice of Sabbath keeping – taking a weekly, quarterly and annual retreat.

As Centering Prayer becomes more consistent in our daily life, we notice our twice-daily prayer times in the silence of Centering Prayer are a kind of daily retreat. An essential in-breath for our day-to-day spiritual life. But one will often discover that a daily practice increases our need and hunger for more time in silence and solitude. To help support our continued evolution and spiritual growth, it is useful to set a day aside each week, or part of a day, for a longer retreat.

This may include taking a walk in a natural area or taking the time for making a home cooked meal. Or listening to or playing music. This allows us to *do* less and *be* more by stepping out of our normal routines and indulging in something we normally don't do – something that will be energizing, relaxing and restorative. Such a weekly "Sabbath" is also a good time to review and reflect on the week that has past, and to plan and envision in a non-stressful way the week to come.

For example, for years, I took Sunday afternoon as my weekly Sabbath. In those afternoons I would drive to my favorite local café, get a coffee and then take an hour long walk in a nearby forest. The first part of the walk was a gentle review of the week that had past. I recalled the events I experienced day-by-day. I noticed where I still had tension or concerns about the week, and let them go in prayer. Then, on the second half of the walk I found myself reviewing the week to come, making plans, offering prayers, and setting intentions. For years, this weekly Sabbath practice served me well.

Each month I would seek to do something similar to my weekly Sabbath. The important factor was to "get out of town." Change the scenery. Do something different, even relaxing. Be renewed in a non-stressful way. On those days, I would often drive three hours to a favorite natural area, like a state park, or a favorite place, like a museum. The point was to simply take time to be – alone or with a beloved. Scheduling monthly one or two-day retreats helps us to replenish and support our inner life and vocational calling.

For those blessed to live near a monastery or a retreat center, many monasteries and retreat centers provide overnight accommodations and "associate programs" to support that monthly intention to be renewed. Many Centering Prayer chapters around the country provide monthly one-day or multi-day Centering Prayer retreats.

An annual ten-day Centering Prayer retreat is both therapeutic and restorative. Such retreats provide a sweep of time to go deep and to simply be in the love of God – a love that has a way of profoundly healing and inspiring us. However long, Centering Prayer retreats reframe the stress and busyness of our life and ministry to such an extent, that upon completion, we often wonder how we ever lived without such a retreat. Longer annual retreats are a planned opportunity for inner renewal, whether it be a ten, seven, or five-day Centering Prayer retreat. Though, it is wise to remember that when it comes to retreats, it is often helpful to start small and build toward a longer time away on retreat.

Retreats aren't merely spiritual. It is important to get our bodies involved. Retreats are an ideal time to eat more cleanly, to exercise more consciously and to enjoy the gift of simply being embodied more fully.

Retreats, whether daily, weekly, monthly, or annually are meant to help support us be more present in the world. We take a brief absence from our worlds of work and family so to be recharged and refreshed to return to love, serve and enjoy our common life in the world.

4 · *Becoming a Contemplative Church*

Before anything else, becoming love in Christ *is* our destination. Being contemplative Christians and becoming a contemplative church is first and foremost about *how* we journey toward the beautiful destination in Christ of an ever-deeper love for God and one another.

No longer just a paradise lost; now, a solitude regained. At first, we feel it inwardly. We know we have been warmed by love itself. And then the miracle happens twice. The silence weds our hearts with others. And the fire of consciously chosen love, hard won in the clouds of unknowing and in the shadows of grace, burns us with a mercy into the flames of wisdom. We become lights for the dimming of fear and the beckoning all of the human family to return home. Such is the grace of the silence.

There is no *one* way to be a contemplative or become a contemplative church. Diversity joyfully abounds, and a shared disposition marks the way of contemplatives. But many of us want to understand what this might look like in our congregation and community. For that reason, I'm hopeful this book helps invite communities of faith to conversations that explore their own unique way of participating in the emerging contemplative revival.

A contemplative friend recently sent me Alan Watts' (1915 – 1973 CE) prophetic and seminal book, *Behold the Spirit*. Reading it, I remembered that Watts wrote this book in the immediate years following World War II. Published in 1947, the book was written for an American Christian church pondering its future. *Behold the Spirit* bears testimony to Watts' far-reaching spiritual gaze and ecclesiastical critique of what the Christian church could and should be. He calls us to return to the Christian roots of contemplative spiritual community. *Behold the Spirit* is in many ways a Protestant, contemplative primer encompassing the sweep of theological history.

Alan Watts may not be that widely known or referenced in Christian circles. He was a British philosopher, writer, and speaker, best known as a mid-century interpreter of Eastern philosophy for a Western audience. Born in England, he moved to the United States in 1938 and began Zen training in New York.

Watts attended Seabury-Western Theological Seminary and became an Episcopal priest in 1945. And in 1950 Watts left "formal church" ministry to move to California, where he joined the faculty of the American Academy of Asian Studies. There Watts continued to write and publish prolifically on spiritual matters. Growing dismayed with Christianity, he left the church. I wonder had he only experienced a contemplative expression of Christianity would he have remained in the church?

Like Thomas Merton (1915 – 1968 CE), Watts similarly spoke to the Christian church about the vital relevance of recapturing the contemplative dimension of Christian life and spirituality. Both men explored the mystical roots of the Western Tradition, and both turned to the East for insights on their personal spiritual journeys.

Watts's book is just now gracefully reaching my life – and the wisdom within it is a clarion call to the Christian church and her pastors. Two years before his death, Watts' wrote a preface for his book which concludes with a compelling and prescient invitation to the Christian church and her leaders:

> "The practical problem is, what are we going to do on Sunday mornings? How are ministers to continue their work? What is to be the use of church buildings, funds, and administrative machinery? Naturally, institutional Christianity will, in its present form, continue to supply the demand which remains for a monarchical [civil] religion. But a considerable number of ministers and even congregations – not to mention millions of reasonably intelligent young people – realize that churches must 'put up or shut up,' and that the chief business of religious facilities and assemblies is to provide a social milieu for religious experience. This is no mere matter of changing the externals – of having rock bands instead of organs and *Kyrie elision* set to jazz, nor even of turning churches into social service centers with the idea that this would be practicing Christianity seven days a week instead of just talking it on Sundays. Indeed, one may well hope that monarchical Christianity will not be practiced, even on Sundays, since the dutiful spirit in which it dispenses charity breeds resentment in the giver and the receiver alike, for when the one gives with reluctance the other receives with guilt. Ministers and their congregations must instead consider what need there may be for churches as temples for contemplation and meditation, stripped of the courthouse furniture of stalls, pews, pulpits, lecterns and other equipment for throwing the Book at captive audiences. They must consider also the

> need for retreat houses and religious communities, and for guidance and instruction in the many forms of spiritual discipline which are conducive to mystical vision [non-dual knowing]."[10]

This vision inspires a way for faith leaders and congregation to practically re-access the wisdom of the contemplative tradition in our time. For congregations re-forming toward becoming a contemplative community, the place to begin is with cultivating a contemplative environment.

Drawing inspiration from others who have gone before us, like Watts, is very useful. So too is focusing on small and practical steps of application – a focus to which we now turn.

5 · *Getting Practical – Start Small and Aim Well*

A congregation that wishes to grow more into a contemplative church, will need to cultivate an awareness of the importance of *becoming* not just *believing*. Not just a *missional* church. But also, a *practicing* church. By practicing, I mean that we ground our life in the kinds of spiritual practices we considered in Chapter Six coupled with the practice of contemplative prayer.

A practicing church begins to understand that we *be* by doing and *do* by being. Psalm 46.10 puts it this way, "*be still and know that I am God.*" Pairing this classic Psalm with the Pauline invitation to "*work out your salvation*" (Philippians 2.12), we can begin to discern an invitation into what I call the environment of spiritual practices.

As we draw a tighter circle around the invitation to cultivate a change toward the contemplative practices, spiritual leaders might begin by shifting focus in three specific areas:

- Shifting the focus from programs to practices.
- Shifting the focus from Sunday worship to a liturgical life together.
- Centering everything in the grace of meditative prayer.

It is also helpful for any faith community becoming more practical on their journey toward contemplative reclamation to agree to start small and aim well in each of these areas, which we will now attempt to do.

Shifting the focus from programs to practices

In every church context I have served, the primary emphasis on potential growth and increased participation was on finding the right programs to draw people into the church, particularly youth and young families. Thus, staff was often hired to create and manage programs. And if staff could not be afforded, such programs fell to the pastor or volunteers to manage.

The challenge with this programmatic model is that it is difficult to keep up with larger churches that can offer programming so much more effectively and robustly due to their expansive financial and volunteer resources. We can all see the chicken and egg dilemma here: If we don't have programs how can we get the people? And if we don't have people, how can we run the programs?

Programs are useful and important for every church community. What I am suggesting is not an either/or, but a return to the core spiritual practices as the foundational reason for being in a spiritual community in the first place. From this center of shared practice, other programs, ministry and priorities flow.

The real power of church life is a deep center of shared, intentional spiritual practices. Here's how one contemplative church in Austin, Texas limits the temptation to be all things to all people through a precise mission statement grounded in spiritual practices:

> "The Church of Conscious Harmony *exists for the sole purpose of facilitating the spiritual journey for people who want to make God devotion the center of their lives while living in the ordinary world without the aid of monastery walls*. As a contemplative Christian community, we encourage and support a life of daily spiritual practice, study and devotion in service to a growing awareness and experience of conscious union with the Living God."[11]

In the absence of shared, intentional spiritual practices, church programming often becomes a solution in search of a problem. Program after program is tried, wearying everyone out, especially the leaders.[12] To me this is a mimicry of our consumer, market-driven economy. The church that can't explain its own existence, often misses its deeper purpose: the inward journey of spiritual healing and transformation.

I often counsel churches, before removing programs, to consider first adding to the menu of current programs, a few key spiritual practices. This might include, for example, launching a Lenten spiritual practices Sunday school paired with a Lenten sermon series. This class might provide a focused overview, educating the congregation on aspects of meditative prayer and contemplative monastic practices. After the class, participants might be encouraged to bring one or more of the practices into their personal life, a rule of life, or practicing *lectio divina*. The class might conclude with a final two-day Centering Prayer retreat at a nearby retreat center.

In time, some of these practices might replace other programs. To further implement a key shift, I recommend introducing select spiritual practices to the leadership board. For example, beginning each board or committee meeting with ten to twenty minutes of silent meditative prayer in a sacred space, following a contemplative liturgy.[13]

Another way of introducing the spiritual practices into a congregation's life is to invite key leaders to participate in a brief *lectio divina* period prior to the Sunday morning worship services. This not only provides a centering point for the congregation, it also has the added benefit of helping the pastor begin the Sunday morning less rushed. For a *lectio* reading, I suggest using the passage of scripture appointed for the sermon as the text for the Sunday morning *lectio divina* period.

No doubt, there are endless ways to incorporate the spiritual practices into a congregation's community life, but the key is to start small and focused, and provide great clarity as to why, what and how it is being done.

Shifting the focus from Sunday worship to a liturgical life together

No matter the style(s) of worship a congregation prefers and expresses, the contemplative dimension calls to the church to shift from being less of a Sunday media event, toward a daily being together in a spirit of worship and prayer.

One way to begin to make this shift is to re-access the sevenfold liturgy of the hours, which is a cornerstone of the monastic rhythm. While gathering seven times a day for prayer or worship would be impractical if not impossible for all but a few large, center-city cathedrals, shifting the mentality of worship from a Sunday media event to a daily, or regularly patterned experience, is a possibility for most congregations. In this way, when it comes to worship, congregations can adopt a small aspect of the monastic ethos.

One way to begin this shift is to introduce Taizé chant into worship. Another way is to introduce the entire congregation to one of the many fine and useful daily lectionaries. Even if congregants are participating alone at home, there is a shared sense of community knowing that others are also partaking as you are. Today, resources abound that make partaking in a daily lectionary reading even more user-friendly. I particularly enjoy the online resource *Pray As You Go*, which pairs a musical reflection and prayer with the daily readings. Another very useful resource is the daily reader, *Give Us This Day* published by the Liturgical Press, or *The Magnificat*.[14]

In addition to building community around the shared praxis of lectionary readings, adding a daily Morning Prayer service, or a Wednesday or Friday evening worship service with time for Centering Prayer or *lectio divina* is an ideal way of weaving the congregation together, deeper than just Sunday morning worship. Attendance may be small at first, but you might also be surprised to discover how frequently visitors from your wider neighborhood are attracted to such offerings.

Centering everything in the grace of meditative prayer

By now, it is not surprising to hear me say (again) that the most necessary practice for spiritual formation and transformation in Christ, is also the mostly missing practice in the life of many of our churches and church leaders. I am not certain about much in life, but there is one thing I am certain of: without a practice of daily meditative prayer, such as Centering Prayer, we will continue to limit our evolution as a species and hinder our fruitfulness and flourishing as a Christian ecclesia.

On what basis do I make such a lofty claim? Well, I simply leave it to your own verification to see the fruit of everything else congregations and leaders have tried in the journey toward abiding in Christ. It seems to me that rather than building everything around the silence and stillness of meditation, we often build our church empires in the name of our own sound and fury. The exhilaration of concertized praise worship, and even the pomp and circumstance of overly dramatized high liturgy – it all reveals the fact that American Christianity has tried it all, *except* the silence.

By center everything in the grace of meditative prayer, I intend to especially include the leader's personal life and daily rhythm of being. It has been my experience that unless pastors and church leaders incorporate a meditative prayer practice into our daily life, the grace of such meditative prayer is less likely to spill over into the wider church community.

One way to begin building everything around the grace of meditative prayer is to attend a five or ten-day Centering Prayer retreat. Contemplative Outreach sponsors many such retreats in many regions of the country and indeed, around the world.[15] Retreats give a participant the personalized time and space to let go of their day-to-day concerns and be renewed in extraordinary ways. Words cannot convey the special graces conveyed on retreats. Retreats can truly be like a vacation for the soul and body – but often less expensive and more enduring in their renewing and healing impact.

As we are grounded more and more in a daily meditative prayer practice, the divine grace of God will begin to take care of the rest. The mystery is that as we consent to God's presence and action in the silence and stillness, unconscious blockages are healed, and new possibilities emerge without us having to lift a finger. It is an amazing grace to watch how seemingly doing nothing, except just sitting for twenty to thirty minutes twice a day, accomplishes so much!

To sum up, the essence of these three shifts in focus can be articulated with three specific action steps:

> First, add contemplative elements to leadership team meetings.
>
> Second, slowly, and in small ways introduce silence and Taizé chant into worship.
>
> Third, start a twice-weekly centering prayer group, and integrate Centering Prayer first into our own life before trying to get it into others.

Adapting these practical ideas for the development of Christian contemplation isn't the only direction we turn for inspiration. For those who wish to see these ideas embodied in spiritual community, consider visiting a living monastery. It is to this invitation that we now briefly turn.

Cultivate a Relationship with a Monastery

A local monastery is a congregation's most precious untapped resource for spiritual development. A living monastery is a compelling witness to the flourishing grace of spiritual practice. Monasteries often reveal the wisdom and fruit of living under the authority of a rule of life, not to mention a spiritual father (Abbot/Prior) or mother (Abbess/Prioress). While this model may be unfamiliar to Protestants, it is not because monasteries lack for spiritual depth.

Many monasteries have oblate or associate programs that encourage participation of local friends and lay folks to engage in a rule of life and begin to partner with them in spiritual practice – not necessarily at the monastery, but at home or church. Associate programs are a wonderful way to slowly become more familiar with the monastic spiritual practices. It is very encouraging to witness the practices and principles lived out by others in real time and real life.

Many monasteries also are equipped to provide overnight lodging for guests and groups who wish to take a retreat with them and engage their daily monastic schedule. Some retreats are "guided" for groups, and other retreats are solo "self-guided" experiences. In time, friendships between a congregation and a monastery may develop through conversation with the Abbot/Abbess and monks/nuns.

These relationships can be life-giving to both the monastery and our spiritual community. Such visits allow the two to support one another in different ways and deepen the harmony and peace in the Body of Christ, supporting our mutual evolution.

Chapter Eight /

Evolving

1 · *The Evolution of Consciousness*

Christians are often afraid of the word *consciousness*, perhaps believing the new age movement has a patent on it. With that in mind, bear in mind that consciousness is allowing you to read this right now! Consciousness is an extraordinary gift to be cherished and cultivated. The subject matter of human consciousness is an immense area, currently experiencing a boom in scholarship and research.[1] In academic circles, consciousness is currently a sexy subject, and rightfully so.[2]

In much of Christian history, pastors, theologians and biblical scholars often understood consciousness in terms of the human mind or heart expressed spiritually with such terms as "the old man," "the new man," or "the flesh." Such biblical categories might provide a sense of certainty, but they also are a dim description of the very broad and complex human experience of consciousness – not to mention an oversimplification of the mystery of the process of inner healing and transformation.

Through the insights of Developmental psychologists such as Aurobindo, Beck, Ferrer, Fowler, Graves, Koberg, Piaget, Washburn, Wilber or Smith, we now have a more nuanced spectrum to understand the spiritual process of maturation and growth into what St. Paul calls, reaching the "*full stature of Christ*" (Ephesians 4.13), and what I believe is a very important aspect of human *flourishing* and transformation.

The spectrum of human development gives us finely tuned definitions to describe the mystery of our transformation process. How? Each of the developmental models articulates and answers the "how" differently, but what they each have in common is the possible unfoldment of consciousness from one level to the next, where, Ken Wilber points out, the lower levels are *both* included *and* transcended. In other words, we integrate the past into the future, the prior to the later, the old into the new, the lower into the higher as we grow.

An analogy for this might be the way we increase our knowledge: we start with the known and move toward the unknown. We first learn the alphabet, then we learn vocabulary. Then we begin to read sentences, and soon we read books. Later we might even write them. The alphabet level is included yet transcended in the book writing level. When you graduate from the eighth grade you don't lose all that primary education, ideally, you integrate your prior education into the new, emerging knowledge gained in high school, and beyond.

We can readily understand this analogy when it comes to knowledge or skills, but we have a more difficult time when it comes to consciousness, often mistakenly believing there is only *one* level of consciousness. Clearly, there are indications that there are more levels of consciousness than we may realize. One example of this spectrum is a basic truth we all experience daily: the distinctions between the states of waking, sleeping and dreaming consciousness.

Different levels of consciousness can help describe the way human behavior functions for individuals and as communities. And if that is true, wouldn't it be wonderful if these levels of human consciousness could be mapped? What if, like the geological record, we could identify the various strata of human consciousness? Strata that might help identify where someone is coming from and the perspective by which they see reality.

Like the now well-documented phases of growth of a human being from fertilization to late-adulthood, what if we could also chart the possible developmental phases of human consciousness? If the map of consciousness is real, wouldn't this developmental map help us clarify what we mean by the spiritual process of sanctification leading to the utmost state of divine union, *theosis*? That kind of mapping, it turns out, is exactly what the gift the Developmentalists have given us.[3]

Developmental models are also useful to explain a great deal of human phenomena – personal and social. The developmental models help us answer pointed questions such as, "why do we find similar fundamentalist mindsets across divergent religions (literalistic scripture interpretation, justification of violence in the name of righteousness)?" Jean Gebser's cultural developmental levels of consciousness may be helpful here. The list starts at the earliest developmental level, moving to deeper (higher) levels in terms of complexity and spiritual development. This cultural development pairs with human psychological development from infancy to late adulthood.

For every age, era and level there are always exceptions to the rule, and those who are forerunners and followers. Such strata or transitions between levels of consciousness are probably more evident at certain "axial" moments in the human record. It goes without saying that these are broad approximations, but this chart is helpful in showing the various stages/eras culturally, and how the stages are mirrored in each developmental lifetime:

Period	Historical Development	Human Development
The Archaic	*Pre-History, 50,000 BCE*	*Infancy*
The Magical	*Ice-Age, 10,000 BCE*	*Three-years old*
The Mythic	*5000 BCE*	*Five-years old*
The Rational	*Axial Age, 500 BCE*	*Twelve-years old*
The Pluralistic	*The Modern age, 1700 CE*	*Forty-years old*
The Integral	*The Postmodern age*	*Sixty-years old*

Current historical scholarship has located the first axial age period occurring around 500 BCE, with the Rational eras reaching a zenith around the Renaissance, Reformation and Enlightenment eras – the foundation stones of the Modern era as we know it. In the mid-1500's, one-thousand years after the emergence of the Rational level, Martin Luther exclaimed that he "was at the dawn of a new era," We are currently in the confluence of an axial age. It is a tectonic-zone of emergence in-between the Pluralistic and Integral levels.

Clearly, a large segment of the population is currently moving beyond a primarily *nationalistic* worldview to a more *worldcentric* view, and in some cases, a *cosmoscentric* worldview. Put another way, as humankind develops, we move from egocentric, to ethnocentric, to worldcentric. Thankfully it seems we are also emerging into the awareness of a fourth: the cosmoscentric perspective. What's also clear is that these transitions, from one level to another, can generate much social and psycho-spiritual friction. Applied to the church, here's a summary, in my own words, of developmentalist pastor Paul Smith's description of religious expressions (i.e. levels of consciousness) possible within the universe of possible churches. Most churches would have one or more of these levels occurring in a ratio of its membership or participants at any given time:

Tribal Church

Ultraconservative, tribal mindset. Marked by fear and survival, biblical superstition, and hyper concerned about apocalyptic doom, and sexual purity, and tribal-kinship bonds among tight knit family groups.

Warrior Church

Fundamentalist, might-makes-right, us versus them mentality. For example, perhaps this level of consciousness is at root what killed Jesus, Gandhi and Martin Luther King, Jr., and what inspires all holy wars and religious violence.

Traditional Church

The mainline church, social groups, patriotic and social religion that unities communities with helpful religious services. An emphasis on appropriate group-think and group behavior. Law and order. Stability. A "join the club membership mentality".

Modern Church

Mainstream, mainline Protestant liberalism. Social action and justice, and a general demythologizing of doctrines, replaces the feeling of love. An emphasis on doing what's right for all.

Postmodern Church

Progressive spirituality that has broken free of theological traditions, but still stays connected to ecclesiastical structures. Beyond the bible mentality, with a focus on wellness and ecumenical harmony. All paths are equal. Diversity and openness are to be defended and celebrated.

Integral Church

"Integral Christianity and church attempt to extricate themselves from these developments by including the best of them and transcending the worst. Rather than rejecting or avoiding beliefs, integral church is at home with beliefs..." A Tapestry. A consciously chosen and woven experience of love. Beyond a collage, toward union.[4]

The value of these levels of consciousness applied to the church is very useful in explaining a diverse range of human behaviors from within those levels and communities. No wonder folks don't just get along in church! No wonder we don't know how to love one another: we are all seeing the world from different levels and states!

However, what is most interesting to me, as it relates to the intentions of this book, is that during the Reformation era, as the level of consciousness moved toward the fullness of the rational expression, Western Protestant Christianity essentially threw out the contemplative state/level because it was presumed "guilty by association" with the less desirable aspects of the pre-rational levels of consciousness, (i.e. magic, mysticism, anti-intellectual) from which some of Christianity was seeking to liberate itself during the Reformation and Enlightenment.

As a result, much of the depth/inner dimension and spiritual practices that cultivated the contemplative state were prematurely thrown out during the Reformation, because they were thought to be from the prior "lower level" of pre-rational consciousness, i.e. pre-Renaissance. On the contrary, the practices weren't levels at all! They were and are spiritual dynamics that operate *within each level.* Ken Wilber calls contemplative practices the *line* within the *level*. In other words, each cultural or consciousness *level* can contain spiritual *lines* within itself expressed according the *level's* energetic imprinting and lens of consciousness – which is why lower *level* consciousness often turns the spiritual practices (*lines*) into abusive distortions of fear, power and control, whereas higher *level* consciousness often uses the spiritual practices (*lines*) to cultivate love, wisdom and increase harmony everywhere, and with everyone.

What the Reformers could never have known then, and what we are re-discovering now, is that the deeper *states* of consciousness (such as those fostered in meditative prayer) can be present in any and all of the *stages* (levels) of consciousness. That is one reason why contemplative mystics pop-up in every level of human consciousness throughout recorded history, and that their critics usually don't understand them.[5] In other words, there can be fundamentalist mystics just as much as there are unitive mystics. The upshot is that contemplative traits and practices can nurture evolution toward deeper/higher stages/levels. Thus, the call to return to the contemplative dimension of Christianity through meditative prayer and the monastic practices can be spoken to all, whatever level of consciousness one may currently be "at", including the Traditional, Modern, Postmodern and Integral. Contemplative practices will serve evolution – from whichever level one begins.

Meditative prayer and contemplative, monastic practices can help tune-in congregations more towards the integral frequency. It seems essential that for more of humanity to evolve toward the unitive/integral and beyond, some type of meditative practice will be necessary. For instance, if I were to locate a crucial turning point in my own development, it would be my rediscovery of the contemplative dimension that rescued me from giving up on my faith as I struggled through the passage between moving from Wilber's Modern to the Postmodern levels, or in Gebser's terms, from the Rational to the Pluralistic.[6] The infusion of contemplative prayer and monastic practices into a larger ratio of human population is currently helping many transcend their prior level of consciousness more quickly, serving their integral growth beyond their current level of consciousness toward the contemplative/unitive, where unexpected flourishing awaits. And this is a very blessed occurrence.

No matter the wisdom and usefulness of the developmental models, let us not think we know everything. Beyond the contemplative, unitive, integral level, surely deeper stages and states exist, by pure grace, that transcend even consciousness itself. The Spirit of God transcends all states and consciousness – and never needs a map of consciousness. With the Spirit of God in the silence, who knows where the journey will take us, if not deeper and deeper into the love of God and the mystery of Christ! We will now explore the importance of human consciousness a little further, so to make the connection between psychological and spiritual depth, especially as it relates to spiritual leadership.

2 · *Serve from a Deeper Place*

Protestant Christianity has heavily emphasized the importance of following Jesus. Perhaps it is time we begin to understand that Jesus was inviting us to *go somewhere.* And that the "somewhere" isn't just a place "up there", but also a *state* or *level of being right here.* A level of consciousness. A different state of being: higher or deeper than our present level. Could it be that Jesus is inviting us to understand (in a profound way) Jesus' mysterious statement that we must be "*born from above*" (John 3.3), from a higher, prior level of consciousness?

Perhaps the most intriguing line in the Gospel of John for spiritual leaders is when Jesus says, *"There is so much more I want to tell you, but you can't bear it now"* (John 16.12). This passage reveals the developmental, emerging, unfolding nature of reality. It is as if Jesus is saying, "This is what you know *now*, but there will be more." As you develop, you will be able to bear it.

These words of Jesus are a call to all of us in spiritual leadership to keep growing ourselves, for there is always more. Not just more to be known and understood theologically, but also more to *be* and *become* it. Paired with Jesus' parable of the soil and sower we see that there is a connection with spiritual growth and depth: "*Other seed fell on rocky ground where it had little soil. It sprang up at once because the soil was not deep*" (Mark 4.5). Depth is an antidote for that which is a passing fad; for that which is temporary; for that which is surface. Depth is a way of connecting consciousness with spiritual development and flourishing.

I have yet to meet a faith leader who deliberately ceased growing. The pastors and spiritual leaders I know and interact with all express a desire to keep growing deeper in God. No one tries to burn out. It just happens, slowly, almost imperceptibly at first. The truth is few pastors go into ministry because they wanted to burnout or run on empty. Pastors go into the ministry of Word and Sacrament because they enjoy what it feels like to "*abide with Christ*" (John 15.4), and to "*participate in the divine nature*" (2 Peter 1.4), and to sing our songs of salvation, and tell our stories of healing with others in the community of faith.

And pastors rarely go to seminary to become effective CEO's of booming churches more like corporations than spiritual communities. And yet this picture is one our culture often presents as the pinnacle of successful ministry. Pastors pastor because, in the words of the Psalmist, they have "*tasted and seen that the Lord is good*" (Psalm 34.8) and wish to share this experience with others, so that they too might know this wondrous state of joy and peace together.

Yet somewhere along the way this awareness may slip. A motivation for ministry may become less about the experience of God's love in Christ, and more about our own or others' needs being met. What then? My belief experience is that the contemplative practices and level of perception restores us to our first love and mystical impulse.

Perhaps we all start out as little mystics, seeing God everywhere and in everyone, awake to the experience that the "world is charged with the grandeur of God" so beautifully conveyed by Gerard Manley Hopkins. Perhaps we all begin as contemplatives, silently in awe of and drawn to the *mysterium tremendum.* Perhaps we all begin our journeys because we once were still and knew that we were also first known?[7]

In the spiritual life, the adjectives higher and deeper are synonymous. Height is depth. Depth is height. Growth in knowledge, wisdom and being is also a growth in depth. And real spirituality is quite integral. Be enticed, and keep going deeper – into love, into the silence and into the unending Presence of Christ. Congregations will be intrigued. Perhaps at first scared. But, this call is the call of the saints: before you, a choice. Do we really want to remain at the level we are at, or do we wish to discover the *more* Jesus hinted?

No one knows where the floor or ceiling of our human development is. The levels keep unfolding, far beyond the integral or unitive level, such as described by Teilhard de Chardin's Omega Point.[8] A disposition of humility and joy is appropriate as we chart out these curious characteristics of consciousness. Surely Jesus' statement "*I am the Way…*" (John 14.6) teaches us that Christ embodied the higher levels of human nature and showed us what those were meant to look like.

Could it be that the answer to the question *What is a fully developed human being supposed to be like?* is this: Jesus. He is referred to as the "new man," and the "second Adam". What is more important for us is that Jesus seems to suggest that it might be possible for others to do some things similarly to what he had done (e.g., John 14.12ff). Perhaps part of the value of understanding the reality of levels of consciousness applied to the church, is that they usefully explain a spectrum of divergent human behaviors within those levels present in most communities. And not only that, the levels invite us to keep growing deeper toward an intuitive, harmonious and non-anxious spiritual leadership.

Chapter Nine/

Flourishing

"Oh, shroud from me the swirling human eddy
That draws us downward, struggle as we might.
Find me that nook of heaven's stillness, heady
With blossom of the poet's pure delight,
Where for the heart both love and friendship flourish,
With godly hands create its bliss and nourish." [1]

– Johann Wolfgang von Goethe

1 · *Re-fill in the Nook of Heaven's Stillness*

In the early Texas spring of 2015, fifteen years after beginning my ministerial vocation, I was serving as a transitional pastor at John Calvin Presbyterian Church in San Antonio, Texas. On my first day at John Calvin, I was cleaning out the file cabinets left by the previous pastor who had faithfully served the John Calvin congregation for eighteen years.

As I cleared out the files, it was as if I was on an archeological dig. The longer I cleaned, the further back in time I went. The cleaning process was like opening a time capsule of the prior twenty years of church leadership trends and resources. I found D. James Kennedy's, *Evangelism Explosion*; Rick Warren's, *Purpose Driven Life* curriculum, and the *How to Be a Contagious Christian* series from Bill Hybels. I found various study guide materials on Christian best sellers – everything from Phillip Yancey's, *Disappointment with God* to Tim Keller's, *The Reason for God.*

Despite trying every bestselling church curriculum available during the last twenty years; despite spending tens of thousands of dollars on two different church consultants over the course of two decades, and despite creating a new contemporary worship service, John Calvin Presbyterian Church steadily declined, leaking over fifty-percent in attendance, membership and giving. By all *external* and numerical measurements, the church had failed to flourish during the 1990's and 2000's. In contrast, during that same twenty-year period several multi-ethnic, non-denominational mega churches neighboring John Calvin Presbyterian were birthed and boomed.

John Calvin's story of mainline congregational decline, or a version like it, can be heard echoed across the country. Over the years, I have heard similar scenarios from pastoral colleagues representing the Protestant spectrum.

When I began my pastoral ministry in the year 2000 at the Frist Presbyterian Church of Flint, I speculated that *if nothing changed in their membership trends*, based on the current demographics of that church *at that time*, in twenty years, I wagered that the active worship attendance of First Presbyterian would decline by at least half. Fresh out of seminary, I can remember pondering what that might mean for my new career, not to mention the future of the church. It was *not* an encouraging thought! Perhaps, like me, the American church, is also pondering the same conclusion.

But, signs of transformation are occurring. For example, during my tenure as Interim pastor at John Calvin Presbyterian Church, I helped integrate Centering Prayer into a weekly small group of the congregation. We also hosted an Advent and Lenten three-day Centering Prayer retreat at a nearby retreat center. Grounded in the silence of Centering Prayer, I also helped lead the Session (church Board) through a revisioning process that included rebranding the church's name to CrossRoads Presbyterian Church and transforming a significant section of their campus into a multi-purpose retreat center.

A further key aspect of their transformation process was partnering with other ethnic congregations looking for a place to gather for worship in the church's neighborhood. Not only did these partnerships make sense from a stewardship perspective, they also supported a missional renewal to the church's neighborhood in ways many of the congregants had long ago stopped doing, since many had moved out to farther flung suburbs. Reviewing my time there, I am convinced that the ethos of Centering Prayer permeated much of the congregation and key leaders and helped open the door to the transformational ideas that emerged over a year long process of discernment and decision.

Yes, it is true, many of our congregations are declining. Perhaps it is for the best – to allow something new to be born, even if it be through unexpected congregations of immigrants and ethnic minorities just starting out on their journeys. For these reasons and opportunities, and so many more, five-hundred years after the founding of the Protestant era, we are invited to ponder our moorings and envision a more creative, life-giving course forward. A course set toward abiding *more deeply.*

It is time to try the one thing most churches have not yet tried: cultivating the nook of heaven's stillness in our lives and congregations. Returning to the monastic practices of silence, stillness and solitude. Trying meditative prayer. Being renourished, not just reformed. Partaking in the unhurried rhythms of grace that infuse us as we consent to simply being still in the Presence through a twice-daily meditative prayer method.[1]

The American Protestant Christian community as a whole, has tried everything else to bolster its missional effectiveness and numerical growth. Everything but the silence. Perhaps it an essential moment to look into the silence for a more complete experience of the Christian life and the unimagined inward flourishing it can bring.

2 · *Nourish, Flourish and Become Love*

It is foolish to remain the same in our *doing* and expect our *being* to change. We cannot change and remain the same. No doubt, it is normal to feel skeptical about what I am suggesting. Many alternatives for *how* have already been tried – the archeological heap of church resources rises high! I recognize that sometimes changing how we do things is like trying to pick up a board that we are standing on – it is impossible. Nevertheless, the truth is we can change – if we move off the board! We can change our being by doing a few things differently.

Paradoxically our *doing* shapes our *being*, and our *being* shapes our *doing*. If we want to *be* different, we need to *do* different. I deeply believe (and have experienced in my own life and ministry) that the answer to the question *how* is to shift our attention to doing meditative prayer paired with the contemplative monastic practices that can transform and deepen our being, as individuals and as communities,

Where for the heart both love and friendship flourish,
With godly hands create its bliss and nourish. [2]

The contemplative dimension is a multidirectional bridge for the reconnection of the Protestant Christian community to its past, present and future. The contemplative dimension reconnects us deeply with much of the spiritual wisdom of both Eastern and Western traditions, even helping heal the enduring wounds of schism. Not only can the contemplative way bind the wounds of our own houses of prayer, the shared practices of silence and stillness also unite us in deeply meaningful ways with our brothers and sisters in the Buddhist, Sufi, and Hindu traditions.

The contemplative dimension even connects us with the "spiritual but not religious" (SBNR), because of their focus on spiritual practices that connect people experientially to love and reverence for the interconnectedness of all life-forms and people on planet earth.

Amazingly, the contemplative dimension also connects us to the non-theistic traditions, since we can agree on the important role of silence in our communal and personal practice – and from this silence, the apophatic impulse arises, recognizing that sometimes the only thing we can really know is that what we don't know anything at all.

The contemplative way quietly feeds those who are hungry for God. It also provides a path for seekers of the good, the true and the beautiful. There is no denying that the contemplative way has guided countless Christians through the past twenty centuries of faith. It is, in the memorable words of Joseph Kopp, "an ascent to the depths."[3]

Surveying the contemplative territory, we see a tapestry of streams flowing and converging. The contemplative dimension is not new. A few of the primary tributaries of the contemplative tradition flow from Jesus to Origen; Mary to Melania the Younger; Evagrius to Cassian; Athanasius to Augustine; Benedict to Theresa of Ávila and John of the Cross; Basil to John Climacus; Gregory the Great to Pseudo-Dionysus; the cells of Mount Saini to the caves of Cappadocia; Jerusalem to Mount Athos; or from the Russian Taiga to Merton's Gethsemane Appalachian forest hermitage.[4] Through it all, the contemplative way has helped Christians connect in deep and life-giving ways with God through Christ by the power of the Holy Spirit in word, sacrament and silence. The contemplative dimension does this in part by cultivating an inward attentiveness through the practices of silence, stillness and solitude.

Such are a few of the reasons to posit that the contemplative dimension has richly imbued Christianity through the centuries with an environment of practices that can, little by little, birth the fruit of the Spirit more fully in our lives, as well as expand our willingness to serve others.[5]

Conclusion /

The Song of Silence

"By day the Lord commands his steadfast love, and at night his song is with me, a prayer to the God of my life."

– Psalm 42.8

"Elected silence, sing to me...and be the music that I care to hear."

– Gerhard Manley Hopkins

"The tao that can be told
is not the eternal Tao.
The name that can be named
is not the eternal Name.
The unnamable is the eternally real.
Naming is the origin
of all particular things.
Free from desire, you realize the mystery.
Caught in desire, you see only the manifestations.
Yet mystery and manifestations
arise from the same source.
This source is called darkness
Darkness within darkness.
The gateway to all understanding."

– Lao-tzu

I'm writing these closing words from the Peter Albertino guest room at New Camaldoli Hermitage, in the Big Sur of California. I'm on the last day of a six-day silent, solo retreat.

After a few days here, it sometimes feels as if the hermitage sits on the edge of the universe, perched as it is, one thousand feet up the coastal hillside overlooking the overwhelmingly majestic Pacific Ocean.[1]

I know the sea is there. I can hear it. But I can't see it. All week, the sea has been hidden by waves of mist and dense fog, lingering like breath over the cedars. When the clouds do part momentarily, it is as if they are the eyelid, revealing the glassy eye of God. A sea of consciousness that seems to see me as I see it. And we stare at each other; with each other, until I seem to disappear in the seeing.

The towering redwoods flourish in the nearby hidden valleys, blanketed by such moisture-rich fog that now veils my view. The mist makes the silence more mysterious. In the fog, I can't tell the difference between the silence of the evergreen forest and the silence of my hermitage room.

In the dark early mornings, and in the dusky hours of early night, I have lit a cedar scented candle. That, along with my hot coffee and room heater have been my chief creature comforts. And I have cherished the meditation time following the vespers service in the sanctuary. The monks light the Eucharistic table candles, ring the meditation bell, and we sink into the silence sitting nearby each other in the milled redwood paneled chapel.

The silence is deep. Sometimes the wooden beams of the redwood ceiling creak in the wind. Otherwise, it is a chamber for the making of the song of silence together. The silent song resonates with decade's worth of prayerful intentions; echoes from the countless souls who have journeyed to this hillside hermitage to disappear into the song of God and become a note lingering in the silence.

In this chamber, the silence seems to hear itself. It sings a song that we can all share in. From time to time, its wordless joy bubbles up in me, and I notice gentle tears streaming down my face. I have no idea why I am crying – it is as if my body is releasing both pain and joy, gratitude and grief. The ancients called it the gift of tears. *Penthos.* Compunction. And it is a gift – a grace that arrives softly like the mountain rain.

Just now, I heard the sanctuary bell calling us to morning Eucharist. I will head out into the fog and listen for the song-chant to find my way there. The song has been sung in every age in diverse ways.

Song. Note. Salt. Seed. Water. Mist. These things act by disappearing and dissolving. A Native American Ute song deeply speaks of this remembrance, interconnectivity and release in the song of silence – our common breathing, praying and being. Like monastics around the world, the Ute people sing in chant form too. Listen closely to their song, and you will hear enduring wisdom:

"In our bones is the rock itself;
in our blood is the river;
our skin contains the shadow
of every living thing we ever came across.
This is what we brought with us long ago."

We have brought with us the ache for silence. And it brings us back to our Source. Our shared song in the silence, as the people of God gathered in churches and fields and living rooms and storefronts all around the planet, is perhaps our last best chance of letting go of all the words that have wounded and barricaded each other out, limiting love in the mists of our fearful grasping to gain or defend.

The song of silence binds us to the void with a quiet joy. But that void is not empty – it overflows with humble, self-giving, other-centered love, drawing us into a deeper relationality; a living choir of notes spun into being from within God's eternal song.

All the more, may the song of silence work its grace, dissolving us into the chorus of love – a song that came here embodied with us long ago in the universe of God's eye, whose blink encompasses eternity and whose tears shine down upon the hills, and forests and mountain lakes, still quickening young women and men to buckle and bow with wonder at the gift of letting go of all that has been, so to discover all that yet might be in the still silences of surrender.

Amen.

"I have a feeling that my boat has struck, down there in the depths, against a great thing. And nothing happens! Nothing...Silence...Waves...Nothing happens? Or has everything happened, and are we standing now, quietly, in the new life?" [1]

– Juan Ramón Jiménez

Afterword /

From the Monastery

Cyprian Consiglio

Even as I write this we have recently witnessed our present pope, Francis I, visit Sweden to commemorate the Reformation. There he acknowledged that the Reformation "helped give greater centrality to sacred Scripture in the church's life." And through that shared hearing of the word of God great steps forward have been taken in the dialogue with the Protestant tradition. So, I am pleased to be a part of this well-worn path between huts of dialogue that Peter Haas introduces in the book, acknowledging also what riches the Catholic tradition might have to offer in return.

I was intrigued by Pastor Haas' statement, in the introduction, that the "Protestant impulse to split away from the Roman Catholic Church" did not end with Luther, Calvin and Knox; and that indeed the splitting has continued for centuries and still persists even to our own day and age. What strikes me as of fundamental importance is the "impulse" itself. What is the seed of truth that drives that "protest" of reformers? Because I often find that impulse and that protest in myself.

I have two reactions whenever I study the era of the Protestant Reformation. First, if history is to be believed, I am appalled at the corruption of the Roman church at the time of the Renaissance and the Reform. I have had a similar reaction when I read the biographies of Leonardo or Michelangelo, and other historical biographies and novels about Renaissance Italy. One can understand why Martin Luther would have considered and taught that Catholicism itself was a corruption of the gospel of Jesus Christ.

I found this phrase of Philip Hughes, in his book *A Popular History of the Reformation,* particularly interesting, that the origins of Luther's convictions lay not just in his own "discovery of the true meaning of the religion of Christ" (which according to him was divinely guided). He also, and maybe especially, drew his convictions from the discovery "in his own personal experience of the ineffectiveness and the mischievousness of Catholicism as a solution offered him for his spiritual troubles."[1]

As a lifelong Catholic myself, and now a professed monk and ordained priest in the tradition, in my own person, in my own body, I too am looking for solutions to the ineffectiveness and mischievousness that I have found in my own tradition, and that is partly why I have been drawn to search for answers outside of the visible boundaries of my own communion as I know it. The good news is that finding solutions in other traditions has led me to discover the same solutions in my own, solutions that are perhaps inchoate, perhaps that had been yet unborn.

So, I sympathize with both the rancor at the Roman church for whatever that corruption was and the desire to return to a pristine articulation and practice of religion. The reformers were disgusted with Catholicism's salvation by works, which had really become practically faith in magic formulas, *Deus ex machina,* what seemed like buying one's way to heaven, especially through the practice of selling indulgences. And, specifically to our subject matter, they saw that monastic life and its contemplative spirituality tended to set apart monastics as more spiritually superior.

Here is a foundational truth: that most of our questions, even if they seem to be about theology, are really at their base anthropological questions. It is this anthropology that went part and parcel along with the "famed Protestant battle cry, 'saved by faith and grace alone,'" that also caused Christians to abandon the "contemplative practices that uniquely help us work out our salvation and participate in Christ's ongoing formation of our inward life."

Germane to this is Tillich's *The Courage to Be.* He points out that in mysticism, can we safely say for those who are drawn to contemplative prayer? – "the individual self strives for a participation in the ground of being which approaches identification." Mystics, he writes further, "draw their power of self-affirmation from the power of being-itself with which they are united."[2]

As my Camaldolese Benedictine confrere, the late Fr. Bruno Barnhart, put it what some think is going on in our day and age is that we are actually (in spite of established churches perhaps) re-awakening (or awakening for the first time) to *our conscious participation in the historical process of the Incarnation.* Bruno calls this the new "sapiential consciousness" and he thought that it is this that will enable us to respond to modernity.[3]

More to my point, part of this new consciousness will be for Christian wisdom in our day and age to articulate a depth anthropology "which integrates the post-modern attainments of radical critical rationality and unconditioned creativity together with the Enlightenment values of human dignity and rights into a view of the human person grounded beneath human consciousness in the non-dual divine mystery."[4] This is part of the 2nd Axial Consciousness, which Pastor Haas also mentions. It is a tall order! But we are up to it, and off to a good start. I certainly see striving for such an articulation and an embodiment of it as well in Peter Haas' marvelous work.

I was particularly attracted to Pastor Haas' proscriptions for the renewal of mainline Christianity. First of all, to shift from "Programs to Practices." We are, oftentimes to our credit, so dreadfully extraverted in Western Christianity. This is what has enabled us to be at the front line of crises and disasters, famines, earthquakes, social justice movements, in a way that I believe the Asian traditions have admired and imitated in contemporary times. (See, for instance, "socially engaged Buddhism.") But our wells often run dry and we appear spiritually bankrupt when face to face with the transformative practices that are so attractive to our friends in the Yoga tradition, or through Zen or some other form of Buddhist meditation.

The classic tension between the active life and the contemplative life accented in Roman Catholicism may be another false dilemma ultimately, but there is a great need to redress the imbalance by re-rooting ourselves in the stream of life giving water that flows from out of the believer's heart (John 7:38) who is none other than the Holy Spirit, so that we may *run and not be weary, walk and not faint* (Isaiah 40:31), and truly give the whole richness of participation in divinity which the apostle Peter tells us is our true inheritance (2 Peter 1:4).

What type of practice then? Pastor Haas lists two, one more communal and the second, at least at first glance, more individual: the shift from Sunday worship to a liturgical life together, and then building on the centering grace of meditative prayer. It is hard to ascertain which of these is primary, but just to see Pastor Haas' embrace of a liturgical spirituality as well as meditative practice was heartening because my own observation has been that the more pessimistic the anthropology gets, the further one gets from both the liturgical traditions and contemplative practices – and vice versa, due not doubt to the same suspicion of works righteousness. My own prejudice here is not only as a Catholic, steeped in liturgical spirituality, but also as a member of a monastic tradition that is both Benedictine and eremitical.

The great gift of the solitary life is the luxurious possibility of cultivating one's own spiritual depths in a subjective, personalized way. What is formative about liturgical spirituality, on the other hand, is that it is always "we" language, and ensures that one stays rooted in the Scripture, the tradition, the community – put simply, in the mind of the church. But how our liturgy takes on a different character, when instead of being an event to attract and propagate it is a moment to commune at depth, with each one bringing to the Table one's own experience of the Word, both in letter and in silent dwelling. This of course is not to mention the transformative experience of shared meditation.

So, regarding both the form that our community will take and the character our communal celebrations, with Peter Haas I ask the question and raise the challenge: What if we started with these common practices, and let it inform and give birth to our programs and our ritual, instead of superimposing a pre-conceived formula? This organic approach will serve us well in the years ahead, when so many of us are rightly questioning our unexamined assumptions and the authority of traditions that do not always continue to serve our evolving understanding of who the human person is in relation to the Divine – our spiritual anthropology.

Our last three popes have been keenly interested in what they called the "new evangelization," in hopes that, as John Paul II stated it, we may proclaim the Gospel of Jesus "[with] a new ardor, new methods, and new expressions." Peter Haas' *Contemplative Church* is surely a welcome partner in this venture.

Cyprian Consiglio, OSB Cam.
New Camaldoli Hermitage
Big Sur, CA

Afterword /

From the Academy

Ilia Delio

In the Letter to the Ephesians the whole of the Gospel is summed up in one short verse: "*May Christ may dwell in your hearts through faith; and that you, being rooted and grounded in love, may be able to comprehend with all the saints what is the breadth and length and height and depth of his love and to know the love of Christ that surpasses knowledge, that you may be filled with all the fullness of God*" (Ephesians 3:17-19).

Peter Traben Haas has plumbed the richness of the contemplative tradition in a way that opens us up to the profound mystery of Christ. Leading us through a comprehensive history of contemplation and its development in various spiritual writers, he has illumined the contemplative dimension of the human person, indicating that contemplation is not for the spiritual elite but the deepest integration of personhood.

In an age which prides itself on scientific achievements, including mapping the human brain, contemplation speaks to us of the uncharted levels of consciousness which reach out to touch the hem of divinity. For Haas, contemplation is as if one is held by a center of infinite space in and beyond time. What is this center of infinite space beyond time but an ultimate center of personal love which we name as God?

Thomas Merton came to this same insight as he stood on the corners of fourth and Walnut Streets in downtown Louisville. "At the center of our being," he wrote, "is a point of pure truth, a point or spark which belongs entirely to God which is never at our disposal, from which God disposes of our lies, which is inaccessible to the fantasies of our own mind or the brutalities of our own will. This little point of nothingness and of absolute poverty is the pure glory of God within us."

The Carmelite philosopher Edith Stein also discovered the profound depth of being in God when she wrote "I do not exist of myself, and of myself I am nothing. Every moment I stand before nothingness, so that every moment I must be dowered anew with being. . . this nothinged being of mine, this frail received being, is being. . .it thirsts not only for endless continuation of its being but for full possession of being." Contemplation is awakening to this deep divine center at the core of life, as the French philosopher Simone Weil wrote: "Whoever says "I" lies."

The German philosopher Martin Heidegger focused on the world of being not as a conceptual argument for God but as an activity immanent in this world, a self-giving presence rather than a transcendent Creator God. We accept without thinking the givenness of the world around us, he said, and most of the things within it. It takes an "emergency," a break in our everyday consciousness to become aware of what is always already there awaiting our response. This is the heart of contemplation, a vision of the inner eye of the heart that sees the truth of reality in its blazing beauty.

To contemplate is to see in a new way, a type of seeing that leads to new ways of loving and thus new levels of acting in the world. As we see so we love, Angela of Foligno wrote, and the more perfectly and purely we see, the more perfectly and purely we love. Teilhard de Chardin spoke of seeing as the heart of evolutionary life. "There is nothing profane below here," he said, "for those who know how to see."

In this respect, he spoke of consciousness and love as two core energies within evolution. Whereas love [or tangential energy] draws together, consciousness [or radial energy] transcends by drawing us beyond the immediate horizon into a new reality, which is a deeper vision of the whole. What we realize, as Haas poignantly indicates, is that contemplation is an evolution of consciousness and love; the kindling of divine-human energies entangled in a mystery of creative transformation and thus self-transcendence.

Contrary to the modern view of the human person as static, fixed and defined, contemplation speaks to us of a much richer process at the heart of the universe itself. What we call the self is not a fixed entity, but a core matrix of relationships whereby deep prayer nurtures an interaction of divine and human energies. Beatrice Bruteau wrote that "our 'I,' our personhood, is not a *product* of God's action, something left over after the action has ceased. Rather it *is* God's action in the very actuality of acting. 'We' are not a thing but an activity. This is why God's activity of ecstatically moving out to us is an act of coinciding with our activity, just as our union with God will be our ecstatically moving out to God as an act of coinciding with God's activity...This activity which we are, and which God is, is the act of creative freedom, of initiative, of self-originated self-giving."

It is precisely this dynamic self that undergirds the importance of Peter Haas' study. Contemplation is necessary for evolving toward a higher level of personhood. Bruteau held that contemplation is the axial point between the individual and the person. An individual she wrote is an individuated existent with a less-complexified consciousness of otherness whereas a person is one who has a higher level of other-centered consciousness.

It is this transcendence of person over the individual that makes possible the communion consciousness of the new creation in Christ. Contemplation leads us to this new awareness of self and other whereby I exist in order that I may give of myself, for it is in giving that I am myself. This differentiated personhood arises out of a deep center within where humanity is held by divinity in utter silence and freedom.

The act of living as persons in communion means living from a deep center of spondic or radiant energy, whereby our act of living unites with another's act of living, and both go on to unite with a third, and so on. To love another, Bruteau states, is a creative act.

We love another not as a static being but insofar as the other is on the point of coming into existence. To love another, therefore, is to co-create the universe, since the whole of the universe is emerging in *this* person. By harnessing the energies of love and consciousness, contemplation becomes an act of the future, deepening within us a personal center of love from which we love freely, deeply and selflessly.

What we realize through the exploration of contemplation and transformation is that each person is a process and a becoming; a protean nature of dynamic energies driven by an inner impulse of divine love. Becoming aware of this love, surrendering to this love and being taken up in this flow of love is the christification of life in the universe.

As Teilhard knew so well: evolution toward Christ Omega requires an inner evolution in love. Contemplation is the key to crossing the threshold of partialities into the future fullness of life.

Sr. Ilia Delio
Connelly Chair in Christian Theology
Villanova University
Philadelphia, PA

Appendix I

You can find further resources at:

www.ContemplativeChristians.com

www.ContemplativeChurch.org

www.ContemplativeChurchNetwork.com

1 · *Selected Contemplative Scripture Passages*

There are many passages of scripture that directly intuit the contemplative disposition and dimension of Christian life and faith. Here are some to provide a starting point:

Matthew 5:8
"The pure in heart will see..."

Matthew 28.20
"I am with you always..."

John 15.4
"Abide in me as I abide in you..."

Romans 8.38
"Nothing can separate you from the love of God in Christ..."

Galatians 2.21
"I, not I, Christ in me..."

Galatians 4.19
"I am in labor pains until Christ is formed in you..."

Ephesians 3.19
"That you may be filled with all the fullness of God..."

Colossians 3.16
"Let the word of Christ dwell in you..."

Ephesians 4.13
"Until you reach the full stature of Christ..."

2 Peter 1.4
"That you might become participants in the divine nature..."

2 · *Sample Contemplative Prayers and Liturgy*

The following prayers are taken from my book *Centering Prayers: A One-Year Daily Companion for Going Deeper into the Love of God:*

God of Mercy:
You who are the first light in the depths of the deep,
shine unexpected blessings upon our life outstretched to you.
Draw us into the silence to feel your closeness,
and send us into the world with attentiveness
to the movement of mercy in-between the extremes of All or Nothing.
Through Christ our Lord we pray.
Amen.

. . .

God, my Counselor:
Imprint Your love upon my heart.
Lead me to walk in Your light.
Guide me in all I do and say so that my words may bear witness to Your way.
With Your Word in my heart, I delight more than in the riches of this world.
I await in Silence for the clarity of Your counsel.
Amen.

. . .

Beloved Source of Life:
We come from you and return to you, and in-between we learn to love.
Thank you for the gift of the human journey.
We wish to use our lifetime to become love.
On behalf of every soul alive or in transition,
we request the fullest experience of love, in this life and the Life beyond life.
Amen.

. . .

Lord Jesus Christ:
I greet you today in silence.
You join yourself to the parts of this human family making us into one whole body.

In this graced fusion, I see in others a part of me and know no stranger.
In you, we are one and there is no other.
We rejoice and suffer together, even in the silence perceiving distant groans.
Amen.

Vespers
Listening in the Silence Together

Welcoming Prayer

Opening Song – Margaret Rizza
"You are the center, you are my life. You are the center lord of my life.

Come lord and guide me, Lord of my life. Send me your Spirit, Lord of my life.

You are the center, Lord of my life."

Listening to Scripture*

"It is no longer I who live, but it is Christ who lives in me. And the life I now live in the flesh I live by faith in the Son of God, who loved me and gave himself for me." - Galatians 2.20

Reflection

Closing Prayer

*Sometimes it takes more than one reading for our minds to slow down enough to be ready to hear God's special message for us; that's why we read the passage three times. During each deepening time of silence, reflect upon the Gospel reading and ask the Holy Spirit to help you discern one thing that speaks to your life.

3 · *Sample Contemplative Retreat Formats and Forms*

Creativity and resources provide unlimited ways for crafting retreat experiences for a congregation. Here are two sample retreats I have led in recent years, with group sizes of 12 – 15 people.

"In Silence and Stillness I Begin Again"
New Year's Retreat Itinerary

Wednesday, December 30

7:00pm	Welcome, Introductions & Overview of Retreat
7:45pm	**Teaching Session A: Guidelines for *Lection Divina* and Centering Prayer**
8:15pm	Compline
8:30pm	Depart in Silence

Thursday, December 31

9:30am	Centering Prayer, *Lectio Divina* and Communion	
10:15am	Break	
10:25am	**Teaching Session B:**	***Resting***
11:15am	Break	
11:25am	**Teaching Session C:**	***Remembering***
12:15pm	Lunch & Afternoon Renewal	
7:00pm	**Teaching Session D:**	***Releasing***
7:30pm	Compline	
8:oopm	Burning Bowl Ceremony	
8:30pm	Closing Prayer & Depart in Silence	

Friday, January 1

9:30am	Centering Prayer, *Lectio Divina* and Communion	
10:15am	Break	
10:25am	***Teaching Session E:***	***Envision***
11:15am	Break	
11:25am	***Teaching Session F:***	***Embody***
12:15pm	Lunch & Afternoon Renewal	
7:00pm	***Teaching Session G:***	***Encounter***
7:30pm	Compline & Depart in Silence	

Saturday, January 2

8:30am	*Lectio Divina* & Communion
	Sharing Circle
	Anointing with Oil and Benediction
10:00am	Farewells, Group Picture and Safe Travels

. . .

Lenten Three Day Centering Prayer Retreat
INFORMATION FOR RETREATANTS

PRAYER ROOM

Please remember that the Prayer Room is a sacred space. Honor the sacred space by:

1. Not wearing watches/timers that beep.
2. Not wearing perfume or aftershave, as the scents may distract others.
3. Leaving food and drinks outside.
4. Removing shoes before entering.
5. Stopping for a moment before entering the circle in order to become conscious of the sacredness of the circle.
6. Entering and exiting only when the door is open. This will ensure that our prayer is not interrupted.
7. If during the prayer, your neighbor falls asleep and begins to snore, you may gently wake them.
8. If you begin to persistently cough during the prayer period, please quietly leave the room. You can re-enter during the meditative walk when the door is opened.

CENTERING PRAYER INSTRUCTIONS

1. Choose a sacred word of 1-2 syllables as the symbol of your intention to consent to God's presence and action within.
2. Sitting comfortably and with eyes closed, settle briefly and silently introduce the sacred word as the symbol of your consent to God's presence and action within.
3. When you notice you are engaged with your thoughts, return ever-so-gently to the sacred word.
4. At the end of the prayer period, remain in silence with eyes closed for a couple minutes.

CENTERING PRAYER

Most periods of Centering Prayer will consist of two periods of 20 minutes duration each. The following is the progression for three periods of Centering Prayer.

1. When everyone is seated in the Prayer Room, the facilitator will ring the prayer bell three times to indicate the beginning of the prayer period.
2. The first reader will slowly read the passage from *Invitation to Love*. After a moment of silence, the 2nd reader (Psalmist) will then slowly read the Psalm. After the readings, the bell is rung once to indicate the beginning of the first prayer period.
3. After twenty minutes, the bell will ring once to indicate that the first twenty-minute prayer period is ending and that the Meditative Walk (see instructions below) will begin after a couple of minutes.
4. After the Meditative Walk, when everyone is seated, the bell will ring once to indicate the beginning of the second period of Centering Prayer.
5. After twenty minutes, the bell will ring once to indicate the end of the second twenty-minute prayer period and we will close the 2nd period of prayer with the Lord's Prayer.
6. Please exit the room reverently and silently.

MEDITATIVE WALK

Between each twenty-minute period of Centering Prayer, you may participate in the Meditative Walk, or remain in prayer. The Meditative Walk allows us to practice extending the silence into the active portion of our daily lives.

1. At the beginning of the retreat, facilitators will demonstrate the Meditative Walk. Depending upon the size of the group, there will be one or two circles.
2. When the bell rings to indicate the end of the twenty-minute prayer, remain in the silence for a couple of minutes. When the leader stands, all rise together then turn right and walk prayerfully using the Sacred Word.
3. When beginning and ending the walk, all participants will rise together and be seated together, to honor those who have chosen to stay in the silence.

VOLUNTEERS NEEDED DURING THE RETREAT

Readers & Grace Giver

During the retreat, retreatants can deepen their experience of community by volunteering to serve the retreat in some way. Each retreatant is asked to volunteer for one or more positions during the retreat.

READERS (*OPEN MIND, OPEN HEART*): The sign-up sheet, a list of readings for each prayer period, and the books to read from (*Invitation to Love* and *Psalms for*

Praying) are located at the back of the Prayer Room. The ***Open Mind, Open Heart*** reader will read the marked passage slowly after the first three bells are rung at the beginning of the prayer period. After a few moments, the ***Psalmist*** will then read the marked Psalm. **Please read SLOWLY**.

GRACE-GIVER: The sign-up sheet for Grace-Giver is also located in the back of the prayer room. The Grace-giver will give the grace before each meal. You may choose your prayer from the provided book, or use one of your own. We will wait to pray until everyone is in the room. After we pray, we will then go get our food.

PERSONAL NEEDS

1. If you have other personal needs, please see Christina or a Shalom retreat center staff member.

SHARING: On the last day of the retreat, retreatants will participate in a group sharing. This is a very important part of the retreat and it is important to attend this session in order to connect with other retreatants and staff and to gain closure on the retreat.

The Evolution of Meditation in the Christian Tradition: From Lectio to Centering

· ***The Evolution of Meditation in the Christian Tradition:*** ***From Lectio to Centering***

The point I'm seeking to make in this brief survey of the evolution of meditation in the Christian tradition is this: *through the influence and practice of lectio divina and the Jesus Prayer, in conjunction with inter-spiritual dialog in the post-Vatican II era, Centering Prayer and Christian meditation provided the first written methods of non-discursive, meditative prayer in Christian history.* What follows, explores why I believe this to be a true and helpful thesis.

In our current usage, the English words meditation and contemplation have come to be used almost synonymously. Thomas Keating begins his modern classic, *Open Mind, Open Heart* with the acknowledgement that there is confusion over the terminology used to describe contemplation, or contemplative prayer and its relationship to meditation. When I first read that statement, I did not realize how accurate and significant his seemingly passing comment was. So, the comment merits further exploration here.[1]

Meditation as the Second Step of Lectio Divina

Today, we normally think of meditation as: *sitting in a prayerful position in silence.* But in previous centuries, the words meditation or meditate, as used in the Christian tradition West and East, traditionally had more to do with reading, listening, reflecting on, or attending to a passage of scripture, rather than silent, contemplative prayer, such as we would today think of in the method of Centering Prayer. [2]

Simply put, at least in the Christian tradition, to meditate meant *to take to heart* what one is *hearing or reading*, particularly in the scriptures.[3] We see this emphasized in the New Testament, with such passages as Mary pondering the words of the Angel Gabriel in her heart (Luke 2. 19, 51), and with the Apostle Paul urging Timothy to take to heart the reading of scripture (1 Timothy 4.15). Christian scholars and monks adapted the Jewish idea of meditation as expressed by the Hebrew term *haga,* which may have included saying the scripture out loud, repeating it to oneself in a quiet manner. This Hebrew term *haga* is often translated into Greek as *meletan*, which meant, "to study or meditate upon." From Greek, this was translated into the Latin *meditari* and *meditatio*, which has as its root the idea of making a soft murmuring sound. From there, it is self-evident that the Latin *mediatio* became the English word meditation. Scholar Janet Ruffing helps us gain a wider perspective on the practice of meditation in *lectio divina*:

> "The Latin word *meditatio* translates the Hebrew word *haga* which denotes recitation of the word of God in a somatic, rhythmic process that facilitates being affected by that word and by God. This ancient Jewish practice of recitation, memorization, and repetition of a word or phrase is found in many other religious traditions. Examples include *dhikr* among the Sufis, mantras among the Hindus, and the 'brief prayer' discovered by John Cassian (c. 360 – 430) in the Egyptian desert and recommended in his *Conferences*. Western monasticism developed this form of meditation through the fourfold organic process of *lectio divina* and later in a musical form in Gregorian chant. Popular piety retained elements of these meditative practices through the recitation of litanies and the rosary. The Greeks translated *haga* with the word *melete,* implying a movement into the depths of the human heart, thereby opening the self to the action of the Spirit. Recitation of the word-prayer in the heart continued in an unbroken lineage in Greek and Russian Hesychasm, where it was known as the Jesus Prayer…."[4]

The practice of meditative readings became foundational for monastic life in the Rule of St. Benedict, who urged monks to savor a word or phase of scripture that opened their heart during the public reading, and to cultivate that feeling in private contemplation.

By the twelfth century, this kind of meditative reading was widely and formally incorporated into the four-fold method of *lectio divina.* As such, it was the second step of the process, *meditatio.* Here is how Guigo the Carthusian describes the process of *lectio divina* in his book, *Ladder of Monks*:

> "One day when I was busy working with my hands I began to think about our spiritual work, and all at once four stages in spiritual exercise came into my mind: reading, meditation, prayer and contemplation. These make a ladder for monks by which they are lifted up from earth to heaven. It has few rungs, yet its length is immense and wonderful, for its lower end rests upon the earth, but its top pierces the clouds and touches heavenly secrets. Reading is the careful study of the Scriptures, concentrating all one's powers on it…Reading seeks for the sweetness of a blessed life, meditation perceives it, prayer asks for it and contemplation tastes it…You can see….how these degrees

> are joined to each other. One precedes another, not only in the order of time but of causality. Reading comes first, and is, at it were, the foundation: it provides the subject matter we must use for meditation. Meditation considers more carefully what is to be sought after; it digs, as it were, for treasure which it finds and reveals, but since it is not in meditation's power to seize upon the treasure, it directs us to prayer. Prayer lifts itself up to God with all its strength, and begs for the treasure it longs for, which is the sweetness of contemplation. Contemplation when it comes reward the labors of the other three; it inebriates the soul with the dew of heavenly sweetness."[5]

What is important to see in Guigo's teaching is that, historically, the idea of meditation in the Christian tradition had more to do with the pondering of a passage of scripture in one's heart, which is quite a bit different from sitting in silent prayer or meditation, as we understand it today. However, here is a key point: the motivation to meditate on scripture is that such meditation might lead one deeper into the silence, into the fourth step of *lectio divina* – which is called, contemplation.

Thus, in the broad monastic tradition of *lectio divina,* meditation was that part of the prayer process initiated and sustained by one's personal efforts. Contemplation, they believed, was God's response to those efforts. *Contemplatio* was the enjoyment of the sweetness gained from pondering and praying the passage of scripture. There was no limit to the depths or heights of what might be happening in that fourth stage of *contemplation*, where one was inebriated "with the dew of heavenly sweetness."[6]

While *lectio divina* is not a practice exclusive to contemplatives, *lectio* may lead one into a restfulness of mind and heart and body that prepares us for the practice of Centering Prayer. In this heart-based prayer of consenting to God's already here presence and action in us, we experience the inward healing and divine therapy that helps us, in theological language, *"live alive to God"* (Romans 6.11). Meditative prayer is simply the golden way to the golden rule (Matthew 6.6; 22.37). It is the means of grace that the Spirit of God uses to help us be *"transformed by the renewing of our minds"* (Romans 12.1).

Meditative prayer is the golden standard of sanctification. Without it, we miss out on the full height and depth, breath and width of the love of God (i.e., Ephesians 3.18). Meditative prayer is how the law of God is written deeply in our hearts. It simply is the Song of Songs. It is the bedroom chamber of surrender to the Spirit.

Meditative prayer is how we connect with the depths and how the depths connect and transform us further into the fullness of Christ (i.e., Ephesians 4.13).

Perhaps an analogy can help illustrate the process. If *lectio divina* is the foyer that leads into the inner rooms of our house of prayer, then meditative prayer is the bedroom chamber that might lead to contemplation. Notice how Guigo describes the effects of the fourth step of *lectio divina,* contemplation, using poetic and devotional rhetoric:

> "So the soul by such burning words inflames its own desire, makes known it state, and by such spells it seeks to call its spouse...but the very meaning of their prayers, does not wait until the longing soul has said all its say, but breaks in upon the middle of its prayer, runs to meet it in all haste, sprinkled with sweet heavenly dew, anointed with the most precious perfumes, and He restores the weary soul. He slakes its thirst, He feeds it hunger. He makes the soul forget all earthly things by making it die to itself He give it new life in a wonderful way, and making it drunk He brings it back to it true senses."[7]

Guigo goes on to describe that, one sign of such contemplation is the gift of tears. Such spontaneous tears are a beautiful expression of grace touching and warming the soul. We need not know why one is crying. We can enjoy the cleansing warmth of the mystery of the divine presence.

Guigo closes his letter with a poignant personal flourish, worth quoting in full for several reasons, not least of which is the clear picture of our journey's end:

> "Now it is time for us to end our letter. Let's beseech the Lord together that at this moment He will lighten the load that weighs us down so that we cannot look up to Him in contemplation, and in days to come remove it altogether, leading us through these degrees from strength to strength, until we come to look upon the God of gods in Zion, where His chosen enjoy the sweetness for divine contemplation, not drop by drop, not now and then, but in an unceasing flow of delight which no one shall take away, an unchanging peace, the peace of God."[8]

A further anecdote that illustrates how meditation related to the practice of *lectio divina,* is St. Augustine's monastic Rule, which predates St. Benedict's famous rule by nearly one hundred years. It is curious to note that Augustine's Rule never once mentions the importance or practice of *wordless* prayer. In fact, Augustine's Rule provided for daily prayer in the monastery, but this corporate and private prayer was to be based on the Psalms. Notice Augustine's specific linking of prayer and *words*: "Consequently, if some wish to pray even outside the scheduled periods, during their free time, they should not be deterred by people who think they have some other task there [in the prayer-room]. When you pray to God in psalms and hymns, the words you speak should be alive in your hearts." [9]

Augustine wrote his Rule in 397 CE at the age of thirty-seven. This is relatively young, even for the early mediaeval era. Augustine was a young Christian too – having just ten years prior experienced his conversion in 386, and baptism in 387. While these two facts may be peripheral to the nature of Augustine's Rule (a rule which in my view is quite focused on external matters, and, to be fair, of no one's fault, does *not* embody a whiff of contemplative ethos), it seems to me, when compared with Augustine's later writings, as well as those of other spiritual writers who followed in Augustine's significant theological wake, that Augustine's relative youth at the time, are revealed in the focus and spiritual thinness of his Rule.

So, to sum up, for most of Christian history the word meditation had more to do with a kind of pondering of scripture. By the late Middle Ages, the meaning of the word meditation began to morph toward the notion of contemplation, which in my view was a happy evolutionary turn, one which we will briefly explore now.

From Meditation to Contemplation

Jean Leclercq (1911 – 1993 CE) has contributed a great deal to our historical and scholarly understanding of meditative prayer and contemplation. In his important, yet all too brief essay, "Ways of Prayer and Contemplation II: Western", Leclercq begins by asserting that the practice of prayer in Western Christianity evolved very little from antiquity until the eleventh century. At that time, Leclercq suggests, a change occurred with the methods of meditation. An evolution inseparable from the decisive influence of monasticism.[10]

Toward the end of the eleventh century onward, a special kind of literature emerged related to prayer, under the simple heading of *meditative prayer*. This prayer literature included collections of spiritual prayers inspired by the model of Augustine's *Confessions,* where the author addressed God in prayer. An example of this development is William of St. Thierry's *Meditative Prayers*.[11] Such texts were meant to be read in the manner of *lectio divina*, providing material for devotional, meditative reading. These were word-based prayers of a devotional nature, meant to cultivate one's attentiveness toward God in all things, which to a certain extent could be described as supporting the overall contemplative life.

Slowly, the Christian practice of meditative prayer began to evolve toward what could be called *methodical prayer*. One example of this historical shift is identified especially by the teaching and mystical writings of the Victorines. Most famously – Hugh of St. Victor (1096 – 1141 CE) and Richard of St. Victor (d. 1173 CE). Richard would go on to influence prominent Christian contemplatives such as Meister Eckhart, St. John of the Cross, and St. Teresa Ávila. The point of remembering this historical fact is that, according to Leclercq, Hugh of St. Victor worked to locate meditation,

> "among the other activities of prayer with more precision than the monastic tradition had previously achieved. This resulted in several series of classifications, which became more and more systematic *but still did not include a method for how to enter into each of these activities*... It was out of these distinctions and schemas that there later developed the beginnings of a method for the practice of meditation and for the activities associated with it." [12]

I find this to be an extraordinary statement. It indicates an evolutionary moment of development in the contemplative tradition within the Western church, and I agree with Leclercq's intuition. In my view, an actual fully developed method of contemplative prayer didn't appear until much later – indeed, not until the twentieth century.

A simple review of two classic texts on mystical theology will also confirm Leclercq's claim. First, review the writings of twentieth century luminary Reginald Garrigou-Lagrange. This masterful and comprehensive two-volume, *The Three Ages of the Interior Life: Prelude of Eternal Life,* set the standard for the study of contemplative spirituality for decades.[13] Yet, in all its masterful discussion on meditation, as well as its retention of the classic distinctions between acquired and infused contemplation, *there is no indication of a non-discursive method of wordless contemplative prayer, such as what is articulated by the* ***method*** *of Centering Prayer.*

Garrigou-Lagrange does discuss the nature of the prayer of quiet, or the prayer of union, which is the closest description I can find to the effects of the method of Centering Prayer, but again, no method is provided. The prayer is described as a grace, effected by the action of the Holy Spirit for spiritual proficients. Such a view was not uncommon for the pre-Vatican II era. Second, a similar conclusion is reached in a survey of a parallel spiritual masterpiece – Adolphe Tanquerey's extraordinary, *The Spiritual Life: A Treatise on Ascetical and Mystical Theology.*[14]

We have covered vast territory very quickly. So, let's listen to another voice to help us summarize the historical aspect we're seeking to bring into perspective. Medieval scholar Amy Hollywood poignantly captures our conversation so far. In Hollywood's comment, we see the weaving together of the meditative, contemplative and mystical traditions, helping us chart the steps from meditative reading (*lectio divina*), to contemplative (mystical) prayer:

> The term mystical came to describe the "stages of contemplation (in Greek, *theoria* and in Latin, *contemplatio*) leading to the vision of God, the vision of God itself, union with God (Greek, *henosis* and Latin, *unitas*), and theology (*theologia*, a Greek term taken over directly into Latin). Early, medieval, and early modern Christian writers referred to all of these things as mystical, and it is to this array of practices – of mystical interpretation of scripture, mystical vision, mystical contemplation, mystical union, and mystical theology – that the substantive term mysticism, which begins to appear in the Western European vernaculars during the seventeenth and eighteenth centuries, refers."[15]

Having briefly reminded ourselves of the evolution of meditation from *lectio divina* to contemplation, let's move now to explore more deeply the place of Centering Prayer within the wider contemplative tradition.

From Contemplation to the Method of Centering Prayer

The current and customary definition of contemplative prayer (or in earlier terminology, mystical prayer) as *wordless* meditation, such as it is practiced today using the method of Centering Prayer, *was essentially unknown as a method or definition in Western Christianity until the mid to late 1980's!* Father Keating calls

Centering Prayer an updating, but I think that is a modest understatement from a very humble teacher.

I don't take the novelty of Centering Prayer as a negative. Nor is Centering Prayer an aberration in the tradition. Quite the contrary. Centering Prayer is a ripe fruit, having been nurtured on the contemplative branch of Christianity through prior centuries. Today, we are the fortunate ones to pluck, take and see how good the fruit is! We have harvested where we did not sow, and the harvest is good, true and beautifully abundant!

To back up the claim that the method of Centering Prayer is a relatively new and post-modern expression of the ancient, medieval and modern contemplative prayer tradition(s), let me start by way of simple illustration: notice the Table of Contents of Oxford University Press' 1986 magisterial and early scholarly-popular reference in the then emerging field of spirituality. The title of the book is, *The Study of Spirituality.* The book collates a broad spectrum of scholars representing various Christian communions.

And yet the Table of Contents lists *no* chapter or extended overview on contemplative prayer, or meditative prayer as a particular method of prayer. The nearest this important modern resource in the field of spirituality studies comes to discussing contemplative prayer, historically understood, is in Kalistos Ware's chapter on the origins of the Jesus Prayer, and also in Andrew Louth's chapters on Hesychism. Edward Yarnold's chapter on the theology of Christian spirituality also hints at contemplation, but his discussion is limited to the mystical prayer of St. Teresa of Ávila and St. John of the Cross, both of whom understood mystical prayer as an indicator of infused contemplation – a state they viewed as *not* available to everyone, and *only* possible after significant ascetic and prayerful preparation (e.g., Teresa's mansions and John's ascent of Mount Caramel).

Such infused contemplation was also closely connected with the experience of the dark night, which may leave one unable to pray using words, feeling dry and barren; aware of nothing spiritual, except perhaps, God's absence. Paradoxically, in the tradition of John of the Cross this nakedness of will and darkness of soul was actually a form of prayer: the prayer of pure faith, stripped of words, ideas and feelings. In this sense, such infused contemplation was probably describing the similar effect that many experience during periods of Centering Prayer, as the sacred word drops away and we are at rest in God.

Here's the simple truth: the method of Centering Prayer is a twenty-first century development. While it shares in the common contemplative, monastic lineage of *lectio divina,* Centering Prayer is a new developmental line. A new branch sprouting off the main-trunk of the tradition.

I view this as a wonderful sign of growth! Like Noah looking for a sprig of green after the flood, we rejoice to see that this new life is pouring into the church in the form of a new meditative prayer method. Some have tried to press the case that a non-discursive, meditative prayer method has always been a part of Christianity. Yet, based on what we have surveyed so far, I don't believe that is a fully accurate statement. It is more honest to say that *through the influence and practice of lectio divina and the Jesus Prayer, in conjunction with inter-spiritual dialog in the post-Vatican II era, Centering Prayer and Christian meditation provided the first written methods of non-discursive, meditative prayer in Christian history.*

There is significant evidence that aspects of discursive prayer existed in prior centuries of Christian spirituality, such as the *contemplatio* step in *lectio divina,* yet as best as I can discern, in all of Christian history, there exists no specific (or simple) *method* of cultivating a twice-a-day, non-discursive, silent meditative prayer practice for the purpose of cultivating and experiencing the contemplative state. This is why I say Centering Prayer is a new development branching off the main-line of the contemplative tradition. Rather than bemoaning this new growth I celebrate it! I rejoice in it! I welcome it with an open mind and an open heart, because for so many today, living under the stress, noise and busyness of post-modern life, the method of Centering Prayer is just the gift needed to help us return to the one necessary thing, which is perhaps our attention and consent to the Presence of God.

I don't think this fact is a negative. It actually points to the historic era we have been witness to: at long last, Western Christianity now has its own method of meditative prayer. No doubt, some practices came close to this method of non-discursive prayer. We immediately think of the *Jesus Prayer* and the fourth step of *lectio divina – contemplatio.* We think of the teaching outlined in the *Cloud of Unknowing,* with its use of one word to pierce the darkness. All these were intimations of a method of contemplative prayer, but none of them, individually or combined, ever envisioned the fullness of a simple, meditative method that led to wordless, contemplative prayer, at least in the written record.

Let me be even more precise. While many refer to the anonymous author of *The Cloud of Unknowing* as a pre-cursor to the method of Centering Prayer, in my study of that beautiful resource – which we will get to in a moment – the only aspect its teaching has in common with the method of Centering Prayer is the idea of taking one, simple word as a means of prayer. Even Basil Pennington, one of the principal founders of the method of Centering Prayer, acknowledges that as one reads *The Cloud of Unknowing,*

> "one is not apt effectively to draw from the text the simple technique the author [of the Cloud] offers. This is not to be wondered at. One will have the same experience reading books on the Jesus Prayer. As the Spiritual Fathers on Mount Athos pointed out to me, no Spiritual Father would seek to teach this method of prayer by a book. It is meant to be handed on personally – tradition...Simply reading it will not usually teach the method." [16]

I too have verified Pennington's observation in my research and have not yet found any written method beyond the simple instructions given for the Jesus Prayer sentence or the general notion of pure prayer or ceaseless prayer, typified in Evagrius, John Cassian and the broad hesychastic tradition. As far as the Christian contemplative tradition is concerned, at least until Centering Prayer or the teaching of John Main, I have not yet found a written method describing the process that may lead one into the state of contemplative prayer. Having said that, it is true that in the sixteenth century, we do see evidence of more detailed descriptions of the journey of prayer from meditation to contemplation in the writings of Teresa and John of the Cross – but no simple method.

We are cautioned by the fact that just because a written method does not appear in the historical record, does not mean that a method did not exist. The assumption is that in certain monastic communities there were spiritual fathers or mothers who did have a method. Presumably, some kind of method was passed on by personal teaching and spiritual guidance. It is also not coincidental that the revival of contemplative, mystical theologians such as Meister Eckhart in the thirteenth century corresponded with the expanding confluence of the increasing Jewish, Muslim and Christian interactions, especially in Spain; not to mention the inevitable similar cross pollination with Buddhist and Hindu spirituality through the crossroads linking India, central Asia, Persia and Eastern Europe.

The Influence of the Cloud of Unknowing and Centering Prayer

Reflecting further on *The Cloud of Unknowing,* we see that we are *not* invited to use one word as a means to meditate, such as the sacred word is used in Centering Prayer, but rather, the one word of the *Cloud* is meant to help us remember God:

> "So when you feel by the grace of God that God is calling you to his work, and you intend to respond, lift your heart to God with humble love. And really mean God who created you, and bought you, and graciously called you to this state of life. And think no other thought of him. It all depends on your desire. A naked intention directed to God, and God alone, is wholly sufficient. If you want this intention summed up in a word, to retain it more easily, take a short word, preferably of one syllable, to do so. The shorter the word the better, begin more like the working of the Spirit. A word like 'God' or 'Love'. Chose which you like, or perhaps some other, so long as it is of one syllable. And fix this word fast to your heart, so that it is always there come what may. It will be your shield and spear in peace and war alike. With this word you will hammer the cloud and the darkness above you. With this word you will suppress all thought under the cloud of forgetting. So much so that if ever you are tempted to think what it is that you are seeking, this one word will be sufficient answer."[17]

Notice that the similarity between the method of Centering Prayer and the Cloud's teaching on the one-syllable word is very evident, but the word's *function* is different. There is also a connection in this passage with Centering Prayer's emphasis on intention and consenting. And, similarly, the general apophatic awareness of the cloud of unknowing, which harmonizes with the contemplative disposition of Centering Prayer, where we are again consenting to the mystery of God, versus trying to control or define God with words.

Having said that, notice also the differences. The one syllable word is used repetitiously, *all* the time, and it is meant as something of an aggressive thought-tool. Notice the *active* action conveyed by these words: a shield, a spear, piercing, suppressing and hammering. This is *not* the passive disposition of "When you notice you are engaged with your thoughts, return ever so gently to your sacred word!"

So it seems that what we have in *The Cloud of Unknowing* is a record of the evolutionary development toward the full contemplative method of meditative prayer that we see coming into further maturity in the method of Centering Prayer. Perhaps the *Cloud* represents a mid-way point on the historical journey to the flourishing of the method of Centering Prayer and non-discursive contemplation.

Yes, it is true, we celebrate the lineage and connection between the *Cloud of Unknowing* and the method of Centering Prayer. Yet, we also wish to celebrate the creative advance into an orthodox novelty that we have been witness to in this generation. The creative work of Fathers Meninger, Pennington and Keating synthesized much of their contemplative, monastic tradition, and birthed a new beginning for Christian spirituality. A new wineskin for new wine. A new meditative method for a new era of going ever deeper into the love of God.

A Nod to Thomas Merton

In the modern era, this fact becomes all the clearer when you search the writings of Thomas Merton, contemplative *par excellence* of the twentieth century. Merton's primary written contribution to the method of Centering Prayer is that, according to Keating, Merton was the reason why the method came to be called "centering" prayer. Yet in all of Merton's vast body of currently published and publicly available work, while you will find beautiful prose about contemplative prayer and its fruits and effects on our spiritual development, as best I can tell, *you will find no simple or practical method of meditative or contemplative prayer.* To be fair, just because the tradition, or a particular writer of that tradition is silent on a method, doesn't mean that there wasn't a method.[18]

As mentioned earlier, perhaps a method was handed down by oral tradition, or kept hidden in the monasteries. I am convinced many were experiencing contemplative prayer but did not describe the method that led to it. Nonetheless, the fact that no one from Augustine to Pseudo-Dionysius, to Aquinas to John of the Cross, to Merton spoke of a simple method of non-discursive meditative prayer is striking. The reason? I have concluded that the simple answer is that there *was no standard written method.* The truth is throughout the whole history of Christianity, as best I can tell, nothing comes close to the simple and elegant, deeply theologically and psychologically informed four-fold guidelines developed by Keating's community, and Keating's supplemental teachings supporting the method.

The Error of Quietism and Its Contrast to the Method of Centering Prayer

Another aspect to the historical development of Centering Prayer is to contrast it to the so called "quietism" of Miguel de Molinos (1628 – 1696 CE).[19] Quietism was condemned by Pope Innocent XI in the papal bull *Coelestis Pastor* of 1687 CE, during the tail-end of the Spanish Inquisition.

Similar to Molinos' teaching, was the French author Jeanne Guyon (1648 – 1717 CE), along with the famed spiritual director and archbishop of Cambrai, François Fénelon (1651 – 1715 CE). Both Guyon and Fénelon taught aspects of quietist ideals, especially as it related to methods of prayer. And, like Molinos, Guyon and Fénelon were also officially condemned by the Church.[20] In the light of modern scholarship, it is increasing evident that their condemnations had less to do with spirituality or contemplative prayer itself, and more to do with the friction of personalities, power-struggles and social dynamics in the court of King Louis XIV.[21]

Even so, what was so offensive about these Quietist teachings that required such a severe condemnation? Unfortunately, like many "heresies", we know of them primarily through the lens of their detractors. In this case, the charge against the Quietists was that they taught that the spiritual journey culminated with our self-annihilation and absorption into god – during this life.

As a result, all worldly interests and pursuits were released, so to constantly and passively be in contemplation. This led to a passivity in life and toward God – an abandonment of the soul, which no longer needed to rely upon anything, including mental prayers, liturgy and scripture. We can see why this kind of experience and teaching would be offensive and threatening to the church hierarchy: it clearly undercut the need for clergy and the role of a clergy-focused sacramental system. While it is true that one can experience union with God in this life, it is incorrect to neglect being a human. As Irenaeus once quipped, the glory of God is a human fully alive.

Here is a summary of Molinos ideas. First, like Teresa of Ávila, there are two ways of approaching God. The first is by meditation and discursive prayer. The second is by pure faith and contemplation. Molinos describes the contrast this way,

> "When the soul already knows the truth…and it has fixed the eyes of its understanding on that truth, seeing it simply with quietude, calm, and silence; when to be convinced it has no

> need of considerations, discourses, or other words; and when the will loves this truth, marvels at it, and enjoys itself in it, this is properly called the prayer of faith, the prayer of quietude, interior recollection, or contemplation."[22]

Molinos goes on to describe these two different kinds of contemplation – acquired and active, in contrast to infused and passive contemplation. This is in essence a re-statement of Teresa's categories. What is more interesting, however, is Molinos' extraordinary development of the experience of interior recollection. In many ways, this has similarities to the modern method of Centering Prayer's invitation to consent to the divine presence and action. And the wisdom of the apophatic tradition of darkness and unknowing. Notice that for Molinos, interior recollection is,

> "faith and silence in the presence of God. You should become used to recollecting yourself in his presence with loving attention, as one who surrenders to and unities with God in reverence, humility, and submission. See him within yourself in the most intimate part of your soul, without form, species, figure, or mode. See him in the general knowledge of loving and obscure faith, without any attributes or distinctions of perfection. Be there with a simple attention, with a tranquil awareness, and full of love for the Lord himself. Resign and surrender yourself into his hands without reflecting on yourself or your own perfection, so that he can arrange and order you according to his approval. Close your senses and put the care for all your good in God by means of solitude and a total forgetting of all the things of this life. Your faith must be pure – without images or species; simple – without discursive prayers; and universal – without any reflection or distinctions."[23]

As far as I am concerned, this passage was so far ahead of its time it is just now timely! It is a beautiful summation of so much of the essence of the contemplative experience. It is clearly wise guidance that comes close to a method. It is not the only occasion in Molinos' writings that edify the reader on the hunt for contemplative wisdom. Molinos may be the most unknown and important contemplative of the Reformation era, and his work clearly anticipates the themes of Jean Pierre de Caussade's famous tract, *The Abandonement to the Divine Presence.*[24]

A Protestant contemporary to Molinos and Guyon is Johannes Kelpius, a German Pietist who journeyed to America in 1694 and settled in Pennsylvania, along the banks of Wissahickon Creek, in what is now the city of Philadelphia.[25] His nearly forgotten book, *A Method of Prayer* reveals a uniquely Protestant perspective on contemplation, grounding it in the tradition of ceaseless prayer and the cultivation of inward silence through devotional meditation, as well as a reliance upon the presence and action of the Holy Spirit.[26] But it is essentially a re-statement of Guyon's ideas. Nor does Kelpius provide a method.

Another historical example of teaching on contemplative prayer is the seventeenth century book, *Sancta Sophia* by Father Augustine Baker, available today under the title, "Contemplative Prayer."[27] Like all the others we have reviewed, Baker does not really provide a simple method, but he does survey the process of moving from meditation to contemplation, and describes the experiences of interior silence and contemplation. Father Baker's teachings are a somewhat modernized expansion on Teresa's scheme, with clear echoes of both Molinos and Guyon's writings.

God-Devotion and the Garden of Silence

The hunger for deeper communion with God runs throughout the blood of our human family. We are awakened by the night and light – and especially the streaming stars of the suspended river Milky Way. Above us, they remind us of something the daylight often helps us forget: that we come from above, and that we can return their, perhaps not physically, but certainly in the silence of our heart.

While certainly not as inspired, I experienced something similar while rummaging through the old library stacks at Princeton Theological Seminary, I was doing research for this book and came across an aged pamphlet with the title, "*The Art of Contemplation.*" The pamphlet was published in India in 1931, and written by J.C. Winslow, a Christian missionary-pastor. It beautifully summarizes what is possible as we continue to deepen our interreligious conversations.

You will hear echoes of *The Cloud of Unknowing* as well as the movement from *lectio divina* into the bliss of contemplation. While Christianity, Buddhism and Hinduism are different flowers in the garden of silence, they are mutually beautiful and fragrant, unique in their own ways. Yet also so similar, when we move beyond our sacred texts and into the paradise of the soul's seeing and being seen, in the silence of sheer love. Here is what I read, standing in the library on a chilly October afternoon. Though cold outside, Winslow's words warmed my heart within:

"The natural and highest object of our concentration will be God Himself or some attribute or aspect of God. Often our previous meditation upon the Scriptures will have supplied us with some such thought of God which may form the point on which to concentrate our thought. The mind, gathered in from all distractions, is now centered upon this one luminous idea which holds it. Toward that idea, that thought of God, with steady but effortless attention, it now gazes quietly, lovingly, aspiringly. Thus attention passes into contemplation. The conscious mind, having done its work of direction, is now almost wholly at rest. There is indeed, until the stage of ecstasy (Samadhi) is reached, a certain consciousness remaining, but it is not sufficient to distract us. The conscious mind has now ceased from all discursive thought, leaving nothing but a 'naked intent stretching unto God.' The fore-conscious is flooded with light, and is the door through which the inflowing power and illumination pass into the unconscious depths of the soul. For the soul is now open to God. The barriers which at ordinary times seem to dim His presence are removed. We reach out towards God, or, as most Indian and much Christian thought would prefer to express, we reach *in* towards God with an eager intent and longing. It is not the reason or thinking faculty which is at work, but the affective...The sense of separateness, the consciousness of 'I' and 'my' disappears, as the Indian bhaktis are ever telling us. We attain the consciousness of being 'yoked' with God. The reality which the mystics experience in such divine communion, which it is to them the most certain of all certainties, baffles description, because it transcends all that ordinary experience with which language is framed to deal. Of these most excellent and divine workings in the soul, says Angela of Foligno, 'man can in no wise speak or even stammer.' Whatever we attempt to predicate of the Supreme Reality, we have to confess that it is utterly inadequate; *neti, neti* – 'Not so, not so.' Yet some language we must use. *Sat, chit, Ananda,* says the Vedantist. 'That which is,' says Augustine. 'Eternal Light,' says Dante. 'Pure love,' says Catherine of Genoa." [28]

I don't believe the process and mystery could be summed up more clearly than that! How beautiful is this tradition! And the experience therein! Wondrously, even in our own era, the voices continue to emerge from the garden of silence, singing their songs of innocence and experience – teachers such as Raimon Panikkar, Bede Griffiths, Basil Pennington, Thomas Keating and John Main, all beautiful souls, now passed on, who continue to call the Christian community back to the silence of love in meditative prayer.

As mentioned earlier, the main point I've been seeking to articulate is that as far as I can discern, there is no written record of a brief, simple, lay-focused method of prayer that can lead to contemplation in the Western philosophical or religious tradition until the twentieth century pioneering, post-Vatican II work of John Main, Thomas Keating, William Meninger and Basil Pennington. All of whom integrated methodological insights from Eastern methods of meditation with their deep Christian theological moorings.

Acknowledgements

Acknowledgements

Few subjects span the sweep of recorded human history like the subject of spirituality, contemplation and monasticism. The literature is immense. A book of this sort – which falls half-way between a general introduction and an academic resource – is not possible without the kind and wise help of many, to whom I express heartfelt gratitude.

Special gratitude to my wife Shannon, for so kindly enduring my endless hours of reading and writing, and for often giving words of encouragement in just the right way. And thanks to Leila Parish, Research Librarian at Austin Presbyterian Theological Seminary and Kate Skrebutenas, Director of Research and Public Services at Princeton Theological Seminary. Both have helped me locate resources I couldn't have found on my own.

I also thank the monks of the New Camaldolese Hermitage in the Big Sur of California, for their joyful hospitality. I've never written more or better, than when I am staying in the #4 St. Albertino guest room, with its unyielding view to the Pacific Ocean. And of course, I am blessed to have had the privilege of personal time and conversation with Father Thomas Keating over the years. I am grateful for his willingness to read my manuscript and provide his encouraging Foreword. So too, I send thanks to Cyprian Consiglio and Ilia Delio, two "rising stars" in the contemplative world, whose conversations and writings have deeply nourished me. And I owe an inexpressible debt of gratitude to my mentor and spiritual father Tim Cook, who demonstrated to me what a contemplative pastor is and what a contemplative church could become.

Lastly, among the unfolding renaissance of contemplative Christianity, one community located in Austin, Texas stands out. It is a church that seeks to embody the monastic ethos and contemplative spiritual practices. This contemplative community is, as best as I can tell, a witness to what a flourishing contemplative, non-denominational church can be in the world. The church's teaching and teachers have helped me grow deeply. The community also provides me with a model that has inspired my pastoral ministry. And I am now deeply blessed to serve with them. So, in part, this book is an acknowledgement of my gratitude to my Austin friends, and an invitation. Whereas St. Augustine, kneeling in a garden long ago heard a boy's distant voice cry out, "*pick up and read*," and Christianity was never the same; perhaps you will hear my mid-life voice crying out from the heart and hills of Texas: *come to Austin and see.*[1]

Bibliography

Selected Bibliography for Further Reading

Centering Prayer

Arico, Carl, *A Taste of Silence: A Guide the Fundamentals of Centering Prayer* (New York: Continuum, 1999).

Bourgeault, Cynthia, *Centering Prayer and Inner Awakening* (Lanham, Maryland: Cowley Publications, 2004).

______, *The Heart of Centering Prayer: Nondual Christianity in Theory and Practice* (Boulder, CO: Shambhala, 2016).

Centering Prayer: In Daily Life and Ministry, ed. Gustave Reininger (New York: Continuum, 2003).

Frenette, David, *The Path of Centering Prayer: Deepening Your Experience of God* (Boulder, CO: Sounds True, Inc., 2012).

Pennington, M. Basil, *Centering Prayer: Renewing An Ancient Christian Prayer Form* (New York: Image Books, 2001).

Pennington, M. Basil, *Daily We Touch Him: Practical Religious Experiences* (Kansas City, MO: Sheed & Ward, 1997).

Thomas Keating

Awakenings (New York: The Crossroad Publishing Company, 1990).

Consenting to God As God Is (New York: Lantern Books, 2016).

Divine Therapy and Addiction: Centering Prayer and the Twelve Steps (New York: Lantern Books, 2009).

Finding Grace at the Center: The Beginning of Centering Prayer (Woodstock, VT: Sky Light Paths Publishing, 2007).

Fruits and Gifts of the Spirit (New York: Lantern Books, 2007).

Intimacy with God: An Introduction to Centering Prayer (New York: The Crossroad Publishing Company, 2012).

Invitation to Love: The Way of Christian Contemplation, 20th Anniversary Edition, (New York: Bloomsbury, 2011).

Manifesting God (New York: Lantern Books, 2005).

Open Mind, Open Heart: The Contemplative Dimension of the Gospel (New York: Continuum, 2002).

Reflections on the Unknowable (New York: Lantern Books, 2014).

The Foundations for Centering Prayer and Christian Contemplative Life: Open Heart, Open Mind; Invitation to Love; The Mystery of Christ (New York: Continnum, 2007).

The Heart of the World: An Introduction to Contemplative Christianity (New York: The Crossroad Publishing Company, 1999).

The Human Condition: Contemplation and Transformation (New York: Paulist Press, 1999).

The Kingdom of God Is Like (New York: The Crossroad Publishing Company, 1993).

John Main

John Main: Essential Writings (Maryknoll, New York: Orbis Books, 2002).

Word Into Silence: A Manual for Christian Meditation, Ed. Laurence Freeman (Norwich, England: The Canterbury Press, 2006).

Thomas Merton

Contemplative Prayer (New York: Image Books, 1996).

The Inner Experience: Notes on Contemplation (San Francisco: Harper Collins Publishers, 2003).

The Springs of Contemplation: A Retreat at the Abbey of Gethsemane (New York: Farrar, Straus, Giroux, 1992).

The Jesus Prayer

Breck, John, *"The Prayer of the Heart: Sacrament of the Presence of God"* in *The Contemplative Path: Reflections on Recovering a Lost Tradition,* ed. E. Rozanne Elder (Kalamazoo, MI: Cistercian Publications, Inc., 1995) 39 – 63.

Gargano, Innocenzo, *Holy Reading: An Introduction to Lectio Divina*, trans. Walter Vitale (Norwich, UK: Canterbury Press, 2007).

Gillet, Lev, *The Jesus Prayer* (Crestwood, NY: St. Vladimir's Seminary Press, 1997).

Goettmann, Alphonse and Rachel, *The Power of the Name: The History and Practices of the Jesus Prayer,* New Revised Edition, (Rollingsford, New Hampshire: Orthodox Research Institute, 2008).

Hall, Thelma, *Too Deep for Words: Rediscovering Lectio Divina* (Mahwah, NJ: Paulist Press, 1988).

Hausherr, Irénée, *The Name of Jesus: The Names of Jesus Used by the Early Christians – The Development of the Jesus Prayer,* trans. Charles Cummings, (Kalamazoo, MI: Cistercian Publications, 1978).

Johnson, Christopher D.L., *The Globalization of Hesychasm and the Jesus Prayer: Contesting Contemplation* (New York: Continuum, 2010).

The Syriac Fathers on Prayer and the Spiritual Life, trans. Sabastian Brock (Kalamazoo, MI: Cistercian Publications, 1987).

The Watchful Mind: Teachings on the Prayer of the Heart by A Monk of Mount Athos (Yonkers, NY: St. Vladimir's Seminary Press, 2014).

The Way of a Pilgrim and *The Pilgrim Continues His Way,* trans. Helen Bacovcin, (New York: Doubleday, 1992).

Ware, Kallistos, *The Power of the Name: The Jesus Prayer in Orthodox Spirituality* (Oxford: SLG Press, 1986).

Theosis

Collins, Paul, M., *Partaking in Divine Nature: Deification and Communion* (London: T&T Clark, 2012); Veli-Matti Karkkainen, *One With God: Salvation as Deification and Justification* (Collegeville, MN: Liturgical Press, 2004).

Litwa, David, M, *Becoming Divine: An Introduction to Deification in Western Culture* (Eugene, OR: Cascade Books, 2013).

Lossky, Vladimir, *In the Image and Likeness of God* (Crestwood, NY: St. Vladimir's Seminary Press, 1974).

Nellas, Panayiotis, *Deification in Christ: Orthodox Perspectives on the Nature of the Human Person* (Yonkers, NY: St. Vladimir's Seminary Press, 1987).

Partakers of the Divine Nature: The History and Development of Deification in the Christian Traditions, ed. Michael J. Christensen and Jeffery A. Wittung (Grand Rapids: Baker Academic, 2011).

Russell, Norman, *Fellow Workers with God: Orthodox Thinking on Theosis* (Yonkers, NY: St. Vladimir's Seminary Press, 2009).

_______, *The Doctrine of Deification in the Greek Patristic Tradition* (Oxford: Oxford University Press, 2004).

Theosis: Deification in Christian Theology, Vol. 1 & 2 in the Princeton Theological Monograph Series #156, eds., Stephen Finlan and Vladimir Kharlamov (Eugene, OR: Pickwick Publications, 2006 & 2011).

Union with Christ: The New Finnish Interpretation of Luther, eds. Carl E. Braaten and Robert W. Jenson (Grand Rapids: William B. Eerdmans Publishing Company, 1998).

Wilbourne, Rankin, *Union With Christ: The Way to Know and Enjoy God* (Colorado Springs, CO: David C. Cook Publishing, 2016).

Bernadette Roberts

The Experience of No-Self: A Contemplative Journey (Albany, NY: State University of New York Press, 1993).

The Path to No-Self: Life at the Center (Albany, NY: State University of New York Press, 1991).

What is Self? A Study of the Spiritual Journey in Terms of Consciousness (Boulder, CO: Sentient Publications, 2005).

The Real Christ (Austin, TX: ContemplativeChristians.com Publishing, 2017).

Meditative Prayer and Contemplation

Augustine, *Soliloquies: Augustine's Inner Dialogue* (New York: New City Press, 2000).

Baker, Augustine. *Contemplative Prayer: Venerable Father Augustine Baker's Teaching Thereon from 'Sancta Sophia,'* ed. by Don B. Weld-Blundell (Lexington, KY: Christ the King Library, 2016 facsimile reprint from the 1906 edition).

Bonaventure: The Soul's Journey into God, The Tree of Life and the Life of St. Francis in The Classics of Western Spirituality: A Library of the Great Spiritual Masters, trans. Ewert Cousins, (Mahwah, New Jersey: Paulist Press, 1978).

Carabine, Deirdre, *The Unknown God: Negative Theology in the Platonic Tradition – Plato to Eriugena* (Eugene, OR: Wipp & Stock, 1995).

Chetwynd, Tom, *Zen & The Kingdom of Heaven: Reflections on the Tradition of Meditation in Christianity and Zen Buddhism* (Somerville, MA: Wisdom Publications, 2001).

Christian Spirituality: Origins to the Twelfth Century, Vol. 16 in the World Spirituality: An Encyclopedic History of the Religious Quest, ed. Bernard McGinn, John Meyendorff, and Jean Leclercq (New York: Crossroad, 1988).

Consiglio, Cyprian, *Prayer in The Cave of The Heart: The Universal Call to Contemplation* (Collegeville, MN: Liturgical Press, 2010).

Consiglio, Cyprian, *Spirit, Soul, Body: Toward an Integral Christian Spirituality* (Collegeville, MN: Liturgical Press, 2015).

Doherty, Catherine de Hueck, *Poustinia: Encountering God in Silence, Solitude and Prayer* (Combermere, ON: Madonna House Publications, 2014).

Finley, James, *Christian Meditation: Experiencing the Presence of God* (San Francisco: Harper Collins, 2005).

Flood, Gavin, *The Truth Within: A History of Inwardness in Christianity, Hinduism, Buddhism* (Oxford: Oxford University Press, 2013).

Foster, Richard J., *Sanctuary of the Soul: Journey into Meditative Prayer* (Downer's Grove, IL: InterVarsity Press, 2011).

Franke, William, ed., *On What Cannot Be Said,* Vol. 1, (Notre Dame, IN: University of Notre Dame, 2007).

Franke, William, *On What Cannot Be Said: Apophatic Discourses in Philosophy, Religion, Literature and the Arts.* Vol 1. "Classic Formulations: (Notre Dame, IN: University of Notre Dame Press, 2007).

Freeman, Laurence et. al., *Journey to the Heart: Christian Contemplation through the Centuries,* ed. Kim Nataraja (Mary Knoll, NY: Orbis Books, 2011).

Goleman, Daniel and Davidson, Richard, *Altered Traits: Science Reveals How Meditation Changes Your Mind, Brain, and Body* (New York: Avery, 2017).
Guyon, Jeanne Marie, *Spiritual Torrents* (Traffic Output Publications, 2016).

Hand, Thomas A., *St. Augustine On Prayer* (Westminster, MD: Newman Press, 1963).

Hansen, Gary Neal, *Kneeling with Giants: Learning to Pray with History's Best Teachers* (Downer's Grove, IL: InterVarsity Press, 2012).

Harris, Paul, *Christian Meditation: Contemplative Prayer for A New Generation* (London: Darton, Longman and Todd, Ltd., 1996).

Healy, Kathleen, *Entering the Cave of the Heart* (New York: Paulist Press, 1986).

Hugh of St. Victor, *Selected Spiritual Writings*, trans. A Religious of C.S.M.V. (London: Faber, 1962).

Iyer, Pico, *The Art of Stillness: Adventures in Going Nowhere* (New York: Simon & Schuster, 2014).

Jacob Holsinger-Sherman, "On the Emerging Field of Contemplative Studies and Its Relationship to the Study of Spirituality" in *Spiritus* 14.2 (Baltimore: John Hopkins University Press).

Johnston, William, *Being In Love: The Practice of Christian Prayer* (New York: Harper and Row, Publishers, 1989).

Kelpius, Johannes *A Method of Prayer* (New York: Harper and Brothers, 1951).

Kenney, John Peter, *Contemplation and Classical Christianity: A Study in Augustine* (Oxford: Oxford University Press, 2013).

Laird, Martin, *A Sunlit Absence: Silence, Awareness, and Contemplation* (Oxford: Oxford University Press, 2011).

Laird, Martin, *Into the Silence Land: A Guide to the Christian Practice of Contemplation* (Oxford: Oxford University Press, 2006).

Leclercq, Jean, "Ways of Prayer and Contemplation II: Western" in Bernard McGinn, John Meyendorff, and Jean Leclercq, eds., *Christian Spirituality: Origins to the Twelfth Century* (London: 1986).

Leclercq, Jean, *The Love of Learning and the Desire for God: A Study of Monastic Culture* (New York: Fordham University Press, 2001).

Lossky, Vladimir, *The Vision of God,* trans. Asheleigh Moorhouse (Crestwood, New York: St. Vladimir's Seminary Press, 1983).

Lynch, Kathleen, *The Sublime Round Tower: An Iconic Call to Contemplative Prayer* (Dublin: The Columba Press, 2013).

Malaval, Francois, *A Simple Method of Raising the Soul to Contemplation: In the Form of a Dialog*. trans. By Lucy Menzies (London: J.M. Dent and Sons, Ltd., 1931).

Maloney, George, *The Prayer of the Heart: The Contemplative Tradition of the Christian East* (Notre Dame, IN: Ave Maria Press, 2008).

Mason, Mary Elizabeth, *Active Life and Contemplative Life: A Study of the Concepts from Plato to the Present* (Milwaukee: The Marquette University Press, 1961).

McWhorter, Matthew R., "Hugh of St. Victor on Contemplative Meditation" in The Heythrop Journal, Vol. LV, 2014 (Oxford: John Wiley and Sons, 2014) 110 – 122.

Meditations on the Life of Christ: An Illustrated Manuscript of the Fourteenth Century, ed. Isa Ragusa and Rosalie B. Green (Princeton: Princeton University Press, 1961).

Merton, Thomas, *"What is Contemplation?"* (Springfield, IL: Templegate Publishers, 1981).

Naranjo, Claudio & Robert E. Ornstein, *On the Psychology of Meditation* (New York: The Viking Press, 1971).

Nemeck, Frances Kelly and Marie Theresa Coombs, *Contemplation* (Eugene: Oregon, Wifp and Stock Publishers, 2001).

Pennington, M. Basil, *A Place Apart: Monastic Prayer and Practice for Everyone* (New York: Image Books, 1985).

Pieper, Josef, *Happiness & Contemplation* (South Bend, IN: St. Augustine's Press, 1998).

Prayer and Contemplation: Studies in Christian and Hindu Spirituality, Vol. 1 (Bangalore, India: Asirvanam Benedictine Monastery, 1980).

Prayer and Thought in Monastic Tradition: Essay in Honor of Benedicta Ward SLG, ed. Santha Bhattacharji, Rowan Williams and Dominic Mattos (New York: T&T Clark Bloomsbury, 2015).

Purity of Heart and Contemplation: A Monastic Dialogue Between Christian and Asian Traditions, ed. Bruno Barnhart's and Joseph H. (New York: Continuum, 2001).

Richard of St. Victor, *Selected Writings on Contemplation*, trans. Clare Kirchberger (New York: Harper) 1957.

Richard of St. Victor, *The Twelve Patriarchs, The Mystical Ark, book of the Trinity,* trans. Grover A. Zinn in The Classics of Western Spirituality (New York: Paulist Press, 1979).

Rohr, Richard, *Silent Compassion: Finding God in Contemplation* (Cincinnati, OH: Franciscan Media, 2014).

Ryrie, Alexander, *Silent Waiting: The Biblical Roots of Contemplative Spirituality* (Norwich, UK: Canterbury Press, 1999).

Ryrie, Alexander, *Wonderful Exchange: An Exploration of Silent Prayer* (New York: Paulist Press, 2003).

Speaking of Silence: Christians and Buddhists on the Contemplative Way, ed. Susand Walker (New York: Paulist Press, 1987).

Špidlík, Tomáš, *The Spirituality of the Christian East: A Systematic Handbook*, trans. Anthony P. Gythiel (Kalamazoo, MI: Cistercian Publications, 1986).

Špidlík, Tomáš, *The Spirituality of the Christian East*, Vol. 2, "Prayer", trans. Anthony P. Gythiel (Kalamazoo, MI: Cistercian Publications, 2005).

Spiritual Disciplines: Papers from the Eranos Yearbooks, Bollingen Series XXX. Vol. 4, ed. Joseph Campbell (Princeton, NJ: Princeton University Press, 1960).

Stead, Christopher, *Philosophy in Christian Antiquity* (Cambridge: Cambridge University Press, 1994).

The Art of Prayer: An Orthodox Anthology, trans. E. Kadloubovsky and G.E.H. Palmer (London: Faber & Faber, 1985).

The Blackwell Companion to Christian Spirituality, ed. Arthur Holder (Oxford: Blackwell Publishers, 2005).

The Cambridge History of Early Christian Literature, ed. France Young, Lewis Ayres and Andrew Louth (Cambridge: Cambridge University Press, 2004).

The Contemplative Path: Reflections on Recovering a Lost Tradition, ed. E. Rozanne Elder (Kalamazoo, MI: Cistercian Publications, Inc., 1995).

The Philokalia: The Complete Text, Volumes 1 – 4, trans. G.E.H. Palmer, Philip Sherrard, Kalistos Ware (London: Faber & Faber, 1979).

The Pursuit of Wisdom: And Other Works by the Author of the Cloud of Unknowing, trans. James A. Walsh (New York: Paulist Press, 1988).

The Practice of the Presence of God: Theology as A Way Of Life, Ed. by Martin Laird and Sheelah Trefle Hidden (New York: Routledge, 2017).

The Syriac Fathers on Prayers and the Spiritual Life, trans. Sebastian Brock (Kalamazoo, MI: Cistercian Publications, 1987).

Ware, Kalistos, "Ways of Prayer and Contemplation I: Eastern" in Bernard McGinn, John Meyendorff, and Jean Leclercq, eds., *Christian Spirituality: Origins to the Twelfth Century* (London:, 1986).

Ware, Kallistos, *The Inner Kingdom: Volume 1 of the Collected Works* (Crestwood, NY: St. Vladimir's Seminary Press, 2000).

Wilber, Ken, *Integral Meditation: Mindfulness as a Path to Grow Up, Wake Up and Show Up in Your Life* (Boulder, CO: Shambhala Publications, 2016).

William of St. Thierry, *On Contemplating God: Prayer Meditations* (Shannon, Ireland: Cistercian Publications, Inc., 1970).

Wright, Robert, *Why Buddhism Is True: The Science and Philosophy of Meditation and Enlightenment* (New York: Simon and Schuster, 2017).

Writings from the Philokalia on Prayer of the Heart, trans. E. Kadloubovsky, ed. Timothy Ware (London: Faber & Faber, 1983).

Your Word Is Fire: The Hasidic Masters on Contemplative Prayer, trans. & ed. Arthur Green and Barry W. Holtz (Woodstock, Vermont: Jewish Lights Publishing, 1993).

Apophatic Spirituality

Carabine, Deidre, *The Unknown God: Negative Theology in the Platonic Tradition, Plato to Eriugena,* (Louvian: Peeters Press, 1995).

Coulter, Dale M., "*Contemplative Life*" in *The Encyclopedia of Christian Civilization, Vol 1.* ed. George Thomas Kurian (Oxford: Wiley-Blackwell, 2011).

Keller, Catherine, *Face of the Deep: A Theology of Becoming* (New York: Routledge, 2003).

Meister Eckhart and the Beguine Mystics: Hadewijch of Brabant, Mechthild of Magdeburg, and Marguerite Porete, ed. Bernard McGinn, (New York: Continnum, 1997).

Mortley, Raoul, *From Word to Silence: The Rise and Fall of Logos,* Vol. 1 (Bonn, Germany: Hanstein, 1986).

Mortley, Raoul, *From Word to Silence: The Way of Negation, Christian and Greek,* Vol. 2 (Bonn, Germany: Hanstein, 1986).

On What Cannot Be Said: Apophatic Discourses in Philosophy, Religion, Literature and the Arts, Vol 1 & 2, ed., William Franke (Notre Dame, IN: University of Notre Dame Press, 2007).

Sells, Michael A., *Mystical Languages of Unsaying* (Chicago: University of Chicago Press, 1994).

The Study of Spirituality, ed. Cheslyn Jones, Geoffrey Wainwright, and Edward Yarnod (Oxford: Oxford University Press, 1986).

Turner, Denys, *The Darkness of God: Negativity in Christian Mysticism* (Cambridge: Cambridge University Press, 1999).

Williams, J.P., *Denying Divinity: Apophasis in the Patristic Christian and Soto Zen Buddhist Traditions* (Oxford: Oxford University Press, 2000).

Spiritual Direction

Hausherr, Irénée, *Spiritual Direction in the Early Christian Church* (Kalamazoo, MI: Cistercian Publications, 1990).

Nemeck, Frances Kelly and Marie Theresa Coombs, *The Way of Spiritual Direction* Collegeville, MN: The Liturgical Press, 1985).

Lectio Divina

Bryan, Jennifer, *Looking Inward: Devotional Reading and the Private Self in Late Medieval England* (Philadelphia: University of Pennsylvania Press, 2008).

Casey, Michael, *Sacred Reading: The Ancient Art of Lectio Divina* (Liguori, MO: Liguori Publications, 1996).

Guigo II, *Ladder of Monks and Twelve Meditations,* trans. Edmund Colledge and James Walsh, (Kalamazoo, MI: Cistercian Publications, 1979).

Hall, Thelma, *Too Deep for Words: Rediscovering Lectio Divina* (New York: Paulist Press, 1988).

Pennington, M. Basil, *Lectio Divina: Renewing the Ancient Practice of Praying the Scriptures* (New York: Crossroad Publishing, 1998).

Studzinski, Raymond, *Reading to Live: The Evolving Practice of Lectio Divina*, Cistercian Studies Series Number Two-Hundred Thirty-One, (Collegeville, MN: Liturgical Press, 2009).

Spiritual Practices

Calhoun, Adele Ahlberg, Spiritual *Disciplines Handbook: Practices that Transform Us* (Downers Grove, IL: InterVarsity Press, 2005).

de Sales, Francis, *Introduction to the Devout Life,* ed. and trans. Allan Ross (Mineola, NY: Dover Publications Inc., 2009).

Driskill, Joseph D., *Protestant Spiritual Exercises: Theology, History and Practice* (Harrisburg, PA: Morehouse Publishing, 1999).

Dykstra, Craig, *Growing in the Life of Faith: Education and Christian Practices* (Louisville: Geneva Press, 1997).

Hadot, Pierre, *Philosophy as a way of life: Spiritual Exercises from Socrates to Foucault*, ed. Arnold I. Davidson, trans. Michael Chase (Malden, MA: Blackwell Publishing, 1995).

James K.A. Smith *You are What You Love: The Spiritual Power of Habit* (Brazos Press: Grand Rapids, MI, 2016).

Lawrence, Bruce B., "Transformation" in *Critical Terms for Religious Studies*, ed., Mark C. Taylor (Chicago: University of Chicago Press, 1998) 334 – 348.

Loyola, Ignatius, *Spiritual Exercises* (New York: Crossroad Publishing Company, 1992).

Paintner, Christine Valters, *The Soul of a Pilgrim: Eight Practices for the Journey Within* (Notre Dame, IN: Sorin Books, 2015).

_______, *The Wisdom of the Body: A Contemplative Journey to Wholeness for Women* (Notre Dame, IN: Sorin Books, 2017).

Practicing Our Faith: A Guide for Conversation, Learning and Growth, eds., Dorothy Bass and Craig Dykstra (San Francisco: Jossey Bass, 1997).

Practicing Theology: Beliefs and Practices in Christian Life (Grand Rapids, MI: Eerdmans, 2002).

Smith, Gordon T., *Called to Be Saints: An Invitation to Christian Maturity* (Downers Grove, IL: InterVarsity Press, 2014).

Smith, James K., *You Are What You Love: The Spiritual Power of Habit* (Grand Rapids, MI: Baker Publishing, 2016).

Steindl-Rast, David, *The Way of Silence: Engaging the Sacred in Daily Life* (Cincinnati, OH: Franciscan Media, 2016).

Stock, Brian, *After Augustine: The Meditative Reader and the Text* (Philadelphia: University of Pennsylvania Press, 2001).

Valantasis, Richard, *Dazzling Bodies: Rethinking Spirituality and Community For*mation (Eugene, OR: Cascade Books, 2014).

New Monasticism

Adams, Ian, *Cave, Refectory, Road: Monastic Rhythms for Contemporary Living* (London: Canterbury Pres, 2010).

Davis, Bruce, *Monastery Without Walls: Daily Life in the Silence* (Lincoln, NE: Authors Choice Press, 2001).

Dekar, Paul R., *Community of the Transfiguration: The Journey of a New Monastic Community* (Eugene, OR: Wipf & Stock, 2008).

Flanagan, Bernadette, *Embracing Solitude: Women and New Monasticism* (Eugene, OR: Cascade Books, 2014).

Grimely, Anthony, and Jonathan Wooding, *Living the Hours: Monastic Spirituality in Everyday Life* (Norwich: Canterbury Pres, 2010).

Markofski, Wes, *New Monasticism and the Transformation of American Evangelicalism* (Oxford: Oxford University Press, 2015).

Martin, Christopher H., *The Restoration Project: A Benedictine Path to Wisdom, Strength, and Love* (Cincinnati, Ohio: Forward Movement, 2013).

McEntee, Rory and Adam Bucko, *The New Monasticism: An Interspiritual Manifesto for Contemplative Living* (Maryknoll, NY: Orbis Books, 2015).

Mobsby, Ian, and Mark Berry, *A New Monastic Handbook: From Vision to Practice* (Norwich, United Kingdom: Canterbury Press, 2014).

Paintner, Christine Valters, *Illuminating the Way: Embracing the Wisdom of Monks and Mystics* (Notre Dame, IN: Sorin Books, 2016).

Tvedten, Brother Benet, *How to Be a Monastic and Not Leave Your Day Job* (Brewster, MA: Paraclete Press, 2011).

Wilson-Hartgrove, Jonathan, *New Monasticism: What It Has to Say to Today's Church* (Grand Rpids, MI: Brazos Press, 2008).

Reformation Era

Calvin, John, *Institutes of the Christian Religion,* Volumes 1 & 2, ed. John T. McNeill, trans. Ford Lewis Battles (Philadelphia: The Westminster Press, 1960).

Evans, G. R., *The Roots of the Reformation: Tradition, Emergence and Rupture* (Downers Grove, IL: InterVarsity Press, 2012).

Lindberg, Carter, *The Third Reformation: Charismatic Movements and the Lutheran Tradition* (Macon, GA: Mercer University Press, 1983).

MacCulloch, Diarmaid, *The Reformation: A History* (New York: The Penguin Group, 2003).

Marty, Martin, *October 31, 1517: Martin Luther and the Day that Changed the World* (Brewster, MA: Paraclete Press, 2016).

McGinn, Bernard, *Mysticism In The Reformation 1500 – 1650, Part 1* in *The Presence of God: A History of Western Christian Mysticism,* Vol 6 (New York: Crossroad, 2016).

Pietists: Selected Writings, ed. Peter C. Erb (New York: Paulist Press, 1983).

Spitz, Lewis W., *The Renaissance and Reformation Movements,* revised edition, Volume 1: The Renaissance and Volume 2: The Reformation (St. Louis, MO: Concordia Publishing House, 1987).

The Complete Fenelon, trans. ed., Robert J. Edmonson and Hal M. Helms (Brewster: MA, Paraclete Press, 2008).

The Reformation in Medieval Perspective, ed. Steven E. Ozment (Chicago, IL: Quadrangle Books, 1971).

Monasticism

Anson, Peter F., *The Call of the Desert: The Solitary Life in the Christian Church* (London: S.P.C.K, 1964).

Athanasius, *The Life of Anthony and the Letter to Marcellinus,* trans. Robert C. Gregg. Classics of Western spirituality (CWS) (New York: Paulist Press, 1980).

Benedict's Dharma: Buddhists Reflect on the Rule of Saint Benedict, ed. Patrick Henry (New York: Continuum, 2001).

Bossy, John, *Christianity in the West, 1400 – 1700* (Oxford: Oxford University Press, 1985).

Brown, Peter, *Society and the Holy in Late Antiquity* (Berkeley, CA: University of California Press, 1989).

Burton-Christie, Douglas, *The Word in the Desert: Scripture and the Quest for Holiness in Early Christian Monasticism* (Oxford: Oxford University Press, 1993).

Casey, Michael, *An Unexciting Life: Reflections on Benedictine Spirituality* (Petersham, MA: St. Bede's Publications, 2005).

Casey, Michael, *Toward God: The Ancient Wisdom of Western Prayer* (Liguori, MO: Triumph Books, 1996).

Chittister, Joan, *The Illumined Life: Monastic Wisdom for Seekers of Light* (Maryknoll, NY: Orbis Books, 2000).

Chittister, Joan, *The Monastery of the Heart: An Invitation to a Meaningful Life* (Katonah, New York: BlueBridge, 2011).

Christie, Douglas E., *The Blue Sapphire of the Mind: Notes for a Contemplative Ecology* (Oxford: Oxford University Press, 2013).

Chryssavgis, John, *In the Heart of the Desert: The Spirituality of the Desert Fathers and Mothers* (Bloomington, IN: World Wisdom, 2008).

Collett, Barry, *"Monasticism"* in *The Oxford Encyclopedia of the Reformation,* ed. Hans J. Hillerbrand, Vol. 3 (Oxford: Oxford University Press, 1996) 78 – 83.

Cummings, Charles, *Monastic Practices* (Collegeville, MN: Liturgical Press, 2008).

Day, Trisha, *Inside the School of Charity: Lessons from the Monastery* (Collegeville, MN: The Liturgical Press, 2009).

Euan Cameron, *The European Reformation* (Oxford: Oxford University Press, 1991).

Evagrius of Pontus: The Greek Ascetic Corpus, trans. Robert T. Sinkewicz (Oxford: Oxford University Press, 2010).

Evagrius Ponticus, *The Praktikos and Chapters on Prayer,* trans. John Eudes Bamberger (Kalamazoo, MI: Cistercian Publications, 1981).

Evans, G.R., *The I.B. Tauris History of Monasticism: The Western Tradition* (London: I.B. Tauris & Co. Ltd., 2016).

Funk, Mary Margaret, *Thoughts Matter: The Practice of The Spiritual Life* (New York: Continuum, 2005).

Funk, Mary Margaret, *Tools Matter: For Practicing the Spiritual Life* (New York: Continuum, 2001).

Gould, Graham, *The Desert Fathers on Monastic Community* (Oxford: Clarendon Press, 1993).

Groeschel, Benedict J., *The Journey Toward God* (Ann Arbor, MI: Servant Publications, 2000).

Haigh, Christopher, et. al., *The English Reformation Revised* (Cambridge: Cambridge University Press, 1987).

Harmless, J. William, "Monasticism," in *The Oxford Handbook of Early Christian Studies*, ed. Susan Ashbrook Harvey and David G. Hunter (Oxford: Oxford University Press, 2008) 493 – 520.

Hugh of Saint-Victor, *Selected Spiritual Writings,* trans. By a Religious of C.S.M.V. (Eugene, OR: Wifp & Stock, 2009).

Kline, Francis, *Lovers of the Place: Monasticism Loose in the Church* (Collegeville, MN: The Liturgical Press, 1997).

Knowles, David, *Christian Monasticism* (New York: World University Library, McGraw-Hill Book Company, 1969).

Lawless, George, *Augustine of Hippo and his Monastic Rule* (Oxford: Clarendon Press, 1987).

Louth, Andrew, *The Wilderness of God* (Nashville, TN: Abingdon Press, 1991).

MacKenney, Richard, *Sixteenth Century Europe: Expansion and Conflict* (New York: St. Martin's Press, 1993)

Merton, Thomas, *The Monastic Journey,* ed. Brother Patrick Hart (Kansas City, MO: Sheed Andrews and McMeel, Inc., 1977).

Merton, Thomas, *The Waters of Siloe* (New York: Hardcourt Brace & Company, 1949).

Mohler, James A., *The Heresy of Monasticism; An Historical Survey* (Staten Island, NY: Alba House, 1971).

Moorhouse, Geoffrey, *The Last Divine Office* (New York: Blue Bridge, 2009).

Palladius of Aspuna, *The Lausiac History,* trans. John Wortley (Collegeville, MN: The Liturgical Press, 2015).

Peters, Greg, *Reforming the Monastery: Protestant Theologies of Religious Life* (Eugene, OR: Cascade, 2014).

Peters, Greg, *The Story of Monasticism: Retrieving an Ancient Tradition for Contemporary Spirituality* (Grand Rapids, MI: Baker Academic, 2015).

Piccardo, Cristiana, *Living Wisdom: The Mission and Transmission of Monasticism,* trans. Erik Varden, (Collegeville, MN: Liturgical Press, 2014).

Pseudo-Macarius, *The Fifty Spiritual Homilies and the Great Letter,* trans., ed. George A. Maloney (New York: Paulist Press, 1992).

Ruffing, Janet K., "Meditation: Christian Perspectives" in *Encyclopedia of Monasticism*, ed. William M. Johnston (Chicago: Fitzroy Dearborn Publishers, 2000) 847 – 850.

Ryrie, Alexander, *The Desert Movement: Fresh Perspectives on the Spirituality of the Desert* (Norwich, UK: Canterbury Press, 2011).

Smith, Cyprian, *The Path of Life: Benedictine Spirituality for Monks and Lay People (*Herefordshire, England: Ampleforth Abbey Press, 2004).

The Book of the Elders: Sayings of the Desert Fathers – A Systematic Collection, trans. John Wortley (Collegeville, MN: The Liturgical Press, 2012).

The Cambridge History of Christianity: Constantine to c. 600, ed. Augustine Casiday and Frederick w. Norris (Cambridge: Cambridge University Press, 2007).

The Desert Fathers, trans. Helen Waddell (New York: Vintage Books, 1998).

The Didascalicon of Hugh of Saint Victor: A Medieval Guide to the Arts, trans. Jerome Taylor (New York: Columbia University Press, 1991).

The Paradise of the Holy Fathers, Vol. 1 & Vol. 2, trans. Wallis Budge (Putty, NSW: St. Shenouda Monastery, 2009).

The Rule of St. Benedict in English, ed. Timothy Fry, OSB (Collegeville, MN: The Liturgical Press, 1982).

The Rule of Taizé in French and English by Brother Rodger (Brewster, MA: Paraclete Press, 2013).

The Sayings of the Desert Fathers: The Alphabetical Collection. trans. Benedicta Ward (London: Mowbrays, 1975).

The Spirituality of Western Christendom, ed. Jean Leclercq (Kalamazoo, MI: Cistercian Publications, 1976).

Thompson, Marjorie, *Soul Feast: An Invitation to the Christian Spiritual Life* (Louisville, KY: Westminster John Knox Press, 2014).

Tickle, Phyllis, *The Great Emergence: How Christianity is Changing and Why* (Grand Rapids, MI: Baker Books, 2008).

Tugwell, Simon, *Ways of Imperfection: An Exploration of Christian Spirituality* (Springfield, IL: Templegate Publishers, 1985).

Vermeirens, Korneel, *Praying with Benedict: Prayer in the Rule of St. Benedict,* trans. Richard Yeo (Kalamazoo, MI: Cistercian Publications, 1999).

Vivian, Tim, *Words to Live By: Journeys in Ancient and Modern Egyptian Monasticism* (Kalamazoo, MI: Cistercian Publications, 2005).

Williams, Rowan, *The Wound of Knowledge: Christian Spirituality from the New Testament to Saint John of the Cross* (Cambridge, MA: Cowley Publications, 1990).

Wolter, Maurus, *The Principles of Monasticism,* translated, edited and annotated by Bernard A. Sause (London: Herder Book Co., 1962).

Workman, Herbert B., *The Evolution of the Monastic Ideal* (Boston: Beacon Press, 1962).

Workman, Herbert B., *The Evolution of the Monastic Ideal: From the Earliest times Down to the Coming of the Friars – A Second Chapter in the History of Christian Renunciation* (Boston: Beacon Press, 1962).

Youings, Joyce, *The Dissolution of the Monasteries* (London: George Allen and Unwin Ltd., 1971).

Asceticism

Asceticism, ed. Vincent L. Wimbush & Richard Valantasis (Oxford: Oxford University Press, 1995).

Flood, Gavin, *The Ascetic Self: Subjectivity, Memory and Tradition* (Cambridge: Cambridge University Press, 2004).

Harpham, Geoffrey Gal, *The Ascetic Imperative in Culture and Criticism* (Chicago: The University of Chicago Press, 1897).

Hermeticisim and the Renaissance, ed. Ingrid Merkel and Allen G. Debus, (Washing: The Folger Shakespeare Library, Folger Books, 1988).

Krawiec, Rebecca, "Asceticism," in *The Oxford Handbook of Early Christian Studies*, ed. Susan Ashbrook Harvey and David G. Hunter (Oxford: Oxford University Press, 2008) 764 – 785.

Lacarrière, Jacques, *The God Possessed,* trans. Roy Monkcom (London: George Allen and Unwin, Ltd., 1963).

Tanquerey, Adolphe, *The Spiritual Life: A Treatise on Ascetical and Mystical Theology,* trans. Herman Branderis, (Charlotte, NC: TAN Books, 2000).

Valantasis, Richard, *Centuries of Holiness: Ancient Spirituality Refracted for a Postmodern Age* (New York: Continnum, 2005).

Valantasis, Richard, *The Making of the Self: Ancient and Modern Asceticism* (Eugene, OR: Cascade Books, 2008).

Consciousness

Beauregard, Mario and Denyse O'Leary, *The Spiritual Brain: A Neuroscientist's Case for the Existence of the Soul* (New York: Harper One, 2007).

Damasio, Antonio, *Self Come to Mind: Constructing the Conscious Brain* (New York: Vintage Books, 2012).

Dispenza, Joe, *Breaking the Habit of Being Yourself: How to Lose Your Mind and Create a New One* (New York: Hay House, Inc., 2012).

Feurestein, Georg, *Structures of Consciousness: The Genius of Jean Gebser – An Introduction and Critique* (Lower Lake, CA: Integral Publishing, 1987).

Gebser, Jean, *The Ever-Present Origin* (Athens, OH: Ohio University Press, 1985).

Helminiak, Daniel A., *Brain, Consciousness, and God: A Lonerganian Integration* (Albany, NY: State University of New York Press, 2015).

Kabat-Zinn, Jon, *Full Catastrophe Living: Using the Wisdom of Your Body and Mind to Face Stress, Pain, and Illness* (Bantam Books: New York, 2013).

McNamara, Patrick, *The Neuroscience of Religious Experience* (Cambridge: Cambridge University Press, 2009).

Thompson, Evan, *Waking, Dreaming, Being: Self and Consciousness in Neuroscience, Meditation, and Philosophy* (Columbia University Press: New York, 2015).

Christian Mysticism

An Introduction to The Medieval Mystics of Europe, ed. Paul Szarmach (Albany, NY: State University of New York Press, 1984).

Arseniev, Nicholas, *Mysticism and The Eastern Church* (Crestwood, NY: St. Vladimir's Seminary Press, 1979).

Borchert, Bruno, *Mysticism: Its History and Challenge* (York Beach, ME, 1994).

Bouyer, Louis, "Mysticism: An Essay on the History of the Word," in *Understanding Mysticism*, ed. Richard Woods (Garden City, NJ: Image Books, 1980) 42 – 55.

Bouyer, Louis, *The Christian Mystery: From Pagan Myth to Christian Mysticism,* trans. Illtyd Trethowan (Petersham, MA: Saint Bede's Publications, 1995).

Clément, Oliver, *The Roots of Christian Mysticism: Texts from the Patristic Era with Commentary,* 2nd Edition. (New York: New City Press, 1993).

Conti, Joseph, *Holistic Christianity: The Vision of Catholic Mysticism* (St. Paul, MN: Paragon House, 2005).

Curtis Hopkins, Emma, *High Mysticism* (New York: Cosimo Classics, 1997).

d'Aquili, Eugene, and Andrew B. Newberg, *The Mystical Mind: Probing the biology of Religious Experience* (Minneapolis, MN: Fortress Press, 1999).

Delio, Ilia, *Crucified Love: Bonaventure's Mysticism of the Crucified Christ* (Quincy, IL: Franciscan Press, 1998).

Dupré, Louis, *Transcendent Selfhood: The Rediscovery of the Inner Life* (New York: The Seabury Press, 1976).

Egan, Harvey D., *An Anthology of Christian Mysticism*, 2nd Ed. (Collegeville, MN: Liturgical Press, 1996).

Egan, Harvey D., *Soundings in the Christian Mystical Tradition* (Collegeville, MN: Liturgical Press, 2010).

Fanning, Steven, *Mystics of the Christian Tradition* (New York: Routledge, 2001).

Fremantle, Anne, *The Protestant Mystics* (Boston: Little, Brown and Company, 1964).

Harpur, James, *Love Burning in the Soul: The Story of the Christian Mystics, from Saint Paul to Thomas Merton* (Boston: New Seeds, 2005).

James, William, *Selected Writings* (New York: Book of the Month Club, 1997).

Lossky, Vladimir, *The Mystical Theology of the Eastern Church* (Crestwood, NY: St. Vladimir's Seminary Press, 1976).

Louth, Andrew, *Origins of the Christian Mystical Tradition: From Plato to Denys* (Oxford: Oxford University Press, 2007).

McColman, Carl, *The Big Book of Christian Mysticism: The Essential Guide to Contemplative Spirituality* (Charlottesville, VA: Hampton Roads Publishing Company, 2010).

The Cambridge Companion to Christian Mysticism, ed. Amy Hollywood and Patricia Z. Beckman (Cambridge, Cambridge University Press, 2012).

The Wiley-Blackwell Companion to Christian Mysticism, ed. Julia A. Lamm (Oxford: Wiley-Blackwell, 2013).

Underhill, Evelyn, *Mysticism* (Stillwell, KA: Digireads.com Publishing, 2005).

Underhill, Evelyn, *The Essentials of Mysticism and Other Essays* (Oxford: One World Publications, 1996).

Understanding Mysticism, Ed. Richard Woods (New York: Image Books, 1980).

Key books:

A New Charter for Monasticism: Proceeding of the Meeting of the Monastic Superiors in the Far East, Bangkok, December 9 to 15, 1968. ed. John Moffit (Notre Dame, IN: University of Notre Dame Press, 1970).

Anonymous, *The Cloud of Unknowing,* (New York: Paulist Press, 1981).

Augustine, *The Confessions,* trans., ed. Philip Burton (New York: Alfred A Knopf, 2001).

Aurobindo, Sri, *The Integral Yoga: Sri Aurobindo's Teaching and Method of Practice* (Twin Lakes, WI: Lotus Press, 2011).

Baisier, Leon, Contemplation Et Vie Contemplative Selon Platon. *New Scholasticism* 1938, 12 (3):302-304.

Beck, Don Edward, and Christopher C. Cowan, *Spiral Dynamics: Mastering Values, Leadership and Change* (Oxford: Blackwell Publishing, 2006).

Biot, Francois, *The Rise of Protestant Monasticism,* trans. W.J. Kerrigan (Baltimore, MD: Helicon, 1963).

Bloesch, Donald G., *Centers of Christian Renewal* (Philadelphia: United Church Press, 1964).

Bloesch, Donald G., Wellsprings of Renewal: Promise in the Christian Communal Life (Grand Rapids, MI: Eerdmans Publishing Company, 1973).

Brooke, Christopher, *The Age of the Cloister: The Story of Monastic Life in the Middle Ages* (Mahwah, NJ: HiddenSpring, 2008).

Bryan, Jennifer, *Looking Inward: Devotional Reading and the Private Self in Late Medieval England* (Philadelphia: University of Pennsylvania Press, 2008).

Butler, Cuthbert, *Western Mysticism: Augustine, Gregory and Bernard on Contemplation and the Contemplative Life* (Mineola, MN: Dover Publications, 2003).

Casey, Michael, *The Undivided Heart: The Western Monastic Approach to Contemplation* (Petersham, Mass. 1994).

Cassian, John, *Conferences,* trans. Colm Luibheid, (New York: Paulist Press, 1985).

Chirban, John, *"Developmental Stages in Easter Orthodox Christianity"* in *Transformations of Consciousness: Conventional and Contemplative Perspectives on Development,* eds., Ken Wilber, Engler, Jack, and Daniel P. Brown (Boston: Shamballa Publications, 1986) 285 – 314.

Dalrymple, William, *From the Holy Mountain: A Journey among the Christians of the Middle East* (New York: Henry Holt and Company, 1997).

de Caussade, Jean Pierre, *The Abandonement to the Divine Presence: With Letters of Father De Caussade on the Practice of Self-Abandonment*, ed. J. Ramiere (San Francisco: CA, Ignatius Press, 2011).

Deck, John N., *Nature, Contemplation and the One: A Study in the Philosophy of Plotinus* Burdett, NY: Larson Publications, 1991).

Delio, Ilia, *Christ In Evolution* (Maryknoll, NY: Orbis Books, 2008).

_____, *The Emergent Christ: Exploring the Meaning of Catholic in an Evolutionary Universe* (Maryknoll, NY: Orbis Books, 2011).

_____, *Making All Things New: Catholicity, Cosmology, Consciousness* (Maryknoll, NY: Orbis Books, 2015).

Encyclopedia Christianity, ed. Geoffrey W. Bromiley (Grand Rapids: Eerdmans, 1999).

Encyclopedia of Ancient Christianity ed. Angelo DiBerardino, Thomas Spidlik, "Contemplation" (Downers Grove, IL: InterVaristy Press Academic, 2014) 606.

Encyclopedia of Ancient Christianity, ed. Angelo Di Berardino (Downers Grove, IL: Intervarsity Press, 2014).

Encyclopedia of Monasticism, ed. William M. Johnston (Chicago: Fitzroy Dearborn Publishers, 2000).

Ferrer, J. N. (2002). *Revisioning transpersonal theory: A participatory vision of human spirituality*. Albany, NY: State University of New York Press.

Festugière, A. J., *Contemplation Et Vie Contemplative Selon Platon Thèse Pour le Doctorat* (*De l'Université de Paris.* J. Vrin. 1936)

Fowler, J. W. *Stages of faith: The psychology of human development and the quest for meaning* (New York: HarperCollins, 1981).

Garrigou-Lagrange, Reginald, *Christian Perfection and Contemplation: According to St. Thomas Aquinas and St. John of the Cross,* trans. Sister M. Timothea Doyle (Charlotte, NC: TAN Books & Publishers, Inc., 2003).

Garrigou-Lagrange, Reginald, *The Three Ages of the Interior Life: Prelude of Eternal Life,* Volume 1 & 2, trans. Sister M. Timothea Doyle (London: Catholic Way Publishing, 2012).

Garrigou-Lagrange, Reginald, *The Three Conversions in the Spiritual Life* (Rockford, IL: TAN Books & Publishers, Inc., 1977).

Hart, Kevin, "Contemplation: Beyond and Behind" in *Springer Science and Business Media*, November 28, 2009.

Heath, Elaine A., *The Mystic Way of Evangelism: A Contemplative Vision for Christian Outreach* (Grand Rapids, MI: Baker Academic, 2008).

Herrman, Arthur, *The Cave and the Light: Plato Versus Aristotle, and the Struggle for the Soul of Western Civilization* (New York: Random House, 2014).

Knowles, David, *Christian Monasticism* (New York: McGraw-Hill Book Company, 1968).

Lacarriere, Jacques, *The God-Possessed* (London: George Allen & Unwin, Ltd., 1963).

Lane, Beldon, *The Solace of Fierce Landscapes: Desert and Mountain Spirituality* (Oxford: Oxford University Press, 1998).

MacCulloch, Diarmaid, *Silence: A Christian History* (New York: Penguin Books, 2013).

MacIntyre, Alasdair, *After Virtue*, Third Edition (Notre Dame: University of Notre Dame Press, 2007).

Maloney, George A., *Inscape: God at the Heart of Matter* (Dennville, NJ: Dimension Books, 1978).

McColman, Carl, *Befriending Silence: Discovering the Gifts of Cistercian Spirituality* (Notre Dame, IN: Ave Maria Press, 2015).

McGinn, Bernard, *The Presence of God: A History of Western Christian Mysticism,* 5 Vols. (New York: Crossroad, 1991).

Meister Eckhart and the Beguine Mystics, ed. Bernard McGinn (New York: Continuum, 1994).

Merton, Thomas, *Invitation to the Monastic Tradition* Vol. 1 – 6: *The Life of Vows,* 6 (Collegeville, MN: Liturgical Press, 2012).

Mohler, James A., *The Heresy of Monasticism: The Christian Monks- Types and Anti-Types* (New York: Alba House, 1971).

Moltmann, Jurgen, *The Spirit of Life: A Universal Affirmation* (Minneapolis: Fortress Press, 1993).

Okholm, Dennis, *Dangerous Passions, Deadly Sins: Learning from the Psychology of Ancient Monks* (Grand Rapids: Brazos Press, 2014).

Okholm, Dennis, *Monk Habits for Everyday People: Benedictine Spirituality for Protestants* (Grand Rapids: Brazos Press, 2007).

Ozment, Steven E., *Mysticism and Dissent: Religious Ideology and Social Protest in the Sixteenth Century* (New Haven, CT: Yale University Press, 1973).

Panikkar, Raimon, *Opera Omnia, Vols. 1 – 12,* (Maryknoll, NY: Orbis Books, 2014).

Peifer, Claude J., *Monastic Spirituality* (New York: Sheed and Ward, 1966).

Peters, Greg, "*Monasticism: Instrument of the Holy Spirit in the Renewal of Today's Church*" in *The Holy Spirit and the Christian Life: Historical, Interdisciplinary and Renewal Perspectives,* ed. Wolfgang Vondey (New York: Palmgrave McMillan, 2014) 41 – 57.

Poulain, Augustin, *The Grace of Interior Prayer* (Caritas Publishin, 2016).

Rohr, Richard, *Eager to Love: The Alternative Way of Francis of Assisi* (Cincinnati, OH: Franciscan Media, 2014).

Sarah, Robert Cardinal, *The Power of Silence: Against the Dictatorship of Noise* (San Fransisco: Igantius Press, 2017).

Schwanda, Tom, "Contemplation" in *Zondervan Dictionary of Christian Spirituality,* ed. Glen G. Scorgie (Grand Rapids, MI: Zondervan, 2011) 370 – 371.

Schwanda, Tom, "'To Gaze on the Beauty of the Lord': The Evangelical Resistance and Retrieval of Contemplation" in *The Journal of Spiritual Formation & Soul Care*, Vol. 7, No. 1, 62 – 84 (La Mirada, CA: Biola University) 2014.

Shannon, William, "Contemplation, Contemplative Prayer" in *The New Dictionary of Catholic Theology* (Collegeville, MN: The Liturgical Press, 1993) 209 – 214.

Smith, Paul R., *Integral Christianity: The Spirit's Call to Evolve* (St. Paul, MN: Paragon House, 2011).

Taylor, Charles, *A Secular Age* (Cambridge, MA: The Belknap Press of Harvard University Press, 2007).

Taylor, Charles, *Sources of the Self: The Making of the Modern Identity* (Cambridge, MA: Harvard University Press, 1989).

The Cambridge Dictionary of Christianity, ed. Daniel Patte (Cambridge: Cambridge University Press, 2011).

The Cambridge History of Early Christian Literature, ed. France Young, Lewis Ayres and Andrew Louth (Cambridge: Cambridge University Press, 2004).

The Encyclopedia of Christian Civilization, ed. George Thomas Kurian (Oxford: Wiley-Blackwell, 2012).

The Innate Capacity: Mysticism, Psychology, and Philosophy, ed. Robert K. C. Forman (Oxford: Oxford University Press, 1998).

The Lion Christian Meditation Collection, compiled by Hannah Ward and Jennifer Wild (Oxford, Lion Books, 2000).

The New Westminster Dictionary of Christian Spirituality, ed. Phillip Sheldrake (Louisville: Westminster John Knox Press, 2013).

The New Westminster Dictionary of Christian Spirituality, ed. Philip Sheldrake (Philadelphia: The Westminster Press, 2013).

The Oxford Dictionary of the Christian Church, ed. F.L. Cross, 3rd Edition Revised, E.A. Livingstone (Oxford: Oxford University Press, 2005).

The Oxford Encyclopedia of the Reformation, ed. Hans J. Hillerbrand (Oxford: Oxford University Press, 1996).

Theologica Germanica, trans. Susanna Winkworth, (Mesa, AZ: Scriptoria Books, 2010).

Tvedten, Brother Benet, *How to Be a Monastic and Not Leave Your Day Job* (Brewster, MA: Paraclete Press, 2011).

Union with Christ: The New Finnish Interpretation of Luther, eds., Carl E. Braaten and Robert W. Jenson (Grand Rapids, MI: William B. Eerdmans Publishing Company, 1998).

Von Balthasar, Hans Urs, *The Glory of the Lord: A Theological Aesthetics*, Vol. IV: *The Realm of Metaphysics in Antiquity* (Edinburgh: T&T Clark, 1989).

Westminster Dictionary of Christian Theology, ed. Allan Richardson and John Bowden, Richard Harries, "Contemplation" (Philadelphia: The Westminster Press, 1983) 121.

Wilber, Ken, *Integral Spirituality: A Startling New Role for Religion in the Modern and Postmodern World* (Boston: Integral Books, 2007).

Wolf, Miroslav, *Flourishing: Why We Need Religion In A Globalized World* (New Haven: Yale University Press, 2015).

Wolter, Maurus, *The Principles of Monasticism,* trans. Bernard A. Sause (London: B. Herder Book Co., 1962).

World Spirituality: An Encyclopedic History of the Religious Quest, vols. 6 – 12, 15 – 22.

Young, Amos, *Pneumatology and the Christian-Buddhist Dialogue* (London: Brill, 2012).

Zondervan Dictionary of Christian Spirituality, ed. Glen G. Scorgie (Grand Rapids: Zondervan, 2011).

Endnotes

Frontspiece quotations

[1] Pierre Teilhard de Chardin, The Divine Milieu, 127-128.

[2] Karl Rahner, *The Practice of Faith: A Handbook of Contemporary Spirituality* (New York: Crossroad, 1983), 22.

Preface

[1] Such as: New Camaldoli Hermitage, California; Snowmass, Colorado; Ghost Ranch, New Mexico; New Melleray Abbey, Iowa; the Oblate Renewal Center, San Antonio, Texas; and Leb Shomea, Sarita, Texas.

[2] Such as www.ContemplativeChristians.com and www.MeditationChapel.org or https://www.facebook.com/groups/ContemplativeChristianity

Opening Quotes

[1] John O'Donohue, *Beauty: The Invisible Embrace: Rediscovering the True Sources of Compassion, Serenity and Hope* (New York: Harper Perennial, 2004), 5.

[2] Pablo Naruda, "I Asked for Silence" in *Extravagaria,* trans. Alastair Reid (New York: Farrar, Straus and Giroux, 1974), 17.

Introduction

[1] Yes, I remember my tears. But I also remember my joy. A joy that has grown in the silence and stillness. A joy that has been born from working out my salvation. I no longer weep because I think something is wrong – with me or with anyone else. I weep because I feel God's love in the silence. I don't resent this axial moment in our civilization. I rejoice for the opportunity to evolve and experience a deeper fruitfulness through the very friction and fault lines that seem to have undone the Christendom we once knew.

[2] The Jesus Prayer is an early Byzantine era Christian method of meditative prayer that can also lead one into contemplation. The Jesus Prayer is a brief and ancient prayer-sentence grounded in scripture. Over the centuries, the Jesus Prayer has had multiple variations, but here below is the current, modern form popularized by such writers as Simeon the New Theologian (949 – 1022 CE), St. Theophan the Recluse (1815 – 1894 CE), and such books as, *The Way of the Pilgrim,* and *The Philokalia*: "*Lord Jesus Christ, Son of God have mercy upon me a sinner.*" For an essential yet brief history of the Jesus Prayer, see Kallistos Ware, "*The Origins of the Jesus Prayer: Diadochus, Gaza, Sinai* in *The Study of Spirituality,* ed. Cheslyn Jones, Geoffrey Wainwright, and Edward Yarnod (Oxford: Oxford University Press, 1986). For a helpful overview of the development and modern adaptation of the Jesus Prayer, see Christopher D.L. Johnson, *The Globalization of Hesychasm and the Jesus*

Prayer: Contesting Contemplation (New York: Continuum, 2010). For an expanded articulation of the Jesus Prayer from within the context of a monastery on Mount Athos see the extraordinary *The Watchful Mind: Teachings on the Prayer of the Heart* by A Monk of Mount Athos (Yonkers, NY: St. Vladimir's Seminary Press, 2014). Here are some of the prayer's biblical roots are Psalm 70.1; John 14.26; Philippians 2. 9 – 10; Acts 4.12 and John 16.23 – 24.

[3] Yes, I'm grateful for all the moments and phases of my journey, especially the brokenhearted ones. But, the truth is, I never felt fully home until I wandered through my unexamined shadows and appointed life-sufferings into the contemplative stream silently and humbly flowing underneath all that we call Christian. The contemplative stream is vibrantly alive, yet mostly hidden within the Christian community. Along the way, I discovered others have also found this way home too, and we have a way of finding one another. Perhaps that is why you picked up this book.

[4] For a helpful overview of the history of such monasteries see, G.R. Evans, *The I.B. Tauris History of Monasticism: The Western Tradition* (London: I.B. Tauris & Co. Ltd., 2016).

[5] For more on this claim, see Chetwynd, Tom, *Zen & The Kingdom of Heaven: Reflections on the Tradition of Meditation in Christianity and Zen Buddhism* (Somerville, MA: Wisdom Publications, 2001), particularly chapter six, "The Line of Christian Spiritual Masters," 95ff.

[6] Karl Rahner, "Christian Living Formerly and Today," in Theological Investigations VII, trans. David Bourke (New York: Herder and Herder, 1971), 15 as quoted in Harvey D. Egan, Soundings in the Christian Mystical Tradition (Collegeville, MN: Liturgical Press, 2010), 338.

Opening Quotes

[1] Wendell Berry, *New Collected Poems* (Counterpoint: Berkeley, CA, 2012), 3.

[2] *McBeth*, Act 5, Scene 5.

Chapter One / Realizing

[1] Thomas Merton, *The Monastic Journey,* Ed. Brother Patrick Hart (Kansas City, MO: Sheed Andrews and McMeel, Inc., 1977), 218 - 223

[2] October 31, 1517 is customarily viewed as the symbolic start of the Reformation: the day Martin Luther posted his ninety-five thesis on the door of All Saints Church in Wittenberg, Germany. The "Ninety-Five Theses on the Power and Efficacy of Indulgences," known in Latin as the *Disputatio pro declaratione virtutis indulgentiarum*. The theses are widely regarded as the initial catalyst for the Protestant Reformation. Among other things, the Theses protests against clerical abuses, especially nepotism, simony, usury, pluralism and the sale of indulgences. The claim that the theses were actually posted on the church door is understood to be more legend than fact. What is certain is that on October 31, 1517 Luther sent a letter to his superiors including the Ninety Five Theses. For a modern reading on the Reformation, see G. R. Evans, *The Roots of the Reformation: Tradition, Emergence and Rupture* (Downers Grove, IL: InterVarsity Press, 2012). It is less commonly known, that two months prior to Luther posting his ninety-five Thesis, on September 4, 1517 when

Luther published a different, equally explosive set of ideas called the *Disputation against Scholastic Theology.*

[3] For an excellent history of the Reformation and its historical and social context see Lewis W. Spitz, *The Renaissance and Reformation Movements,* revised edition, Volume 1: The Renaissance and Volume 2: The Reformation (St. Louis, MO: Concordia Publishing House, 1987). See also Dennis E. Tamburello's essay on "The Protestant Reformers on Mysticism" in *The Wiley-Blackwell Companion to Christian Mysticism,* ed. Julia A. Lamm (Oxford: Wiley-Blackwell, 2013) and Edward Howells essay "Early Modern Reformations" in *The Cambridge Companion to Christian Mysticism*, ed. Amy Hollywood and Patricia Z. Beckman (Cambridge, Cambridge University Press, 2012).

[4] For a helpful overview of this thesis see Heiko A. Oberman's excellent article "*Simul Gemitus et Raptus: Luther and Mysticism*" in *The Reformation in Medieval Perspective,* ed. Steven E. Ozment (Chicago, IL: Quadrangle Books, 1971), 219 – 251. See also Diarmaid MacCulloch, *Silence: A Christian History* (New York: Penguin Books, 2013), particularly chapter six, "The Protestant Reformation," 127ff. And for a useful essay on the theological basis of the monastic ethos from a Protestant perspective see Part Three in Francois Biot, *The Rise of Protestant Monasticism,* trans. W.J. Kerrigan (Baltimore, MD: Helicon, 1963), 107ff. For a similar treatment of many of the themes I will be exploring see Anthony Grimley and Johnathan M. Wooding, *Living the Hours: Monastic Spirituality in Everyday Life* (Norwich: Canterbury Press, 2010).

[5] The Reformation wasn't all bad. The Reformers called the church back to the bedrock truth that living the Christian life does not save us, but *how* we live is the fruit of our salvation in Christ. In theological terms, the Reformers were saying that justification is not contingent upon sanctification. Union with God is not contingent upon a spiritual journey toward God, but in Christ, union is our grace-given starting point from which we can continue to abide and bear spiritual fruit. Having said that, it is easy to see that the Reformer's principal critique of monastic life and contemplative spirituality was that it tended to set apart monastics as more superior to ordinary lay folk. To the Reformers, this division was based on, among other things, a false idea they called works-righteousness. For an excellent treatment of this see Greg Peters, *The Story of Monasticism: Retrieving an Ancient Tradition for Contemporary Spirituality* (Grand Rapids, MI: Baker Academic, 2015) especially chapter twelve, "The Reformers and Counter-Reformers," 205ff, and chapter thirteen, "Protestants and Monasticism after the Reformation," 224ff.

[6] Lewis W. Spitz, *The Renaissance and Reformation Movements,* revised edition, Volume 1: The Renaissance and Volume 2: The Reformation (St. Louis, MO: Concordia Publishing House, 1987), 318.

[7] The Quakers are the most renowned movement, but other Protestant communities also focused on the importance of inward spiritual life. Note for example (in no particular order) the books: *Epistle on Mixed Life*; *Scale of Perfection; Contemplations on the Dread and Love of God; The Prickling of Love; Piers Plowman; The Chastening of God's Children; A Talking of the Love of God; Imitation of Christ; Spiritual Espousals; The Mirror of the Blessed Life of Jesus Christ; The Mirror of Recluses; The Orchard of Sion; The Book of Vices and Virtues; The Seven Points of True Love and Everlasting Wisdom; The Tree and Twelve Fruits,* et. al. 3

[8] Carter Lindberg among others, develops the logic of Martin Luther's *extra nos in Christo* in the light of Johannes Tauler's mystical language which provides the vehicle for expressing Luther's justification theology. Lindberg notes that Luther understood , "the destruction of human self-righteousness and the establishment upon this of what is *extra nos in Christo* as the experiential movement away from all self-concern and inner complacency toward the grace of Christ." These scholars keenly point out that "Luther transferred the mystical function of ecstatic love (*amor extatiens*) to faith using the notion of being outside or beyond oneself (*extra se*) to characterize justification by faith. In oneself the person is nothing but a sinner, but outside oneself in faith in Christ the person is at the same time righteous. For Luther this moving outside oneself is not a silent interior event but rather occurs in the knowledge of faith in which the person's being is disclosed before God (*coram Deo*) by the Word. Thus the mystic *extra now* is a key to the correct understanding of the forensic understanding of Luther's doctrine of justification." Carter Lindberg, *The Third Reformation: Charismatic Movements and the Lutheran Tradition* (Macon, GA: Mercer University Press, 1983), 30. Pair Lindberg's idea with how Martin Luther puts it: "By faith a Christian is caught up beyond himself into God. By love a Christian descends beneath himself into his neighbor. Yet one always remains in God and in God's love..." Martin Luther, *The Babylonian Captivity of the Church, 1520* LW 36, 39.

[9] For a very current review of the Reformers views on monasticism see, Greg Peters, *Reforming the Monastery: Protestant Theologies of the Religious Life* (Eugene, OR: Cascade Books, 2014), particularly chapter one, "The Protestant Reformers," 19ff.

[10] Lewis W. Spitz, *The Renaissance and Reformation Movements,* revised edition, Volume 1: The Renaissance and Volume 2: The Reformation (St. Louis, MO: Concordia Publishing House, 1987), 316.

[11] See Lewis W. Spitz, *The Renaissance and Reformation Movements,* revised edition, Volume 1: The Renaissance and Volume 2: The Reformation (St. Louis, MO: Concordia Publishing House, 1987), 316 – 317 for a review of the attempted monastic reforms.

[12] Martin Luther, *Luther's Works: Table Talk.* Vol. 54. ed. and trans. Theodore G. Tappert (Philadelphia: Fortress Press, 1967), 312.

[13] *Wittenberg Articles, XV* accessed from [http://www.welsne.org/data/uploads/2013/2013_pastoralconference_wittenbergarticles.pdf] on September 7, 2016.

[14] The Protestant impulse to split away from the Roman Catholic Church in the mid-Renaissance era did not cease with Martin Luther (1483 – 1546 CE), John Calvin (1509 – 1564 CE), or John Knox (1532 – 1572 CE). The splitting continued centuries thereafter, and persists even to this moment. As a result of such ongoing rifts and splits, depth and wholeness are not words that come to mind to describe the quality, mood or status of our current Protestant communities. For a good picture of how Reformation era Protestants unfolded in the American context see Sydney E. Ahlstrom, *A Religious History of the American People* (New Haven, CT: Yale University Press, 1972) and Mark A. Noll, *America's God: From Jonathan Edwards to Abraham Lincoln* (Oxford: Oxford University Press, 2002).

[15] For more in-depth treatment of these Protestant-Monastic remnants, see Greg Peters, *The Story of Monasticism: Retrieving an Ancient Tradition for Contemporary Spirituality* (Grand Rapids, MI: Baker Academic, 2015), especially chapter twelve, "The Reformers

and Counter-Reformers," 205ff, and chapter thirteen, "Protestants and Monasticism after the Reformation," 224ff.

[16] Also associated with this were the Moravians, first inspired by Czech Reformer Jan Hus (c. 1369 – 1415). For more background on these historical developments, see Francois Biot, *The Rise of Protestant Monasticism,* trans. W.J. Kerrigan (Baltimore, MD: Helicon, 1963), especially Part Two, "Trial Communities and Monastic Renaissance" 65ff.

[17] See especially Bonhoeffer's *Life Together.*

[18] For the Evangelical avoidance of contemplation as a remedy, see Tom Schwanda, "'To Gaze on the Beauty of the Lord': The Evangelical Resistance and Retrieval of Contemplation" in *The Journal of Spiritual Formation & Soul Care*, Vol. 7, No. 1, 62 – 84 (La Mirada, CA: Biola University, 2014).

[19] For more on the Nones, see Linda A. Mercadante, *Belief without Borders: Inside the Minds of the Spiritual but not Religious* (Oxford: Oxford University Press, 2014). And, for more on New Monasticism see Ian Mobsby and Mark Berry, *A New Monastic Handbook: From Vision to Practice* (Norwich, United Kingdom: Canterbury Press, 2014). Or, Rory McEntee and Adam Bucko, *The New Monasticism: An Interspiritual Manifesto for Contemplative Living* (Maryknoll, NY: Orbis Books, 2015).

[20] Interestingly, the closest experience most pastors will have to a monastery is the modern seminary, but even that has become heavily oriented toward academic formation, often lacking opportunities and mentors in spiritual and sapiential formation.

[21] See for example Wilson-Hartgrove, Jonathan, *New Monasticism: What It Has to Say to Today's Church* (Grand Rapids, MI: Brazos Press, 2008), or Rory McEntee and Adam Bucko, *The New Monasticism: An Interspiritual Manifesto for Contemplative Living* (Maryknoll, NY: Orbis Books, 2015). See also the work of Thomas Keating or Richard J. Foster. See also Thom S. Rainer, *Autopsy of a Deceased Church: 12 Ways to Keep Yours Alive* (Nashville: B&H Publishing, 2014); Thom and Joani Schultz, *Why Nobody Wants to God to Church Anymore: And How 4 Acts of Love Will Make Your Church Irresistible* (Loveland, CO: Group Publishing, 2013.

[22] The vast and growing literature on the subject is expanding exponentially. Of the many books and articles available on the subject of meditation and neuroscience, one of the most compelling and accessible is Evan Thompson's *Waking, Dreaming, Being: Self and Consciousness in Neuroscience, Meditation, and Philosophy* (Columbia University Press: New York, 2015).

[23] See for example, Mario Beauregard and Denyse O'Leary, *The Spiritual Brain: A Neuroscientist's Case for the Existence of the Soul* (New York: Harper One, 2007) and Patrick McNamara, *The Neuroscience of Religious Experience* (Cambridge: Cambridge University Press, 2009). See also the very helpful book by Daniel Goleman and Richard J. Davidson, *Altered Traits: Science Reveals How Meditation Chances Your Mind, Brain, and Body* (New York: Avery, 2017).

[24] Jon Kabat-Zinn, *Full Catastrophe Living: Using the Wisdom of Your Body and Mind to Face Stress, Pain, and Illness* (Bantam Books: New York, 2013).

[25] See for example, Daniel Goleman and Richard J. Davidson, *Altered Traits: Science Reveals How Meditation Changes Your Mind, Brain and Body* (New York: Penguin Random House, 2017). See: https://centerhealthyminds.org/.

[26] For example, *Contemplative Practices in Higher Education* by Daniel Barbezat and Mirabai Bush. And *Contemplative Learning and Inquiry across Disciplines,* Eds. Ollen Gunnlaugson, Edward Sarath, and Charles Scott State University of New York Pres: Albany, 2014) and Jacob Holsinger-Sherman's essay, "On the Emerging Field of Contemplative Studies and Its Relationship to the Study of Spirituality" in Spiritus 14.2 (Baltimore: John Hopkins University Press).

[27] On a scholarly level, the convergence can be seen in the "mindfulness" revolution, articulated by such thoughts leaders as Jon Kabat-Zinn, known for his bestselling book *Full Catastrophe Living* and Mindfulness-Based Stress Reduction program at the University of Massachusetts Medical Center. Similarly, we can also point to Dr. David Davidson's bestseller *The Emotional Life of Your Brain* and work at The Center for Investigating Healthy Minds at the University of Madison. The mindfulness revolution is impacting multiple disciplines, such as the work of through the work of The Center for Contemplative Mind in Society, whose founders Daniel P. Barbezat and Mirabai Bush book *Contemplative Practices in Higher Education: Powerful methods to transform teaching and learning* connects mindfulness with the field of education. The convergence can be seen in the "consciousness" revolution, articulated by a host of scholars such as Baroness Susan Greenfield, Antonio Damasio and Evan Thompson, whose book *Waking, Dreaming, Being* is perhaps one of the most important books on the subject of neuroscience and meditation in decades. On a popular spiritual level, authors such as Thomas Keating, Mark Nepo, Thích Nhất Hạnh, and Elkhart Tolle have deeply and beautifully articulated not only the methods of meditative prayer, but also personally embody the contemplative way of being, representing the spiritual spectrum from Roman Catholicism (Keating), Buddhism (Nepo, Hanh), to spiritual but not religious (Tolle).

[28] See the 2015 Pew Research Center findings on decreased church attendance and the decline of Christianity. [http://www.pewresearch.org/fact-tank/2015/05/12/5-key-findings-u-s-religious-landscape/] accessed July 21, 2016. Also, Diana Butler-Bass, *Christianity after Religion: The End of Church and the Birth of A New Spiritual Awakening* (Harper Collins: New York, 2013). Or Phyllis Tickle, *The Great Emergence: How Christianity is Changing and Why* (Baker Books: Grand Rapids, MI, 2008). Tickle along with others such as Karen Armstrong's *The Great Transformation: The Beginning of our Religious Traditions* (Random House: New York, 2006) have helped the church see the big-picture of epochal changes, along the lines of what Karl Jasper introduced in his groundbreaking book *The Origin and Goal of History* published in 1949. Like sociological archeologists, certain strata of time and human consciousness can be discerned as structures unfolding in global meme like fashion. The important question today is discerning what is unfolding now?

[29] Martin Luther was significantly inspired by the contemplative, mystical book *The Theologica Germanica of Martin Luther: The Classics of Western Spirituality*, (Mahwah, New Jersey: Paulist Press, 1980), 54. Next to the bible and Augustine, Luther thought "no other booked taught him more about God, Christ, humankind and what all things are." For a specific example of the importance of the contemplative and mystical dimension and its impact on the Reformation and vice versa see the helpful book by Jennifer Bryan, *Looking Inward: Devotional Reading and the Private Self in Late Medieval England* (Philadelphia:

University of Pennsylvania Press, 2008), 14. In Bryan's *Looking Inward*, I found a particularly insightful quotation: "Augustine's emphasis on returning to 'the inner man' never really ceased to affect medieval theology. His ideas were taken up with particular enthusiasm by twelfth-century spiritual writers, particularly Cistercians such as Bernard of Clairvaux and Aelred of Rievaulx. The notion of self-concentration and self-examination as prerequisites to mystical experience, to self-knowledge and knowledge of God, was one of the defining themes of that period's intellectual life." For more on the influence of mysticism and the contemplative dimension's influence on the Reformation see Steven Fanning,'s chapter IV "Mystics In Early Modern Europe: The Reformation, The Efflorescence of Mysticism in Spain and France" in Fanning's book, *Mystics of the Christian Tradition* (New York: Routledge, 2001), 139ff. And for an overall, excellent and brief background story on monasticism see Christopher Brooke, *The Age of the Cloister: The Story of Monastic Life in the Middle Ages* (Mahwah, NJ: Hidden Spring, 2008).

[30] By depth dimension, I mean that process and goal described by the term *theosis.* Thankfully, a recovery of the theological importance of *theosis* is occurring in the Reformed community. Note the particular work of the Finnish theologians in the helpful book *Union with Christ: The New Finnish Interpretation of Luther,* eds. Carl E. Braaten and Robert W. Jenson (Grand Rapids: William B. Eerdmans Publishing Company, 1998).

[31] Martin Laird, *Into the Silent Land: A Guide to the Christian Practice of Contemplation* (Oxford: Oxford University Press, 2006), 4, 15, 10, 77.

[32] *The Rule of Taizé in French and English* by Brother Rodger (Brewster, MA: Paraclete Press, 2013).

[33] *The Contemplative Path: Reflections on Recovering a Lost Tradition,* ed. E. Rozanne Elder (Kalamazoo, MI: Cistercian Publications, Inc., 1995), 12.

[34] Maurice Nicoll, *Psychological Commentaries on the Teachings of Gurdjieff and Ouspensky,* Vol. 1 (Boston, MA: Weiser Books, 1996), 154.

[35] By again, I am thinking of Thomas Cahill's wonderful book, *How the Irish Saved Civilization: The Untold Story of Ireland's Heroic Role from the Fall of Rome to the Rise of Medieval Europe,* which makes the point how the monastic communities safe-guarded the western intellectual tradition, while the rest of Europe dissolved in the so called dark ages.

[36] A more complete list would expand to at least these: *Fasting, Humility, Lectio Divina, Prayer of the Hours, a Rule of Life, Self-Observation, Silence, Simplicity, Solitude, Spiritual direction and friendship, Stability, Stillness, Work,* which are technically related to the threefold classic vows of *Obedience, Poverty* and *Chastity.*

[37] One of the most important gifts the monastic tradition has given Christianity, is a focused way of life within the monastic setting. Through this intentional spiritual life in community, the church was able to identify the "ordinary milestones" of a Christian's spiritual development. For example, it became very clear that the spiritual journey started with some sort of conversion; continued with a period of training and reformation of life, including practical and ascetic disciplines that helped purify one's heart, mind, and body. After a time, this purification led one to a season of illumination and deepened understanding, where one often began to see visible spiritual fruits, such as increased love, joy or peace in one's life. This season of illumination could then culminate in the Unitive state, which is another

way of saying the "contemplative state." The terms are essentially synonymous; however it is important to recognize that while one may have contemplative experiences, one may not yet be in the Unitive state. It is understood that while experiences are temporary, states are more permanent. It is also important to remember that on the spiritual journey we don't work for results. We simply say "Yes" to God, and let God carry us further along in the great River of Life to wherever our unique destiny is to lead us. The practices help us remember to say both Yes to God and No to that which we are invited to let go of.

[38] Georges Friedmann, *La Puissance et la Sagesse* (Paris: Galimard, 1970) 359 cited in Pierre Hadot, *Philosophy as a way of life: Spiritual Exercises from Socrates to Foucault*, ed. Arnold I. Davidson, trans. Michael Chase (Malden, MA: Blackwell Publishing, 1995), 81.

[39] Benedicta Ward, ed. *The Saying of the Desert Fathers* (London: A.R. Mowbray, 1975), 8.

[40] See Philippians 4. 1 – 12.

[41] Quoted in Christopher Bamford, *An Endless Trace: The passionate pursuit of wisdom in the west* (Codhill Press: New Palz, New York, 2003), 222, 212.

[42] See John of the Cross, *The Living Flame of Love* http://www.saintsbooks.net/books ; Teresa of Ávila, *The Interior Castle*, chapter II [http://www.sacred-texts.com/chr/tic/tic18.htm]; Frances De Sales, *Treatise On The Love of God,* chapter XIII [http://www.ccel.org/ccel/desales/love].

Chapter Two / *Needing*

[1] For a helpful overview of this claim, see Phillip Jenkins, *The Next Christendom* (New York: Oxford University Press, 2002).

[2] For a very helpful survey of the historical trends of the "spiritual but not religious" movement in America see Robert C. Fuller, *Spiritual but Not Religious: Understanding Unchurched America* (Oxford: Oxford University Press, 2001).

[3] Globally, 2014, 2015, 2016 were the hottest years on record, each surpassing the prior. It is beyond refute that rising sea levels and extreme weather intensify our mutual predicament and, in the coming decades, will significantly confront and challenge our way of being, as individuals and as a human community living together on planet earth. We are redlining in every measurable statistic, from soil-depletion; to increasing levels of toxicity of the oceans; to the evaporation of glaciers and the resulting reduction of clean water for a third of the earth's population.

[4] See the writings of John of the Cross in *Selected Writings,* Classics of Western Spirituality, ed. Kieran Kavanaugh and Ernest E. Larkin (New York: Paulist Press, 1987). For a psychological application of these ideas see Gerald May, *The Dark Night of the Soul: A Psychiatrist Explores the Connection between Darkness and Spiritual Growth* (San Francisco: HarperSanFransisco, 2010).

[5] Keating develops this phrase extensively thorough out his writings.

[6] I am not the only observer who has drawn the connection. Professor Elaine A. Heath also describes the similarity: "The dark night is here, even now. While the sun sets on Christendom in the West, the saints, mystics and martyrs beckon to the church as a great cloud of witnesses, calling us to transformation. The church will persevere through the night and emerge alive on the other side, not because of church programs, but because God's love has kept [us]. But to get there, we need the wisdom of the mystics…" Elaine A. Heath, *The Mystic Way of Evangelism: A Contemplative Vision for Christian Outreach* (Grand Rapids, MI: Baker Academic, 2008), 27.

[7] Similarly, lost among Luther's *sola's* was the important dimension of depth and height that calls us forward in development toward *theosis*. Finnish Lutheran scholars have "rediscovered" the importance of Theosis in Luther's traditional understanding of Justification by faith alone. *Union with Christ: The New Finnish Interpretation of Luther,* eds. Carl E. Braaten and Robert W. Jenson (Grand Rapids: William B. Eerdmans Publishing Company, 1998). See also the classic work by Vladimir Lossky, *In the Image and Likeness of God* (Crestwood, NY: St. Vladimir's Seminary Press, 1974).

[8] For example, *Theosis: Deification in Christian Theology,* Vol. 1 & 2 in the Princeton Theological Monograph Series #156, ed., Stephen Finlan and Vladimir Kharlamov (Eugene, OR: Pickwick Publications, 2006 & 2011); *Partakers of the Divine Nature: The History and Development of Deification in the Christian Traditions,* ed. Michael J. Christensen and Jeffery A. Wittung (Grand Rapids: Baker Academic, 2011); Paul M. Collins, *Partaking in Divine Nature: Deification and Communion* (London: T&T Clark, 2012); Veli-Matti Karkkainen, *One With God: Salvation as Deification and Justification* (Collegeville, MN: Liturgical Press, 2004); Norman Russell, *Fellow Workers with God: Orthodox Thinking on Theosis* (Yonkers, NY: St. Vladimir's Seminary Press, 2009); Panayiotis Nellas, *Deification in Christ: Orthodox Perspectives on the Nature of the Human Person* (Yonkers, NY: St. Vladimir's Seminary Press, 1987); Norman Russell, *The Doctrine of Deification in the Greek Patristic Tradition* (Oxford: Oxford University Press, 2004).

[9] See Ilia Delio, *Making All Things New: Catholicity, Cosmology, Consciousness* (Maryknoll, NY: Orbis Books, 2015).

[10] In the quantum world, when a butterfly flaps its wings in the Amazon forest its flutter may trigger a tsunami in Taiwan. Or when a butterfly doesn't flap its wings in the Amazon forest its stillness in the quantum entanglement may trigger a blizzard in Kansas.

[11] For a more positive take on things, see Steven Pinker's extraordinary book *Enlightenment Now: The Case for Reason, Science, Humanism and Progress* (New York: Viking, 2018).

[12] Two extraordinary new books on silence are must-reads. First is Sarah, Robert Cardinal, *The Power of Silence: Against the Dictatorship of Noise* (San Fransisco: Igantius Press, 2017). Next is, George Prochnik's recent book, *In Pursuit of Silence: Listening for Meaning in a World of Noise* is a delightful tour of the complexities of noise in our culture. He concludes his book with a beautiful invitation arising from his interwoven definitions of noise, sound and silence: "The French philosopher Maurice Merleau-Ponty writes in his last book that perception is differentiation, while forgetting is non-differentiation. Earlier I took my stab at a definition of noise: sound that gets into your head and won't go away. It might be enjoyable or not enjoyable, but noise is sound that makes us, for the time it is there, cease to distinguish between the beings and objects outside us. Noise enables us to

forget the larger world. Conversely, if I were to hazard a definition of silence, I would describe it as the particular equilibrium of sound and quiet that catalyzes our powers of perception. Quiet is distinguished because it enables differentiation, and the more we observe the distinction between things, the less mental space we have for our isolate selves. It is not chance that even when we are talking about quieting our own voices, we speak of "observing" silence," as though just by being silent we create something to behold beyond the self. What's unknown, then, is the world around us; what's missing is our awareness that we don't know. Silence as a state of expectancy, a species of attention, is a key back into the garden of innocence. We may not stay. But God knows we listen for the sound of that opening." George Prochnik, *In Pursuit of Silence: Listening for Meaning in a World of Noise* (New York: Doubleday, 2010) 293.

[13] Cited in George Prochnik, *In Pursuit of Silence: Listening for Meaning in a World of Noise* (New York: Doubleday, 2010) 86.

[14] Ibid., 87.

[15] Raimon Pannikar, *The Rhythm of Being*, 323.

[16] Susan Cain's excellent book, *Quiet: The Power of Introverts in a World that Can't Stop Talking* helps us see the intrinsic, creative value of *not* being noisy. With a simple list, she suggests that without introverts and without quiet, our world-culture would be devoid of such important discoveries as the theory of gravity, and such cultural gifts as Charlie Brown and Harry Potter. Susan Cain, *Quiet: The Power of Introverts in a World that Can't Stop Talking* (New York: Crow Publishers, 2012), 5.

[17] World Population Prospectus, The 2015 Revision: Key Findings and Advance Tables. (New York: United Nations, Department of Economic and Social Affairs, Population Division), 2015.

http://esa.un.org/unpd/wpp/Publications/Files/Key_Findings_WPP_2015.pdf. Accessed August 22, 2015.

Today, Tokyo is the world's largest megacity, with 37 million people. The fastest growing megacity is Lagos, Nigeria. With a current population of 11 million, Lagos is projected to expand to 19 million by 2025. Indeed, half of the global population growth over the next forty years is projected to occur in Africa, which is currently on pace to more than triple its present population, topping four billion people by the end of this century.

[18] See for example Al Gore, *The Future: Six Drivers of Global Change* (New York: Random House, 2013).

[19] From now until 2050, half of the world's population growth is expected to be concentrated in nine countries: India, Nigeria, Pakistan, Democratic Republic of the Congo, Ethiopia, United Republic of Tanzania, United States of America, Indonesia and Uganda. Meanwhile by 2050, Europe's population will decrease from its 2015 levels. Contributing to this global population growth, is the rising ceiling of life expectancy. Globally, life expectancy at birth is projected to rise from seventy years in 2015 to seventy-seven years in 2050, and to eighty-three years in 2100.

[20] See Jon Kabat-Zinn, *Full Catastrophe Living: Using the Wisdom of Your Body and Mind to Face Stress, Pain and Illness* (New York: Bantam Books, 2013), 288ff.

[21] Data obtained from the web site https://gsmaintelligence.com/ accessed on July 30, 2018.

[22] For a Christian perspective on the importance and implications of evolutionary theory see the work of Ilia Delio, particularly *Making All Things New: Catholicity, Cosmology, Consciousness* (Maryknoll, NY: Orbis Books, 2015) and *The Unbearable Wholeness of Being: God, Evolution and the Power of Love* (Maryknoll, NY: Orbis Books, 2013).

[23] One example of how human consciousness is evolving with an increasing perspective on the nature of our existence, is our view of cosmology. Just twenty-six years after Martin Luther posted his ninety-five theses on the church doors in Wittenburg, Nicolas Copernicus published *De revolutionibus orbium coelestium (On the Revolutions of the Heavenly Spheres),* presenting a mathematical model of a sun-centered universe. This book "started" a scientific reformation that has slowly shifted our common conception away from what was, at the time, the dominant world view: an earth centered universe. Humankind has continued to expand our knowledge and understanding of the universe in profound ways since then. Of particular note are Edwin Hubble's cosmological observations in 1921 from the Hooker Telescope at the Mount Wilson Observatory in California. Hubble, drawing upon the insights of Georges Lemaître, observed the Redshift effect between nebula, revealing the expanding nature of the universe described in what has become known as Hubble's' Law. Appropriately, one of the most significant efforts of human endeavor that has forever changed our ability to see the universe we live in bears Hubble's name: the Hubble Telescope – a witness to the human spirit questing for its source. The telescope is, at this very moment, still capturing light and allowing us to see beyond sight the glory the heavens are telling. The implications of Copernicus' sun centered solar system sent unprecedented shock waves through Christianity, and indeed all of the monotheistic traditions. While our cosmology may have evolved since Copernicus, and while Christianity has completely adapted to the sun-centered reality of our solar system in theory, much of Christian theology and liturgical language, including our interpretation of scripture is still shaped by an earth centered view. This shows up most clearly in our theology of and language about God, who is often spoken of as dwelling "up there." It is evident in the popular conception of heaven being a place above the sky and hell being a place beneath the earth. In truth, Christianity has yet to integrate the massive shift of perspective that the expanding universe presents to us. No one can look at the images of earth from outer space and not be deeply moved by a sense of oneness, and reverence for our planet. All the more so when we look at images from the Hubble Telescope, revealing our own solar system, the Milky Way, awash as speck of light in an ocean of other systems. We have not yet evolved our religions of the book to the spiritual story the universe is declaring.

[24] Confucius and Lao-Tse were living in China; the Upanishads and Buddha; in Iran Zarathustra; in Palestine the prophets made their appearance from Elijah by way of Isaiah and Jeremiah; in Greece the appearance of Homer, of the philosophers Parmenides, Heraclitus and Plato, and the tragedies of Thucydides and Archimedes.

[25] See Charles Taylor, *A Secular Age* (Cambridge, MA: Harvard University Press, 2007).

[26] Phyllis Tickle's *The Great Emergence* aptly diagnoses the situation Christianity is facing. Tickle shows how major cultural shifts have occurred every 500 years, and compares the Great Reformation of the sixteenth century to the Great Emergence of the 21st Century.

It is an important historical survey, but the book lacks an answer to the question *so now what?* The book concludes with one brief page entitled "future possibilities," yet it leaves the reader, and especially the church, devoid of any next practical steps. See also Robert N. Bellah's magisterial *Religion in Human Evolution: From the Paleolithic to the Axial Age* (Cambridge, MA: The Belknap Press of Harvard University, 2011).

[27] Richard Madsen, "The Future of Transcendence" in *The Axial Age and Its Consequences, ed* Robert N. Bellah and Hans Joas (Cambridge, MA: The Belknap Press of Harvard University Press, 2012), 444.

[28] Richard Madsen, "The Future of Transcendence" in *The Axial Age and Its Consequences, ed* Robert N. Bellah and Hans Joas (Cambridge, MA: The Belknap Press of Harvard University Press, 2012), 444 – 445.

[29] If you are seeking a place to start in integrating evolutionary, developmental ideas into your frame of reference, I invite you to explore the following resources: Paul Smith, *Integral Christianity: The Spirit's Call to Evolve;* Jim Marion, *The Death of the Mythic God: The Rise of Evolutionary Spirituality;* Ilia Delio, *Making All Things News: Catholicity, Cosmology, Consciousness;* Cletus Wessels, *The Holy Web: Church and the New Universe Story.*

[30] See also Brother Benet Tvedten, *How to Be a Monastic and Not Leave Your Day Job* (Brewster, MA: Paraclete Press, 2011); Wes Markofski, *New Monasticism and the Transformation of American Evangelicalism* (Oxford: Oxford University Press, 2015); Ian Mobsby and Mark Berry, *A New Monastic Handbook: From Vision to Practice* (Norwich: Canterbury Press, 2014); Paul R. Dekar, *Community of the Transfiguration: The Journey of a New Monastic Community* (Eugene, OR: Cascade Books, 2008); Rory McEntee and Adam Bucko, *The New Monasticism: An Interspiritual Manifest for Contemplative Living* (Maryknoll, NY: Orbis Press, 2015); Christopher H. Martin, *The Restoration Project: A Benedictine Path to Wisdom, Strength, and Love* (Cincinnati, OH: Forward Movement, 2013); Anthony Grimley and Johnathan M. Wooding, *Living the Hours: Monastic Spirituality in Everyday Life* (Norwich: Canterbury Press, 2010).

[31] For a brief but helpful history of the recent influencers shaping new monasticism see Bernadette Flanagan, *Embracing Solitude: Women and New Monasticism* (Eugene, OR: Cascade Books, 2014), especially, 12ff.

[32] *Reveal: Where Are You?* (Barrington, IL: Willow Creek Association, 2008). The study revealed, among many things, that a quarter of the "close to Christ" and "Christ-centered" described themselves as spiritually "stalled" or "dissatisfied" with the role of the church in their spiritual growth. And nearly a quarter of the "stalled" segment and 63 percent of the "dissatisfied" segment had contemplated leaving the church.

[33] This admission became all the more tragic and telling in the light of Hybles' resignation, after allegations of sexual impropriety, again revealing a connection between a leader's lack of focus on spiritual depth, while maintaining a hyper attention on growth and success.

[34] Bill Hybles, "If I Were Planting a Church Today" interview by Cally Parkinson and Greg Hawkins in *Worship Leader,* May/June, 2013. Also accessed online at https://exponential.org/bill-hybels-how-i-would-plant-a-church-today/. Theologically and experientially,

a Centering Prayer practice helps reveal that Christ is *always* at the center – indeed, Christ is the center.

[35] See http://www.practicetribe.com.

[36] Phyllis Tickle, *The Great Emergence: How Christianity is Changing and Why* (Baker Books: Grand Rapids, MI, 2008), 159.
[37] Protestant mystics such as Karlstadt, Muntzer, Schwenckfeld and others, see Carter Lindberg, *The Third Reformation: Charismatic Movements and the Lutheran Tradition* (Macon, GA: Mercer University Press, 1983), particularly chapter One, "The Reformation of the Sixteenth Century" and the essay on "Luther and Experience: German Mysticism," 25ff.

[38] Luther and Calvin were not alone either in their appreciation of the contemplative/mystical dimension. Among the Lutherans, such stalwarts as Johann Arndt, Jakob Boehme, Valentin Weigel and Count von Zinzendorf stand with them. Among the Calvinists, Pierre Poiret and Gerhard Tersteegen. Among the Anglicans, William Law, William Blake, and the fathers of the Oxford renewal movement, Cardinal Newman and Pusey. Prior to the Reformation, and even fueling its popular unfolding, such contemplatives and mystics as Meister Eckhart, Johannes Tauler, and the *Devotio Moderna* communities clearly paved the way for the development of key themes that the Reformers cultivated and adapted for their own purposes. In unique ways, each of these spiritual teachers helped infuse contemplation into an over-rationalized church. See, *Theologica Germanica,* trans. Susanna Winkworth, (Mesa, AZ: Scriptoria Books, 2010).

[39] For more on the secularization theory and its critique, see especially Charles Taylor, particularly his *A Secular Age* (Cambridge, MA: Harvard University Press, 2007) and the writings of Mark C. Taylor, particularly *After God* (Chicago: The University of Chicago Press, 2007). See also Charles E. Winquist's essay on "Person" in *Critical Terms for Religious Studies,* ed. Mark C. Taylor (Chicago: University of Chicago Press, 1998), 225 – 238. Winquist notes that, "Paradoxically, the Reformation enfranchised the concept of the self by putting the self into question." The Reformation was an evolutionary unfolding in human consciousness, which came to be expressed primarily in the rise of democracy and the freedom of the individual, and the dignity of human rights and equality for all.

[40] See for example, Carter Lindberg, *The Third Reformation: Charismatic Movements and the Lutheran Tradition* (Macon, GA: Mercer University Press, 1983), and especially Donald G. Bloesch, excellent and brief summary of Protestant spiritual communities Wellsprings of Renewal: Promise in the Christian Communal Life (Grand Rapids, MI: Eerdmans Publishing Company, 1973), particularly chapter Four, "Attempts to Recover Community Life" and chapter five, "The Community Revival in Europe." And Edward Howells' useful essay, "Early Modern Reformations" in *The Cambridge Companion to Christian Mysticism,* ed. Amy Hollywood and Patricia Z. Beckman (Cambridge, Cambridge University Press, 2012), 114 – 134.

[41] See especially the luminously helpful book by Arthur Herrman, *The Cave and the Light: Plato Versus Aristotle, and the Struggle for the Soul of Western Civilization* (New York: Random House, 2014).

[42] For an authoritative survey of the historical eclipse of the contemplative see Louis *Dupré, Passage to Modernity: An Essay in the Hermeneutics of Nature and Culture* (New Haven: Yale University Press, 1993).

[43] This is not the first time the church has gone deeper in order to move forward. Let's briefly consider the well documented fact that the Reformation was empowered by mystical, contemplative theology. Church historian and scholar Steven E. Ozment has written an exceptional overview of the connections between the contemplative/mystical dimensions of Christianity and the Reformation movements. In Ozment's *Mysticism and Dissent: Religious Ideology and Social Protest in the Sixteenth Century*, he suggests that, "The mystical way of salvation is paradigmatic of the operative value judgements. According to Eckhart and Tauler, true self-realization entails the suspension of normal rational and volitional activities, a shutting down of the regular processes of the soul. The latter are immobilized and cut off from the external world. For a moment, the soul surrenders its accustomed routine and takes refuge in its self-sufficient inner ground. With the collapse of the normal activities of the soul follows...the irrelevance of everything the visible world has to offer, whether it be of good or of ill. One is above popes and kings, beyond sacraments and laws, immune to worldly praise and condemnation. Even if the experience (or the theory) does not issue in dissent, reform, or revolutionary activity, it uniquely drives home the ideological prerequisite for such, viz. an understanding of the penultimate character of all worldly power and authority. In the mystical traditions, quietism is no less negative a judgement on established power than violent revolution. Mystical salvation is the discovery of the final power and authority of the Self within one's own self. Medieval mystical writings uniquely contain the raw material of dissent..." Steven E. Ozment, *Mysticism and Dissent: Religious Ideology and Social Protest in the Sixteenth Century* (New Haven, CT: Yale University Press, 1973), 12. For more in depth background on these important historical, social and theological themes, see also L.W. Spitz, *The Renaissance and Reformation Movements,* Vol. 2 (Saint Louis: Concordia Publishing House, 1987); Heiko A. Oberman, *The Harvest of Medieval Theology* (Cambridge, MA: Harvard University Press, 1963), and Heiko A.Oberman, "The Shape of Late Medieval Thought: The Birthpangs of the Modern Era," in Archive for Reformation History, Vol. 64, December, 1973, 13 – 33.

[44] For an insightful overview on why the Protestant Reformers opposed Monasticism, see Dennis Okholm, *Monk Habits for Everyday People: Benedictine Spirituality for Protestants* (Grand Rapids: Brazos Press, 2007), particularly "Historical Afterword," the closing essay in the book, 115 – 129.

[45] Commenting on Calvin's doctrine of union, Ronald Wallace reflects on this beautiful, important, yet often overlooked Reformed perspective: "The nature and reality of this 'mystical union' of the Church with Christ in human nature or flesh Calvin regards as one of the great mysteries of the Gospel. It is a real and substantial union by which believers living 'out of themselves' thus live in Christ. By means of it Christ becomes 'of one substance' with us and we become 'bone of His bone and flesh of His flesh.' Yet it is at the same time essentially a spiritual union effected by the power of the Holy Ghost in such a way that there is no 'gross mixture' of Christ and ourselves. Moreover, this union is effected by faith alone and cannot be experienced apart from faith. Yet it is effected also by the Sacraments, which are given to faith and which must be regarded as concrete and visible means whereby we are brought into this union." Ronald S. Wallace, *Calvin's Doctrine of Christian Life* (Eugene, OR: Wipf and Stock Publishers, 1997), 17 – 18.

[46] Martin Luther, *Luther's Works*, Vol.26, *Commentary on Galatians*, ed. J. J. Pelikan, H. C. Oswald & H. T. Lehmann [CD-ROM] (Saint Louis: Concordia Publishing House, 1999), 168.

[47] John Calvin, *Institutes of the Christian Religion,* ed. John T. McNeill, trans. Ford Lewis Battles, 3.11.10 (Philadelphia: The Westminster Press, 1960), 736 – 737. For more on Calvin's doctrine of Christian life see Ronald S. Wallace, *Calvin's Doctrine of Christian Life* (Eugene, OR: Wipf and Stock Publishers, 1997) and John H. Leith's *John Calvin's Doctrine of the Christian Life* (Louisville, KY: Westminster/John Knox Press, 1989). Calvin believed that a union with God through Christ occurred, but he disagreed with Osiander, who taught that it was a union of essence. Rather, Calvin taught that we are united to Christ by the secret energy of the Holy Spirit.

[48] Cited in Ronald S. Wallace, *Calvin's Doctrine of Christian Life* (Eugene, OR: Wipf and Stock Publishers, 1997), 17.

Opening Quotes

[1] Plotinus, *The Essential Plotinus.* trans. E. O'Brian (Indianapolis: IN, 1964), 42.

[2] Anonymous, *Meditations on The Tarot: A Journey into Christian Hermeticisim* (Jeremy P. archer / Penguin: New York, 2020), 37.

Chapter Three / *Defining*

[1] The concept of inwardness was famously developed by Emmerson whose conception of the spiritual life was based on three interrelated principles: inwardness, unity and right action. Inwardness to Emmerson was "the awareness of and reverence for the unique though, perception, intuition, and emotional response that define our experience." See Ralph Waldo Emerson, *The Spiritual Emerson: Essential Writings,* ed. David M. Robinson (Boston: Beacon Press, 2003), 2ff. The history of inwardness is beautifully explored by Charles Taylor in his classic *Sources of the Self: The Making of the Modern Identity* (Cambridge, MA: Harvard University Press, 1989).

[2] For a delightful overview of spiritual trajectory of inwardness in multiple traditions see Gavin Flood, *The Truth Within: A History of Inwardness in Christianity, Hinduism, Buddhism* (Oxford: Oxford University Press, 2013).

[3] St. Augustine, *Confessions,* 7: xvii.

[4] St. Augustine intimated this is his sermons on the Eucharist, such as "What you receive is what you yourselves are" (Sermon, 229a.2) and "Be what you can see and receive what you are" (Sermon 272).

[5] Interestingly, just change the vowels and "I con-sent" becomes "I can-sit."

[6] Adapted from Cyprian Consiglio, *Prayer in The Cave of The Heart: The Universal Call to Contemplation* (Collegeville, MN: Liturgical Press, 2010), 50.

[7] For an insightful and brief essay on this see Bruno Barnhart's and Joseph H. Wong's *Introduction* in the book *Purity of Heart and Contemplation: A Monastic Dialogue Between Christian and Asian Traditions* (New York: Continuum, 2001), especially pages 4 – 5.

[8] See Tom Chetwynd, *Zen and The Kingdom of Heaven: Reflections on the Tradition of Meditation in Christianity and Zen Buddhism* (Somerville, MA: Wisdom Publications, 2001) for an excellent comparison, especially chapters 4 – 7.

[9] For a helpful treatment on both Meditation and Contemplation see Michael Casey, *Toward God: The Ancient Wisdom of Western Prayer* (Liguori, MO: Triumph Books, 1996), as well as Casey's, *The Undivided Heart: The Western Monastic Approach to Contemplation* (Petersham, Mass. 1994).

[10] For a very helpful overview of contemplative prayer, meditation and Centering Prayer see Basil Pennington's masterful *Daily We Touch Him: Practical Religious Experiences* (Kansas City, MO: Sheed & Ward, 1997), particularly chapters 2 – 5.

[11] See the *Catechism of the Catholic Church*, 2nd ed. (Vatican: Libreria Editrice Vaicana,1997).

[12] Anonymous, *Meditations on The Tarot: A Journey into Christian Hermeticisim* (New York: Jeremy P. archer / Penguin, 2002), 456.

[13] The main point I am seeking to convey is that, over the centuries, contemplation has become more than simply "thinking about God." While contemplation involves theology, it is not seeking to be a branch of theological inquiry. In essence, contemplation is the practical art of theology: the perception and deepening experience of God and self through the cultivation of one's purity of heart (Matthew 5.8). After centuries of faith seeking understanding, by the twenty-first century much of what we mean by doing theology or thinking about God is limited to the term *theoretical* spirituality, in contrast to the invitation of the contemplative way, which is best conveyed by the term *participative* spirituality. Perhaps these terms can update the older, classical categories of dogmatic theology and mystical theology.

[14] Francis de Sales, *Treatise on the Love of God*, Book VI, chapter 3.

[15] Ibid.

[16] For an incomparable overview of contemplation see Butler, Cuthbert, *Western Mysticism: Augustine, Gregory and Bernard on Contemplation and the Contemplative Life* (Mineola, MN: Dover Publications, 2003).

[20] For a lovely overview of the history of Christian contemplation, see Kathleen Lynch's helpful chapter, "The Crown of Contemplative Prayer" in her book, *The Sublime Round Tower: An Iconic Call to Contemplative Prayer* (Dublin: Thc Columba Prcss, 2013).

[21] John Cassian, *Conferences* 10, 7.

[22] Ibid., 9, 25

[23] Ibid., 9, 35.

[24] Thomas Aquinas, *Summa Theologica,* II-II, 180, a. 3 & 4 (Benziger Bros.: New York, 1948).

[25] John of the Cross, *The Dark Night*, Chapter 17, 2.

[26] St. John of the Cross, *The Dark Night,* Book II, Chapter 18.

[27] John of the Cross, *The Ascent of Mount Carmel,* 125.

[28] Also called mystical union. In Teresa's model there were four degrees or stages of mystical union: 1.) Incomplete mystical union, or the prayer of quiet or supernatural recollection. 2). Full or semi-ecstatic union. 3. Ecstatic union, or ecstasy. 4). Transforming or deifying union, or spiritual marriage of the soul with God. In fact, the monastic tradition has multiple ways of speaking about the same kinds of experiences in prayer, such as: The prayer in secret, The prayer of the heart, The prayer of pure faith, The prayer of simplicity, The prayer of silence, The prayer of simple regard, Active recollection, and Acquired contemplation.

[29] Let's make the point even clearer. What I am seeking to articulate is that at the same time contemplation is open to anyone, there is a distinction in function beyond semantics between concentration, meditation and contemplation. No doubt the concepts are fluid, even now evolving through cultural usage and shaped by communities of practioners.

[30] An important fact to acknowledge is that monastics and monasteries aren't necessarily contemplatives, and contemplatives are not necessarily monastics. In fact, many monastic communities are so busy praying the psalms that they don't create space for communal silent prayer. Silent prayer is left for the individual monk, alone in his or her room. Both historically, and in the present time, it is less common for monastic communities to gather together for periods of meditative, wordless, contemplative prayer. The primary prayer methods in monasteries tend to be the Prayer of the Hours, which is scripture based, and the meditative prayer that arises during the practice of *lectio divina*. While silence is an essential atmosphere in every monastery that does not mean that the monks are practicing wordless, contemplative prayer as a whole or even as individuals.

[31] *Catechism of the Catholic Church*, 2nd ed. (Vatican: Libreria Editrice Vaicana, 1997), 872.

[32] Richard Rohr, *Silent Compassion: Finding God in Contemplation* (Cincinnati, OH: Franciscan Media, 2014), 54.

[33] Thomas Merton, *"What is Contemplation?"* (Springfield, IL: Templegate Publishers, 1981), 36 – 39.

[34] Daniel P. Barbezat and Mirabai Bush, Contemplative Practices in Higher Education: *Powerful Methods to Transform Teaching and Learning* (San Fransisco: Jossey-Bass, 2014), 21.

[35] Josef Sudbrack, *"Contemplation"* in *Encyclopedia Christianity, A – D* (Grand Rapids: Eerdmans, 1999), 677 – 678.

[36] Raimon Panikkar, *Blessed Simplicity,* 45.

[37] Putting all this together, I appreciate how Denis Renevey summarized contemplation as: 1). A private cultivation of a loving relationship with God. 2). A humble receptivity to the

scrutiny of God. And 3). An awareness or desire for the journey into God. See Denis Renevey, "Mysticism and the Vernacular" in *The Wiley-Blackwell Companion to Christian Mysticism*, ed. Julia A. Lamm (West Sussex, UK: Wiley-Blackwell, 2013), 565.

[38] For an extraordinary overview of the place of contemplation in Christian mysticism see Friedrich Heiler's comprehensive essay, "Contemplation in Christian Mysticism" in *Spiritual Disciplines: Papers from the Eranos Yearbooks,* Bollingen Series XXX. Vol. 4, ed. Joseph Campbell (Princeton, NJ: Princeton University Press, 1960).

Chapter Four / *Deepening*

[1] For exceptional treatment of these women, see the series "Classics of Western Spirituality". For example, Marguerite Porete, *Mirror of Simple Souls,* trans. Ellen L. Babinsky (New York: Paulist Press, 1993).

[2] Origen, *Commentary on the Song of Songs.*

[3] Cited in Harvey D. Egan, *An Anthology of Christian Mysticism*, 2nd ed. (Collegeville, MN: Liturgical Press, 1996), 26.

[4] William Harmless, *Desert Christians: An Introduction to the Literature of Early Monasticism* (Oxford: Oxford University Press, 2004), 351.

[5] Basil Pennington, *Daily We Touch Him: Practical Religious Experiences* (Kansas City, MO: Sheed & Ward, 1997), particularly chapters 2 – 5.

[6] For further discussion on this early monastic literature, see Andrew Louth, "The Literature of the Monastic Movement" in *The Cambridge History of Early Christian Literature*, ed. France Young, Lewis Ayres and Andrew Louth (Cambridge: Cambridge University Press, 2004), 373 – 381, especially pp. 373 – 376.

[7] Evagrius, *De oration* 57, trans. William Harmless.

[8] Evagrius, *De oration* 35.

[9] William Harmless, *Desert Christians: An Introduction to the Literature of Early Monasticism* (Oxford: Oxford University Press, 2004), 352.

[10] Evagrius, *Sekemmata* 27.

[11] Evagrius, *Scholia in Psalm* 126.2.

[12] William Harmless summarizes the process like this: "We can piece together Evagrius's basic view. During pure prayer, the purified mind sees itself, its truest self, and its true state. And the self that it sees is luminous. But that luminosity which permits it to see itself is the divine light. In seeing itself as luminosity, as light like sapphire or sky blue, the mind discovers its Godlikeness. At the same time, it sees and knows by seeing – indirectly, as in a mirror – the uncreated, immaterial light that God is. That is why for Evagrius prayer is at once a moment of self-discovery and an encounter with ultimate mystery: 'Prayer is the state of the mind that comes to be from the single-light of the Holy Trinity.'" William

Harmless, *Desert Christians: An Introduction to the Literature of Early Monasticism* (Oxford: Oxford University Press, 2004), 354, citing Evagrius's *Skemmata* 27.

[13] William Harmless, *Desert Christians: An Introduction to the Literature of Early Monasticism* (Oxford: Oxford University Press, 2004), 393.

[14] John Cassian, *Conferences* 10.13.1-2, trans. Boniface Ramsey, Ancient Christian Writers, The Works of the Fathers in Translation, No. 57 (New York: Newman Press, 1997), 385 – 386; though I quoted Harmless' version of the translated text by Colin Luibheid in the CWS 1985 version. See William Harmless, *Desert Christians: An Introduction to the Literature of Early Monasticism* (Oxford: Oxford University Press, 2004), 393 – 394.

[15] John Cassian, *Conferences* 10.10.2, trans. Boniface Ramsey, Ancient Christian Writers, The Works of the Fathers in Translation, No. 57 (New York: Newman Press, 1997), 379.

[16] William Harmless, *Desert Christians: An Introduction to the Literature of Early Monasticism* (Oxford: Oxford University Press, 2004), 396.

[17] John Cassian, *Conferences* 10.11.6, trans. Boniface Ramsey, Ancient Christian Writers, The Works of the Fathers in Translation, No. 57 (New York: Newman Press, 1997), 385.

[18] Harmless summarizes Cassian's multiple statements and quotations about this state in one profound paragraph. For Cassian, these spiritual peak experiences are: "brief, passing; they are graced, not earned, given as the secret and hidden dispensation of God; they feel like out-of-body experiences, or like awakening from a deep sleep; one sees earthly realities as mere smoke and an empty shadow and glimpses the future; one's mind tastes enlightenment, an infusion of heavenly light, while one's heart brims and gushes forth as from a most abundant fountain." William Harmless, *Desert Christians: An Introduction to the Literature of Early Monasticism* (Oxford: Oxford University Press, 2004), 397.

[19] John Cassian, *Conferences* 9.15.2, trans. Boniface Ramsey, Ancient Christian Writers, The Works of the Fathers in Translation, No. 57 (New York: Newman Press, 1997), 339.

[20] *Conferences* 9.15.2.

[21] *Conferences,* 9.2.

[22] Columba Steward, "Benedictine Monasticism and Mysticism" in *The Wiley-Blackwell Companion to Christian Mysticism*, ed. Julia A. Lamm (West Sussex, UK: Wiley-Blackwell, 2013), 222.

[23] For an informative commentary on the Confessions see James J. O'Donnell, *Augustine Confessions:* Commentary on Books 1 – 7, II (Oxford: Clarendon Press, 1992).

[24] Yet Augustine ultimately grew doubtful about the appropriateness of a purely contemplative life.

[25] *Confessions*, Book 7, 10.

[26] *Confessions*, Book 7, 17.

[27] See St. Gregory the Great, *Homilies, Ezekiel 2.2.8.*

[28] Also, Gregory's *Dialogues* and *Moralia on Job* are compendiums of ascetical and mystical theology.

[29] *Moralia* 6.42.

[30] Columba Stewart, "Benedictine Monasticism and Mysticism" in *The Wiley-Blackwell Companion to Christian Mysticism*, ed. Julia A. Lamm (West Sussex, UK: Wiley-Blackwell, 2013) 229. For the original text, see Gregory's *Homilies on Ezekiel* I. 10, 29, II.1.16 – 18. II.5.9.

[31] Gregory the Great, *Life of Moses.* Emphasis mine.

[32] For a helpful overview of Hugh's perspective on contemplation see, Matthew R. McWhorter's essay, "Hugh of St. Victor on Contemplative Meditation" in The Heythrop Journal, Vol. LV, (Oxford: John Wiley and Sons, 2014), 110 – 122.

[33] Perhaps this new phase of awakening is a nod to the influence of Augustine.

[34] Grover Zinn helps us understand the immense contribution the Victorines made to the contemplative tradition and its wider interpretation of mystical theology and experience: "The contemplative experience represents humankind's original non-discursive inner awareness of God's presence. As created, humans had three 'eyes': the eye of the understanding to see divine things; the eye of reason to see the self within; the eye of sense to behold the world. In the fall the eye of the understanding was blinded, reason was weakened, and only sense remained intact. Christ represents a new second 'external' approach to God to humans. Calling people outwardly and healing them through the sacraments, Christ shows the way and provides the goal for the contemplative's quest. Hugh, like Richard later, likens the image of God within to a mirror that is obscured by sin and cleansed by discipline with result that the presence of God again shines within the individual through the image beheld by the eyes of the understanding. The ecstatic, unific, and transforming aspects of the contemplative experience can be seen in the iconography of the stages of illumination. Illumination overcomes ignorance, which Hugh depicts as a person breaking a vase, thus representing the fragmentation of knowledge in the fall. The first stage, cognition or thought, gazes at a book open to the words of Genesis 1:1. Which indicates that the purified mind can now again read the 'book' of the created world. Meditation, which Hugh understands as concentrated attention to a single matter and as a state of withdrawn interiorized reflection, begins to gather up the pieces of the shattered vase. Finally, contemplation, symbolized by a craftsman, melts the fragments with the flame of divine love and sends the liquid into…Christ in the center…where the lost likeness to God is recovered….In this image, Hugh captures multiple aspects of contemplation: passage beyond one's ordinary state (ecstasy), reforming of the lost image/likeness, and unification with Christ, the center." Grover A. Zinn, *The Regular Canons* in Bernard McGinn, John Meyendorff, and Jean Leclercq (eds.), *Christian Spirituality: Origins to the Twelfth Century* (New York: Crossroad Publishing Company, 1988), 222 – 223.

[35] Dale M. Coulter, "Contemplative Life," in *The Encyclopedia of Christian Civilization*, ed. George Thomas Kurian (Oxford: Wiley-Blackwell, 2012), 598.

[36] Grover A. Zinn, *The Regular Canons* in Bernard McGinn, John Meyendorff, and Jean Leclercq (eds.), *Christian Spirituality: Origins to the Twelfth Century* (New York: Crossroad Publishing Company, 1988), 225 – 226. Zinn expertly summarizes that for Richard, contemplation is a, "distinctive mode of awareness, a beholding defined by inherent qualities, not by the object contemplated....the degree of contemplation id defined by the way something becomes known...Contemplation itself is defined as a beholding with wonder and amazement in an expansive, intuitive grasp of things. It is non-discursive and non-analytical; it is awareness in a state of complete inner quiet, rest and reception. There are three modes of contemplation: (1) enlargement of the mind, (2) raising up of the mind, and (3) alienation of the mind or ecstasy. Enlargement of the mind is the fruit of human effort, a kind of contemplation that can be learned...Raising up of the mind involves human effort and divine grace together, the latter granting a visionary experience to the mystic...Alienation of the mind, or ecstasy, is the third mode and has three causes: greatness of devotion, greatness of wonder, and greatness of exultation. In the first, the fire of divine love is kindled with such force that ecstasy results. In the second, a visionary experience impels the mind to an ecstatic state. In the third, the mind becomes inebriated with an interior sweetness that leads to ecstasy. In each of these cases there is something that can be called a 'trigger' that initiates a breakthrough to a special level of awareness."

[37] I adapted this quip from Steven Fanning, *Mystics of the Christian Tradition* (New York: Routledge, 2001), 139.

[38] For a very helpful and concise overview of Christian mysticism, see Julia A. Lamm's introductory essay "A Guide to Christian Mysticism" in *The Wiley-Blackwell Companion to Christian Mysticism*, ed. Julia A. Lamm (West Sussex, UK: Wiley-Blackwell, 2013), 1 – 23. And also Oliver Clément, *The Roots of Christian Mysticism: Texts from the Patristic Era with Commentary*, 2nd Edition. (New York: New City Press, 1993). And the incomparable Butler, Cuthbert, *Western Mysticism: Augustine, Gregory and Bernard on Contemplation and the Contemplative Life* (Mineola, MN: Dover Publications, 2003).

[39] For an overview, see David B. Perrin's excellent and comprehensive essay "Mysticism" in *The Blackwell Companion to Christian Spirituality*, ed. Arthur Holder (Oxford: Blackwell Publishers, 2005), 442 – 458, and also Harvey D. Egan, *Soundings in the Christian Mystical Tradition* (Collegeville, MN: Liturgical Press, 2010), or Carl McColman, *The Big Book of Christian Mysticism: The Essential Guide to Contemplative Spirituality* (Charlottesville, VA: Hampton Roads Publishing Company, 2010).

[40] For a helpful essay on the role of mysticism leading up to the Reformation see Lewis W. Spitz's chapter two, "The Church in Crisis," subheading "Mysticism" in his book *The Renaissance and Reformation Movements,* revised edition, Volume 1: The Renaissance (St. Louis, MO: Concordia Publishing House, 1987), beginning on page 38.

[41] Karl Rahner, *The Practice of Faith: A Handbook of Contemporary Spirituality* (New York: Crossroad, 1983), 22.

[42] Alongside this renaissance, has also followed a robust and critical scholarly conversation, not always in support of mystical experiences. Consider such watershed works as: Steven T. Katz's collection of essays in *Mysticism and Philosophical Analysis* (London: Sheldon Press, 1978); Wayne Proudfoot, *Religious Experience* (Berkeley: University of California Press, 1985).

[43] Christian mysticism is essentially an updated term for what was known in the Roman Catholic Church as "mystical theology."

[44] Bernard McGinn, *The Presence of God: A History of Western Christian Mysticism,* 5 Vols. (New York: Crossroad, 1991).

[45] For an example of McGinn's influence and the renewal of mysticism studies, see the comprehensive collection of essays on mysticism and Christian history available in *The Wiley-Blackwell Companion to Christian Mysticism*, ed. Julia A. Lamm (West Sussex, UK: Wiley-Blackwell, 2013).

[46] In 1902, William James famously delineated four aspects of religious mystical experiences. They are: 1). Ineffable. 2). Noetic. 3). Transitory. 4). Passive. See William James, *Varieties of Religious Experience,* "Mysticism," Lectures XVI and XVII. Similarly, in 1910, Evelyn Underhill characterized the four aspects of true mysticism as: 1). Practical. 2). Transcendental. 3). Mystic as Lover. 4). Divine Union as goal. See Evelyn Underhill, *Mysticism,* Part One, chapter four "The Characteristics of Mysticism."

[47] For a good example of this, see Adolphe Tanquerey, *The Spiritual Life: A Treatise on Ascetical and Mystical Theology,* trans. Herman Branderis, (Charlotte, NC: TAN Books, 2000). And *The Graces of Interior Prayer* by Father Augustin Poulain.

[48] See Leigh Eric Schmidt's important historical overview in his essay "Mysticism in the Anglo-American World" in *The Wiley-Blackwell Companion to Christian Mysticism*, ed. Julia A. Lamm (West Sussex, UK: Wiley-Blackwell, 2013), 452 – 472.

[49] For more on this see Louis Bouyer's essay "Mysticism: An Essay on the History of the Word," in *Understanding Mysticism*, ed. Richard Woods (Garden City, NJ: Image Books, 1980), 42 – 55.

[50] For more on this see, Louis Bouyer's classic work, *The Christian Mystery: From Pagan Myth to Christian Mysticism.* Bouyer provides four chapters of essential reading for anyone wishing to get a deeper grasp on the history of Christian contemplation, and its relationship with Christian mysticism. Bouyer's four succinct chapters are a much faster read than Bernard McGinn's multi-volume masterpiece on the history of Christian mysticism. You will be blessed to read Bouyer, starting with chapter fourteen, "*Mystical Contemplation According to the Father*"; chapter fifteen, "*Philosophy and Mysticism*"; chapter sixteen, "*The Development of Mysticism in the Church Fathers*", and finally chapter seventeen, "*The Development of Mysticism in the Medieval West.*"

[51] Bernard McGinn, *The Presence of God: A History of Western Christian Mysticism,* Vol 3: *The Flowering of Mysticism: Men and Women in the New Mysticism, 1200 – 1350* (New York: Crossroad, 1998), 26.

[52] Ibid. Evelyn Underhill also reflects beautifully on the meaning of the word mysticism: "One of the most abused words in the English language, it has been used in different and often mutually exclusive senses by religion, poetry and philosophy: has been claimed as an excuse for every kind of occultism, diluted transcendentalism, vapid symbolism, religious sentimentality and bad metaphysics. On the other hand, it has freely been employed as a term of contempt...It is much to be hoped that it may be restored sooner or later to its old meaning, as the science or art of the spiritual life" (Evelyn Underhill, *Mysticism,* xiv).

[53] For a meaningful scholarly conversation on the emergence of the innateness of mysticism, see *The Innate Capacity: Mysticism, Psychology and Philosophy*, ed Robert K. C. Forman (Oxford: Oxford University Press, 1998).

[54] See Pseudo-Dionysius, *Mystical Theology.*

[55] *Dark Night of the Soul, II, 23, 11.*

[56] For example, Marguerite Porete, *Mirror of Simple Souls,* trans. Ellen L. Babinsky (New York: Paulist Press, 1993).

[57] William Franke, *On What Cannot Be Said: Apophatic Discourses in Philosophy, Religion, Literature, and the Arts,* Vol. 1 Classic Formulations, ed. William Franke, (Notre Dame, IN: University of Notre Dame Press, 2007), 5.

[58] For more background on the apophatic tradition and its relationship to mystical theology see Andrew Louth's excellent essay "Apophatic and Cataphatic Theology" in *The Cambridge Companion to Christian Mysticism*, ed. Amy Hollywood and Patricia Z. Beckman (Cambridge, Cambridge University Press, 2012), 137 – 146.

[59] It is important to note that mysticism can be both *apophatic* (the way of negation) and *kataphatic* (the way of affirmation). Where apophatic theology describes what God is *not*, kataphatic theology describes what God *is. Apophatic,* referring to the way of negation as it relates to speaking about God, was formally introduced into Christian theology in the early sixth-century by the anonymous author known as Pseudo-Dionysius. However, the apophatic tradition pre-dated Christianity. The roots of the apophatic perspective can be found in both the Hebrew Scriptures and in Greek philosophy. For our purposes here, William Franke, provides an ideal summary of *apophasis,* especially as it relates to Christian mysticism: "In its original employment, 'apophasis' is simply the Greek word for 'negation.' Neoplatonists, followed by monotheistic writers, extend the term to mean the negation of speech...vis-à-vis what exceeds all possibilities of expression whatsoever: for them apophatic discourses consist in words that negate themselves in order to evoke what is beyond words – and indeed beyond the limits of language altogether...Apophasis also carries a more potent, theological sense of negation that is informed ultimately by the divine transcendence: it indicates an utter incapacity of language to grasp what infinitely exceeds it, a predicament of being surpassed irremediably by what it cannot say, 'Apophasis' reads etymologically, moreover, as 'away from speak' or 'saying *away*' (*apo,* 'from' or 'away from'; *phasis,* 'assertion,' from *phemi,* 'assert' or 'say'), and this points in the direction of *un*saying and ultimately of silence as virtuosities of language that tend to underlie and subvert any discursively articulable meaning. The ultimate apophatic expression is silence, a silence that stretches in tension toward...what cannot be said. Only this negation of saying by silence 'says'...what cannot be said. Nevertheless, apophasis constitutes a paradoxically rich and various genre of discourse. The methods and modes of silence are legion, and numerous new forms of expression of it burst forth in almost every period of cultural history." Excerpted from William Franke, *On What Cannot Be Said: Apophatic Discourses in Philosophy, Religion, Literature, and the Arts,* Vol. 1 Classic Formulations, ed. William Franke, (Notre Dame, IN: University of Notre Dame Press, 2007), 2.

[60] John Ruusbroec, *The Adornment of Spiritual Marriage.*

[61] See Bernadette Roberts, *The Path to No-Self: Life at the Center* (Albany, NY: State University of New York Press, 1991) and Bernadette Roberts, *The Experience of No-Self: A Contemplative Journey,* Revised Edition (Albany, NY: State University of New York Press, 1993).

[62] Bernadette Roberts, *The Experience of No-Self: A Contemplative Journey,* Revised Edition (Albany, NY: State University of New York Press, 1993), 209 – 211.

[63] Catherine de Hueck Doherty, *Poustinia: Encountering God in Silence, Solitude and Prayer* (Combermere, ON: Madonna House Publications, 2001).

[64] As we review the treasures of the Christian mystics and their experiences with contemplative prayer, I wish to at least mention two other major themes that the mystical dimension of Christianity has woven together throughout the centuries: *union* and *ascent.* Each of these important and related themes is further explored in such excellent compendiums as Denys Turner's, *The Darkness of God* and William Franke's two volume anthology, *On What Cannot Be Said.* Useful launching pads for deeper study of this essential subject of universal spiritual experience.

Chapter Five / *Centering*

[1] Bernard McGinn, "*The Intersection of Time and Eternity*" in Insights: The Faculty Journal of Austin Seminary, Spring, 2011 Vol. 126, No. 2, 6.

[2] The phrase center comes to circumference is inspired by a statement G.I. Gurdjieff is recorded to have said at a Christmas talk.

[3] See maxim two from *The Book of Twenty-Four Philosophers*: http://themathesontrust.org/papSeers/metaphysics/XXIV-A4.pdf. Accessed September 28, 2015.

[4] Meister Eckhart, *Latin Sermon LV.3.*

[5] Marguerite Porete, *Mirror of Simple Souls,* trans. Ellen L. Babinsky (New York: Paulist Press, 1993).

[6] Grover A. Zinn, *The Regular Canons* in Bernard McGinn, John Meyendorff, and Jean Leclercq, eds., *Christian Spirituality: Origins to the Twelfth Century* (New York: Crossroads Publishing, 1986), 223.

[7] Thomas Keating, *Spirituality, Contemplation and Transformation: Writings on Center Prayer* (New York: Lantern Books, 2008), 2 – 3.

[8] *Conferences,* 132.

[9] *Praktikos,* 75.

Opening Quotes

[1] Alasdair MacIntyre, *After Virtue*, Third Edition (Notre Dame: University of Notre Dame Press, 2007), 263.

---

[2] Brendan Freeman, *Come and See: The Monastic Way for Today (*Trappist, KY: Cistercian Publications, 2010), 22.

Chapter Six / *Practicing*

[1] For a few examples of the vastness of the subject see Andrew Louth, *The Wilderness of God* (Nashville, TN: Abingdon Press, 1991) and *The Paradise of the Holy Fathers,* Vol. 1 and Vol. 2, trans. E.A. Wallis Budge (St. Shenouda Coptic Orthodox Monastery: Putty, NSW, 2009).

[2] For a beautiful and insightfully brief history of early monasticism see Helen Waddell's introductory essay in *The Desert Fathers,* trans. Helen Waddell (New York: Vintage Books, 1998), 3 – 29. For fine modern overviews, see also Alexander Ryrie, *The Desert Movement: Fresh Perspectives on the Spirituality of the Desert* (Norwich, UK: Canterbury Press, 2011. And John Chryssavgis, *In the Heart of the Desert: The Spirituality of the Desert Fathers and Mothers* (Bloomington, IN: World Wisdom, 2008).

[3] The most famous of monastic rules is St. Benedict's, but Romulad's is briefer. Rule can readily be found on the Internet such as at: https://en.wikipedia.org/wiki/Romuald.

[4] For a similar book that invites the church to integrate a rule of life and key monastic practices, see Anthony Grimley and Johnathan M. Wooding, *Living the Hours: Monastic Spirituality in Everyday Life* (Norwich: Canterbury Press, 2010).

[5] In recent years, several books have helped congregations explore the spiritual practices, such as Marjorie Thompson's *Soul Feast: An Invitation to the Christian Spiritual Life* (Louisville, KY: Westminster John Knox Press, 2014) and Charles Cummings *Monastic Practices* (Collegeville, MN: Liturgical Press, 2008). I particularly like Bruce Davis, *Monastery without Walls: Daily Life in the Silence* (Lincoln, NE: Authors Choice Press, 2001).

[6] *Rule of Benedict,* 48.4, 10, 14, 17, 22.

[7] Guigo II, *Ladder of Monks and Twelve Meditations,* trans. Edmund Colledge and James Walsh, (Kalamazoo, MI: Cistercian Publications, 1979).

[8] Janet K. Ruffing, "Meditation: Christian Perspectives" in *Encyclopedia of Monasticism*, ed. William M. Johnston (Chicago: Fitzroy Dearborn Publishers, 2000), 849.

[9] Tomáš Josef Špidlík, *The Spirituality of the Christian East.*

[10] In my experience, starting *lectio divina* is easier if it is added to a previously existing group, class or worship. Creating a new brief twenty minute *lectio* service an hour prior to the start of the main Sunday morning worship service. In my context, we were able to use the church's chapel. This provided a sacred space that was quiet and also felt connected to the community's overall life of worship. At 8:00am I rang the meditation bell, briefly welcomed the participants, opened with a brief prayer and began reading the selected passage in the manner of *lectio divina.* For me, this meant inviting all to close our eyes, to sit comfortably and at ease, while I began to read the passage four times, with increasing silence in-between each reading. At the conclusion of the fourth reading and silence, I rang the bell and closed with the Lord's Prayer. I then invited the participants to briefly share a word

they heard that spoke to them from their listening. I sometimes invited them to keep their eyes closed for the time of sharing, to keep the focus on the word that was heard, rather than on the one who heard it. As a further resource for exploring this important and foundational level of *lectio,* I recommend two books on the subject, which in my view, are the essential modern works on *lectio divina:* Michael Casey, *Sacred Reading: The Ancient Art of Lectio Divina* and M. Basil Pennington, *Lectio Divina: Renewing the Ancient Practice of Praying the Scriptures.*

[11] For an excellent side by side comparison between Benedict's Rule and Bonhoeffer's Rule for his house-seminary, see Greg Peter, *The Story of Monasticism: Retrieving An Ancient Tradition for Contemporary Spirituality* (Grand Rapids, MI: Baker Academic, 2015), 233ff.

[12] See for example, Elsie Mckee, *John Calvin: Writings on Pastoral Piety,* The Classics of Western Spirituality, (Mahwah, NJ: Paulist Press, 2001).

[13] One way to partake in this trend, might be to introduce a morning prayer on Tuesdays and Thursdays, for example. It doesn't have to be a long service, perhaps twenty to thirty minutes. Use part of the chapel or sanctuary, wherever quiet reverence can be maintained. Keep the service simple by focusing on scripture readings. Perhaps include a Taizé type song chant and brief prayer, and consider including time for Centering Prayer and Eucharist. Contemporary artists such as Margaret Rizza, David Haas and Dana Cunningham provide further musical resources to draw upon. Their music conveys the gift of setting the appropriate background music without needing to be center stage. Their music is ideal for helping folks gently adjust to the silence and prepare their heart for worship.

[14] "*A King inside who listens" The Essential Rumi* trans. Coleman Banks (New York: Harper San Francisco, 1995), 321.

[15] St. Basil, *Regulae fusius tractatae* PG 31, 920C – 921B.

[16] *Shaking the Pumpkin,* trans. Jerome Rothenberg (New York: Doubleday, 1972), 363.

[17] M. Basil Pennington, *Lectio Divina: Renewing the Ancient Practice of Praying the Scriptures (*New York: Crossroad Publishing, 1998), 12.

[18] Variously attributed to Abba Moses and Jon Cassian. For more see, *The Sayings of the Desert Fathers,* trans. Benedicta Ward (Kalamazoo, MI: Cistercian Publications, 2006).

[19] Abraham of Nathpar, in *The Syriac Fathers on Prayer and the Spiritual Life,* trans. Sabastian Brock (Kalamazoo, MI: Cistercian Publications, 1987), Section 4, 193.

[20] Sebastian Brock, *The Luminous Eye: The Spiritual World Vision of Saint Ephrem the Syrian* (Kalamazoo, MI: Cistercian Publications, 1992), 79.

[21] John Climacus, *Ladder of Divine Ascent,* Step 27.

[22] Brendan Freeman, *Come and See: The Monastic Way for Today* (Collegeville, MN: Liturgical Press, 2010), 86.

[23] Brendan Freeman, *Come and See: The Monastic Way for Today* (Collegeville, MN: Liturgical Press, 2010), 86.

[24] Try it just for thirty minutes in the morning and evening, and instead of watching or listening to your normal program(s), take rest with God in the silence. Perhaps try *lectio divina* in the silence, or just watch the sunrise or sunset. Or, take a silent walk in a nearby park, simply being with the earth's silence and natural sounds. If the silence is too much at first, try a resource such as www.PrayAsYouGo.com to gently introduce the silence accompanied by music or scripture reading.

[25] Along these lines, Contemplative Cyprian Smith offers this beautiful reflection on the nature of silence, and its value: "Out of a silent heart, steeped in God, freed from the clamoring's of selfish desire, a true Word can sometimes come forth, comforting the lonely, healing the wounded, enlightening the perplexed. But then it is not we who are speaking, but the supreme Word, spoken out of the depths of the Father. The depths themselves, however, whether in the Father or in ourselves, are perpetually silent. There is no Word without a silence from which it emerges and to which it finally returns." Cyprian Smith, *The Path of Life: Benedictine Spirituality for Monks and Lay People* (Herefordshire, England: Ampleforth Abbey Press, 2004), 72 – 73.

[26] Cited in M. Basil Pennington, *A Place Apart: Monastic Prayer and Practice for Everyone* (New York: Image Books, 1985), 52.

[27] Perhaps consider inviting the congregation to take a moment of silence at the beginning of the worship service, after the morning greeting, but before the morning call to worship. In the various contexts I have served, after the morning greeting and announcements, I often say the following:

> *"Again, thank you for making the decision to come to church today, to be the body of Christ at John Calvin Presbyterian Church. Let's take a moment in the silence to prepare our hearts for worship. Ask the Holy Spirit to bless you for what you need today."*

After about thirty seconds, I conclude the silence by saying *Amen.* I then say,

> *Let's stand, and give our hearts to song.*

[28] Isaac of Nineveh, *Early Fathers from the Philokalia,* 206.

[29] One way to begin practicing simplicity is by creating a more open space for prayer and worship in our home or church. Monastic simplicity is expressed in embodied ways – from how the church is designed to how our office is set up. Other ways to introduce the value of simplicity is to plan an all church spring cleaning day in Lent, or a church rummage sale. The point is, little by little, we can simplify aspects of our life. Small changes can have a big impact.

[30] *Against Heresies*, Book 5.

[31] See Peter Brown, *Society and the Holy in Late Antiquity* (Berkeley, CA: University of California Press, 1989), 114. While spiritual hunger played its part in this migration, perhaps widespread unemployment also impacted the willingness of individuals to leave the city for a different experience of communal life.

[32] Thomas Merton, *Contemplation in a World of Action* (New York: Doubleday, 1971), 36.

[33] On a practical level, cultivating solitude in our busy and crowded lifestyles is a challenge, requiring intentional efforts. For example, try creating space in our daily schedule for solitude. For some, this might be the morning commute in the car. For others, it might mean waking up thirty minutes before the rest of the household gets up. If your job allows, it is also useful to take time out during the day. Perhaps you can slip away at 10:00am or 3:00pm to a quiet room or vacant hallway with a pleasant view. Take five minutes of solitude and silence. Breathe into your body and reconnect with your heart. What I'm staying is that you don't have to go to a monastery to experience solitude, although it might be helpful to schedule a personal Sabbath, weekly; a personal retreat day, monthly, and an extended retreat, annually. Building these practical actions into your life will convey the benefits of this monastic practice without too much disruption.

[34] *The Philokalia: The Complete Text,* Volumes 1 – 4, trans. G.E.H. Palmer, Philip Sherrard, Kalistos Ware (London: Faber & Faber, 1979).

[35] Perhaps explore a "taste and see" moment with the congregation right before the sermon or homily. Invite them to take a few breathes, to sink into their hearts, to feel what they are feeling, and to request that the time of study and listening to the message be profitable. There are many practical ways to cultivate stillness as well – such as creating a small meditation garden adjacent to the sanctuary. Or, dimming the lights and sound. These are practical signals that create an opportunity for parishioners to experience the gift of stillness in community.

[36] If you are looking for a monastery to visit where you can see and experience many of these spiritual practices lived out in community, here are six exceptional models located in North America:

New Camaldoli Hermitage, Big Sur, California
St. Benedict's, Snowmass, Colorado
New Melleray Abbey, Dubuque, Iowa
St. Gregory's Monastery, Three Rivers, Michigan
Abbey of Gethsemane, Trappist, Kentucky
St. Joseph's Abbey, Spencer, Massachusetts

[37] Consider James K.A. Smith's recent approach apply "practices" and habits to worship in his book *You are What You Love: The Spiritual Power of Habit* (Brazos Press: Grand Rapids, MI, 2016).

[38] Alasdair MacIntyre, *After Virtue*, Third Edition (Notre Dame: University of Notre Dame Press, 2007) xvi. For a social-cultural perspective, there is much wisdom in Robert N. Bellah's classic *Habits of the Heart: Individualism and Commitment in American Life* (Berkley, CA: University of California Press, 2008).

[39] For a very helpful, current and accessible overview of monasticism and desert spirituality see Alexander Ryrie, *The Desert Movement: Fresh Perspectives on the Spirituality of the Desert* (Norwich, UK: Canterbury Press, 2011). See also Columba Stewart's, OSB excellent historical essay, *"Rethinking the History of Monasticism East and West: A Modest tour d'horizon"* in *Prayer and Thought in Monastic Tradition: Essay in Honour of Benedicta Ward* SLG, ed. Santha Bhattacharji, Rowan Williams and Dominic Mattos (New York:

T&T Clark Bloomsbury, 2015), 3 – 16. Andrew Louth invariably is a masterful guide in all things monastic, and his many articles on the history of monastic themes are readily available in English, and invaluable, such as *"The Literature of the Monastic Movement"* in *The Cambridge History of Early Christian Literature*, ed. France Young, Lewis Ayres and Andrew Louth (Cambridge: Cambridge University Press, 2004), 373 – 381.

[40] Yet the origins of Christian monasticism are not as crisply delineated as once thought. It turns out that there is an extensive and diverse background to the monastic impulse, perhaps shaped by such social movements as the Jewish Essenes; the Jewish Therapeutae, the monks of Syria and the *apotaktikoi* (the renouncers) of Egypt. Some have even drawn clear connections between Buddhist influences integrated in Judaism, such as the Quran community at the Dead Sea, as well as the seeming spontaneous emergence of Desert monasticism in Christianity, flowing out of Eastern influences pollinating in and through the ancient city of Alexandria. For more on this fascinating idea see Tom Chetwynd, *Zen & The Kingdom of Heaven: Reflections on the Tradition of Meditation in Christianity and Zen Buddhism* (Somerville, MA: Wisdom Publications, 2001), especially chapter Four, "The Story of Christian Meditation" 71ff.

[41] "Saint Anthony is sometimes considered the first monk, but there were others before him. There were already ascetic pagan hermits (the *Therapeutae*) and loosely organized cenobitic communities were described by the Hellenized Jewish philosopher Philo of Alexandria in the 1st century AD as long established in the harsh environment of Lake Mareotis and in other less accessible regions. Philo opined that "this class of persons may be met with in many places, for both Greece and barbarian countries want to enjoy whatever is perfectly good." Christian ascetics such as Thecla had likewise retreated to isolated locations at the outskirts of cities. Anthony is notable for having decided to surpass this tradition and headed out into the desert proper. He left for the alkaline Nitrian Desert (later the location of the noted monasteries of Nitria, Kellia, and Scetis) on the edge of the Western Desertabout fifty-nine miles west of Alexandria. He remained there for 13 years." Cited from https://en.wikipedia.org/wiki/Anthony_the_Great Accessed May 17, 2016.

[42] See Dale M. Coulter, "Contemplative Life," in *The Encyclopedia of Christian Civilization*, ed. George Thomas Kurian (Oxford: Wiley-Blackwell, 2012), 597 – 598.

[43] For a delightful, yet sometimes depressing travelogue of this region and how it has changed since the early founding of its monastic communities see William Dalrymple, *From the Holy Mountain: A Journey among the Christians of the Middle East* (New York: Henry Holt and Company, 1997). Today, the regional birthplaces of Christian monasticism (Egypt, Palestine, Syria, Persia, and Cappadocia) are no longer Christian territories.

[44] For an excellent and brief overview of the decline and renewal of monasticism in the Western Church see Barry Collett, *"Monasticism"* in *The Oxford Encyclopedia of the Reformation,* ed. Hans J. Hillerbrand, Vol. 3 (Oxford: Oxford University Press, 1996,), 78 – 83.

[45] For an excellent overview of this period of English history see Joyce Youings, *The Dissolution of the Monasteries* (London: George Allen and Unwin Ltd., 1971).

[46] See Amy Hollywood, "Introduction" in *The Cambridge Companion to Christian Mysticism,* ed. by Amy Hollywood and Patricia Z. Beckman (Cambridge: Cambridge University Press, 2012), 32.

[47] Along these lines, Abbot Francis Kline, a modern contemplative monk, envisions a new era of Christianity infused with the ancient monastic charism. He concludes his beautiful book, *Lovers of the Place: Monasticism Loose in the Church* with this important reflection in the light of Vatican II and the *Lumen gentium,* on the future place of monasticism in the church: "Monasticism, as one of the earliest and perhaps the most fruitful charism in the long history of the reconfigured church, should be the first to stand up and be counted in this reconfigured assembly. Our response should be to return to the Church what we have been given. With all the gifts intact, and after years of formation, at least some should return to the Church in an act of self-giving for the sake of the kingdom of God. If the Church can point herself onto a road of such different direction, so can monasticism follow without losing an iota of the monastic charism except what the heat of the gospel can burn away." Francis Kline, *Lovers of the Place: Monasticism Loose in the Church* (Collegeville, MN: The Liturgical Press, 1997), 123.

[48] Timothy Ware, ed. *The Art of Prayer: An Orthodox Anthology* (London: Faber & Faber, 1971), 192.

[49] John Calvin, *Institutes of the Christian Religion,* ed. John T. McNeill, trans. Ford Lewis Battles, 3.11.10 (Philadelphia: The Westminster Press, 1960), 689 – 690.

[50] John Cassian, *Conferences IX.2.*

[51] When our belief-tank runs dry, or starts to get gummed up with doubt or contradictory information and ideas, if we don't soon discover the useful grace that the spiritual practices hold us while we grow, we may find ourselves feeling like we have lost our faith altogether.

[52] Visit a contemplative monastery for a day (or a week!) and discover how the depth of Christian life is flourishing in community. Explore the treasures therein that have the capacity to sustain us and take us beyond our saturation point of self into the depth of ever-expanding spiritual growth. Even better, integrate the wisdom and contemplative practices of the monastery into your daily life and into your local church. As you recover these forgotten treasures, you and your church community will never be the same.

Chapter Seven / *Becoming*

[1] For Keating's teaching on the method of Centering Prayer:

- *Open Mind, Open Heart: The Contemplative Dimension of the Gospel*
- *Foundations for Centering Prayer and the Christian Contemplative Life*

For Keating's teaching on the contemplative dimension of Christianity:

- *Intimacy with God: An Introduction to Centering Prayer*
- *The Heart of the World: An Introduction to Contemplative Christianity*

For Keating's model of infusing the contemplative dimension into the liturgical life of the church, read:

- *The Mystery of Christ: The Liturgy as Spiritual Experience*

---

[2] See http://www.contemplativeoutreach.org/product/spiritual-journey-series-part-i-developing-centering-prayer-and-spiritual-journey-dvd.

[3] Thomas Keating, *The Human Condition: Contemplation and Transformation* (New York: Paulist Press, 1999), 17.

[4] For a vivid example of the usefulness of the idea of programs for happiness and the power of Centering Prayer as therapy, see the connection to addictions in Thomas Keating, *Divine Therapy and Addiction: Centering Prayer and the Twelve Steps* (New York: Lantern Books, 2009).

[5] Thomas Keating, *Invitation to Love: The Way of Christian Contemplation, 20th Anniversary Edition,* (New York: Bloomsbury, 2011), 153.

[6] Personal notes from a group discussion during a Christian Mysticism retreat with Bernadette Roberts in Fullerton, CA., November 2010.

[7] Thomas Keating, *Open Mind, Open Heart: The Contemplative Dimension of the Gospel* (New York: Continuum, 2002), 13.

[8] Thomas Keating, *Manifesting God* (New York: Lantern Books, 2005), 93.

[9] Keating summarizes the profound opportunity this way, "Along with the invitation to repent – to change the direction in which we are looking for happiness – comes Jesus' invitation to submit to the Divine Therapy: If you want to be free, he suggests, if you want to heal your relationship with God, with others and yourself, enter your inner room – the office, where the Divine Therapy takes place. Close the door so you don't run away. Quiet your interior dialogue so that you can listen to what the Spirit is saying to you." Thomas Keating, *Manifesting God* (New York: Lantern Books, 2005).

[10] Allan Watts, *Behold the Spirit: A Study in the Necessity of Mystical Religion* (New York: Random House, 1971), xx – xxi.

[11] http://consciousharmony.org/about/overview/.

[12] Shifting the focus from programs to becoming a gathering place for doing communal spiritual practices, relieves pressure for having to be all things to all people, and alleviates the need to structure programs around demographics or interest groups.

[13] Ambiance is key. It is helpful to dim the room lights, and set the room so that the chairs are placed in a semi-circle, facing each other – like two parentheses:

(·)

In the center, place a small and low table and put a Christ candle there, reminding all that Christ holds the center. As you begin, perhaps ring a prayer bell and invite a participant to light the Christ candle saying something along the lines of, "We light this Christ candle a symbol of God's loving presence, in the Name of the Father, Son and Holy Spirit." Since most aren't comfortable with much silence at first, perhaps use quiet background music, such as the piano solos of Dana Cunningham. The liturgical schedule for the meeting could go something like this:

Opening Prayer

Lectio Divina with increasing silence

Sharing What Was Heard in *Lectio*

Time for Silence and Stillness

A Brief Taizé Chant or Doxology

Closing Prayer

Adjourn to Committee Meeting Carrying Christ Candle

[14] https://www.giveusthisday.org/.

[15] To see a listing of current retreats, visit http://www.contemplativeoutreach.org/category/category/retreats.

Chapter Eight / *Evolving*

[1] Any book on spiritual flourishing would be incomplete without looking specifically at the field of spiritual (or integral) development. The developmentalists provide a model of human consciousness that identifies the existence of common, patterned processes and expressions, especially as it relates to of psycho-spiritual growth. And most importantly, the growth unfolds in stages. Such developmental models can help us understand the well-traveled phases on the journey into further flourishing. While there are many developmental writers (Sri Aurobindo, Don Beck, Austin Ferrer, James Fowler, Paul Smith, Michael Washburn, Ken Wilber, et al), Paul Smith's framework stands out for me as particularly relevant to our interests because Smith developed his model from within a Christian congregational context. Anyone interested in exploring Smith's ideas further should give a careful reading of his extraordinary book *Integral Christianity: The Spirit's Call to Evolve.*

The primary works to consider are (in no particular order):

- Ken Wilber, *Integral Spirituality: A Startling New Role for Religion in the Modern and Postmodern World* (Boston: Integral Books, 2007).
- _________, *The Religion of Tomorrow: A Vision for the Future of the Great Traditions* (Boulder: Shambhala, 2017).
- Sri Aurobindo, *The Integral Yoga: Sri Aurobindo's Teaching and Method of Practice* (Twin Lakes, WI: Lotus Press, 2011).
- Paul R. Smith, *Integral Christianity: The Spirit's Call to Evolve* (St. Paul, MN: Paragon House, 2011).
- Raimon Panikkar, *Opera Omnia* (Maryknoll, NY: Orbis Books, 2014).
- Jim Marion, *The Death of the Mythic God* (Charlottesville, VA: Hampton Roads, 2004).
- Michael Washburn, *The Ego and the Dynamic Ground: A Transpersonal Theory of Human Development* (Albany: State University of New York Press, 1995).
- Jorge N. Ferrer, *Revisioning transpersonal theory: A participatory vision of human spirituality* (Albany, NY: State University of New York Press, 2002).

- James Fowler, *Stages of faith: The psychology of human development and the quest for meaning* (New York, NY: HarperCollins, 1982).
- Peter Feldmeier, *The Developing Christian: Spiritual Growth Through the Life Cycle* (Mahwah, NJ: Paulist Press, 2007).
- Don Edward Beck and Christopher C. Cowan, *Spiral Dynamics: Mastering Values, Leadership and Change* (Oxford: Blackwell Publishing, 2006).

[2] Among the vast literature, see for example, *The Blackwell Companion to Consciousness*, ed. Max Velmans and Susan Schneider (Oxford: Blackwell Publishing, 2007).

[3]For more on the Reformation as a dawn of a new era, see Lewis W. Spitz, *The Renaissance and Reformation Movements,* revised edition, Volume 1: The Renaissance and Volume 2: The Reformation (St. Louis, MO: Concordia Publishing House, 1987), 301. And for cosmological view, see David Christian, *Maps of Time: An Introduction to Big History* (Berkeley, CA: University of California Press, Ltd., 2005) or Sean Carroll, *The Big Picture: On the Origins of Life, Meaning, and the Universe Itself* (New York: Dutton, 2016).

[4] Paul R. Smith, *Integral Christianity: The Spirit's Call to Evolve* (St. Paul, MN: Paragon House, 2011), 235.

[5] For an excellent article on the developmental stages in the Easter Orthodox community, with a view to the contemplative, see John Chirban, *"Developmental Stages in Easter Orthodox Christianity*" in *Transformations of Consciousness: Conventional and Contemplative Perspectives on Development,* eds., Ken Wilber, Jack Engler and Daniel P. Brown (Boston: Shamballa Publications, 1986), 285 – 314.

[6] Psychologically, some Developmentalists locate the contemplative/mystical practices during the middle-age of life, spanning from about forty to sixty-five years old. I agree with that general assessment, but also believe that the contemplative line is operative throughout one's entire lifetime, and is especially accessible in childhood, but is often quickly forgotten by adolescence – at least in much of Western culture. In fact, what is experienced during midlife is often a *rediscovery* or a second naiveté, returning the fully rational adult back to their life-giving earlier mystical and unitive experiences from childhood. Whereas in childhood, they were not fully developed rationally, now in mid-life, they are, and that fact makes the shift a very fruitful opportunity. This developmental perspective adds new dimensions to what Jesus said: that in order to enter the kingdom of heaven, *"you must become like little children"* (Mark 10.15). Such emergence of growth or development is not particularly a new idea. Moving backward from the recent toward the ancient: We can see it in Darwin's theories. We can see it in Bunyan's, *Pilgrim's Progress*. We can see it in Theresa of Ávila's, *Interior Mansions.* We can see it in John Climacus' *Ladder of Ascent*. We can see it in the story of Jacob's ladder in Book of Genesis. Why then would we not recognize that sanctification also has a patterned process to it, with discernable and distinct Lines (i.e. moral, intellectual, spiritual) and Levels (infant, adolescent, etc.) of development?

[7] Psalm 46.10.

[8] In this we only need to reference the work of Pierre Teilhard de Chardin, and especially his recent illuminative interpreters such as Beatrice Bruteau and Ilia Delio. For more on this, see Ilia Delio, *From Teilhard to Omega: Co-Creating an Unfinished Universe* (Mary Knoll, NY: Orbis Books, 2015); Ilia Delio, *Making All Things New: Catholicity, Cosmology, Consciousness* (Mary Knoll, NY: Orbis Books, 2015); or Beatrice Bruteau, *Evolution toward Divinity: Teilhard de Chardin and the Hindu Traditions* (Wheaton, IL: Theosophical Publishing House, 1974).

Opening Quotes

[1] The poet in *Faust, Prelude in the Theatre* by Johan Wolfgang von Goethe, trans. Walter Arndt and ed. By Cyrus Hamilin (Norton & Company: New York, 2001), 4.

Chapter Nine / *Flourishing*

[1] "The unhurried rhythms of grace" is an adaptation of Eugene Peterson's translation of Matthew 11.29 in The Message, "the unforced rhythms of grace."

[2] Johan Wolfgang von Goethe, trans. Walter Arndt and ed. By Cyrus Hamilin (Norton & Company: New York, 2001), 4.

[3] Joseph Kopp, *Teilhard de Chardin: A New Synthesis of Evolution* (Deus Books, 1968), 32.

[4] Essential reading for understanding the depth and breadth of the philosophic tradition and its shaping of mystical/contemplative theology, is Deirdre Carabine's, *The Unknown God: Negative Theology in the Platonic Tradition – Plato to Eriugena* (Eugene, OR: Wipf & Stock, 1995). For an excellent summary, see Ilia Delio's essay "Mysticism: Metaphysical Foundations and the Monastic Quest for God" in her book *Crucified Love: Bonaventure's Mysticism of the Crucified Christ* (Quincy, IL: Franciscan Press, 1998), 173 – 202.

[5] For a helpful overview that bears this claim out see Ana Maria Bidegain and Juan Sanchez, "Contemplation, Contemplative Prayer and Life," *The Cambridge Dictionary of Christianity,* ed. Daniel Patte (Cambridge: Cambridge University Press, 2011), 276 – 277.

Conclusion / *The Song of Silence*

[1] The ocean is an unseen liquid presence. I know it is there, like one knows silk curtains are blowing through an open window in a distant room. I can feel the ocean's majesty; sense it just staring back at me from the void – a stretching silver eye of endlessness, hiding the ages and wrinkles of the planet, beneath the sea's at once taught then tumultuous surface. The ocean remembers. The sea has a lineage whose history dwarfs the stories of humankind, both our words and silence; our being and becoming. I have been given fleeting moments when the sea has appeared to me, suddenly, and then just as fast, disappeared again by the shifting clouds of mist. At first, I felt disappointed, even frustrated. The ocean view is, in part, what makes this place so sacred for me. But slowly, after a couple of days, I came to love the metaphor the earth, sea and sky were offering me at midlife on this retreat: learning to be present to whatever is occurring in each moment. Not fidgeting or

wanting something to change. Just sinking into the stillness of Is-ness. Letting go of resistance. Releasing my need to for anything to be different or clearer.

Ending Quote

[1] Juan Ramón Jiménez, trans. By Robert Bly.

Afterword / *From the Monastery*

[1] Philip Hughes, *A Popular History of the Reformation*, 91.

[2] Paul Tillich, *The Courage to Be*, 157.

[3] Bruno Barnhart, *The Future of Wisdom,* 136.

[4] Ibid, 150.

Appendix / *The Evolution of Centering Prayer*

[1] For an insightful and creative history of contemplative methods in Christianity, see Tom Chetwynd, *Zen & The Kingdom of Heaven: Reflections on the Tradition of Meditation in Christianity and Zen Buddhism* (Somerville, MA: Wisdom Publications, 2001), chapter six, "The Line of Christian Spiritual Masters", 95ff.

[2] A good example of the development of the concept and practice of contemplation in our current understanding in contrast to the fourteenth century is the classic work *Meditations on the Life of Christ.* In this classic, we see a clear distinction between meditation and contemplation. This contrast is also evident in the widely influential, seventeenth century book *Sancta Sophia* by Father Augustine Baker, published today under the title "Contemplative Prayer." See *Meditations on the Life of Christ: An Illustrated Manuscript of the Fourteenth Century,* ed. Isa Ragusa and Rosalie B. Green (Princeton: Princeton University Press, 1961); and Augustine Baker, *Contemplative Prayer: Venerable Father Augustine Baker's Teaching Thereon from 'Sancta Sophia',* ed. by Don B. Weld-Blundell (Lexington, KY: Christ the King Library, 2016 facsimile reprint from the 1906 edition).

[3] Note Janet K. Ruffing's wise comment: "In the Christian tradition the term *meditation* currently refers to the entire process of contemplative prayer. Under the influence of various forms of meditation characteristic especially of Buddhism and Hinduism, the term has recently been reappropriated in a Christian context to designate a similar spectrum of processes and practices long taught in the Western monastic tradition. These had become obscured since the 16th century by restricting the term *meditation* to activities of thinking, reflecting, reasoning, imagining, and resolving. Thus, within classical Christian texts the word *meditation* might refer to one among many practices that promote contemplative experience. In a broader sense the term denotes any practice for focusing intention and attention that disposes the seeker to be aware of the Divine Presence and as a result to become receptive to transformation of consciousness and action." cited from, Janet K. Ruffing, "Meditation: Christian Perspectives" in *Encyclopedia of Monasticism*, ed. William M. Johnston (Chicago: Fitzroy Dearborn Publishers, 2000), 847 – 848.

[4] Janet K. Ruffing, "Meditation: Christian Perspectives" in *Encyclopedia of Monasticism*, ed. William M. Johnston (Chicago: Fitzroy Dearborn Publishers, 2000), 848.

[5] Guigo II, *The Ladder of Monks and Twelve Meditations,* trans. E. Colledge and T. Walsh (London, 1976), II, n.2 – 14, 81 – 96.

[6] Scholar Jennifer Bryan shines insight on the practice of *lectio divina* in its historical context. She writes, "It is worth recalling too that many of the emerging modes of devotional reading emphasized a subjective encounter with the text – an emphasis that made private experience primary, even if it did not preclude public reading. The practices associated with Franciscan visual meditation, for example, encouraged readers to use the text as a starting point for independent, interactive meditation and prayer, so that even public readings would produce private experience. As Brian Stock has argued, vernacular reading practices across Europe after the fourteenth century were mainly derived from the tradition of *lection spiritualis,* a subset of the traditional monastic practice of *lectio divina* centered not on a biblical text but on the reader's emotional response and spiritual progress. Whereas *lectio divina* – conceived of as one kind of ascetic experience among many – depended on 'the recreation of the biblical text through oral reading and recitations', to be followed by prayer and meditation, *lectio spiritualis* could take place entirely in silence. While *lectio divina* helped the reader to slowly internalize the biblical text, creating a more exact correspondence between reading and prayer, *lectio spiritualis* emphasized the subjective words and images that might arise in the reader's mind both during and after the textual encounter." Jennifer Bryan, *Looking Inward: Devotional Reading and the Private Self in Late Medieval England* (Philadelphia: University of Pennsylvania Press, 2008), 14.

[7] Guigo II, *Ladder of Monks and Twelve Meditations,* trans. Edmund Colledge and James Walsh, (Kalamazoo, MI: Cistercian Publications, 1979), 74.

[8] Guigo II, *Ladder of Monks and Twelve Meditations,* trans. Edmund Colledge and James Walsh, (Kalamazoo, MI: Cistercian Publications, 1979), 86.

[9] George Lawless, *Augustine of Hippo and his Monastic Rule* (Oxford: Clarendon Press, 1987), 85.

[10] Jean Leclercq, "Ways of Prayer and Contemplation II: Western" in Bernard McGinn, John Meyendorff, and Jean Leclercq (eds.), *Christian Spirituality: Origins to the Twelfth Century* (London: 1986), 415.

[11] See William of St. Thierry, *On Contemplating God: Prayer Meditations* (Shannon, Ireland: Cistercian Publications, Inc., 1970).

[12] Jean Leclercq, "Ways of Prayer and Contemplation II: Western" in Bernard McGinn, John Meyendorff, and Jean Leclercq (eds.), *Christian Spirituality: Origins to the Twelfth Century* (London: 1986), 424. Emphasis added.

[13] Reginald Garrigou-Lagrange, *The Three Ages of the Interior Life: Prelude of Eternal Life,* Volume 1 & 2, trans. Sister M. Timothea Doyle (London: Catholic Way Publishing, 2012). And also, Reginald Garrigou-Lagrange, *The Three Conversions in the Spiritual Life* (Rockford, IL: TAN Books & Publishers, Inc., 1977); and Reginald Garrigou-Lagrange, *Christian Perfection and Contemplation: According to St. Thomas Aquinas and St. John*

of the Cross, trans. Sister M. Timothea Doyle (Charlotte, NC: TAN Books & Publishers, Inc., 2003).

[14] Adolphe Tanquerey, *The Spiritual Life: A Treatise on Ascetical and Mystical Theology,* trans. Herman Branderis, (Charlotte, NC: TAN Books, 2000).

[15] Amy Hollywood, "Introduction" in *The Cambridge Companion to Christian Mysticism,* ed. by Amy Hollywood and Patricia Z. Beckman (Cambridge: Cambridge University Press, 2012), 6.

[16] M. Basil Pennington, *Daily We Touch Him: Practical Religious Experiences* (Kansas City, MO: Sheed & Ward, 1997), 30 – 31.

[17] Anonymous, *The Cloud of Unknowing,* trans. Clifton Wolters (New York: Penguin Book, 1973), 61 – 62.

[18] One of Merton's most comprehensive books on the contemplative tradition is Thomas Merton, *The Inner Experience: Notes on Contemplation* (San Francisco: Harper Collins Publishers, 2003) and also Thomas Merton, *Contemplative Prayer* (New York: Image Books, 1996).

[19] An excellent resource is now available to help understand the actual dynamics behind the Quietist controversy. It turns out the controversy had less to do with spirituality and more to do with politics and power struggles. See Miguel de Molinos, *The Spiritual Guide*, ed. and trans. Robert P Baird, (New York: Paulist Press, 2010).

[20] Here too we are blessed by modern scholarship to provide an insightful overview and introduction to the writings and influence of Guyon and Fenelon. See especially, *Jeanne Guyon: Selected Writings*, ed. and trans. Dianne Guenin-Lelle and Ronney Mourad, in Classics of Western Spirituality Series (New York: Paulist Press, 2011) and *The Complete Fenelon*, trans. ed., Robert J. Edmonson and Hal M. Helms (Brewster: MA, Paraclete Press, 2008).

[21] For more on the social aspects behind the Quietist controversy in France, see *Jeanne Guyon: Selected Writings*, ed. and trans. Dianne Guenin-Lelle and Ronney Mourad, in Classics of Western Spirituality Series (New York: Paulist Press, 2011), 13 – 18.

[22] Miguel de Molinos, *The Spiritual Guide*, ed. and trans. Robert P Baird, (New York: Paulist Press, 2010), 57.

[23] Miguel de Molinos, *The Spiritual Guide*, ed. and trans. Robert P Baird, (New York: Paulist Press, 2010), 81 – 82. Guyon's method is virtually the same. For example, see *A Short Method of Prayer and Other Writings* (Peabody, MA: Hendrickson Publishers, Inc., 2005). What is fascinating to me, is to study the lineage of Guyon's influence, which included such early Protestant movements as the Methodists, Pietists and especially the Quakers. John Wesley supposedly said that one could "search many centuries to find another woman who was such a pattern of true holiness." Another influential work of Guyon's is, *Spiritual Torrents* (Traffic Output Publications, 2016).

[24] Jean Pierre de Caussade, *The Abandonement to the Divine Presence* (London: Catholic Way Publishing, 2013).

[25] For a basic overview of the Pietists see *Pietists: Selected Writings,* ed. Peter C. Erb (New York: Paulist Press, 1983).

[26] See the rare book, *Johannes Kelpius, A Method of Prayer* (New York: Harper & Brothers) 1951. For more on Kelpius' Pietist community in Pennsylvania see *The Diarium of Magister Johanenes Kelpius,* available online in multiple formats.

[27] Augustine Baker, *Contemplative Prayer: Venerable Father Augustine Baker's Teaching Thereon from 'Sancta Sophia,'* ed. by Don B. Weld-Blundell (Lexington, KY: Christ the King Library, 2016 facsimile reprint from the 1906 edition).

[28] J.C. Winslow, *The Art of Contemplation* (Calcutta, India: Y.M.C.A Press, 1931), 30 – 32. Pamphlet book.

Acknowledgments

[1] I am referring to the Church of Conscious Harmony: A Contemplative Christian Community in Austin, Texas. I describe this contemplative spiritual community at length in chapter five of my book *The God Who Is Here: A Contemplative Guide to Renewing Your Relationship with God and the Church* (New York: Lantern Books, 2010). I see Austin as a New Alexandria for the third millennium of inter-spiritual conversation and collaboration The New Alexandria in part because of the global impact and connection of such influences as the ACL Festival and the SXSW Festival. Such festivals, in the age of the internet, are physical gathering places/spaces/events, perhaps providing a similar function as the ancient libraries and scholastic communities of the past.

Made in the USA
Columbia, SC
08 October 2018